REPAIRING
APPLIANCES

TIME
LIFE ®
BOOKS

Other Publications:

PLANET EARTH
COLLECTOR'S LIBRARY OF THE CIVIL WAR
LIBRARY OF HEALTH
CLASSICS OF THE OLD WEST
THE EPIC OF FLIGHT
THE GOOD COOK
THE SEAFARERS
THE ENCYCLOPEDIA OF COLLECTIBLES
THE GREAT CITIES
WORLD WAR II
THE WORLD'S WILD PLACES
THE TIME-LIFE LIBRARY OF BOATING
HUMAN BEHAVIOR
THE ART OF SEWING
THE OLD WEST
THE EMERGENCE OF MAN
THE AMERICAN WILDERNESS
THE TIME-LIFE ENCYCLOPEDIA OF GARDENING
LIFE LIBRARY OF PHOTOGRAPHY
THIS FABULOUS CENTURY
FOODS OF THE WORLD
TIME-LIFE LIBRARY OF AMERICA
TIME-LIFE LIBRARY OF ART
GREAT AGES OF MAN
LIFE SCIENCE LIBRARY
THE LIFE HISTORY OF THE UNITED STATES
TIME READING PROGRAM
LIFE NATURE LIBRARY
LIFE WORLD LIBRARY
FAMILY LIBRARY:
    HOW THINGS WORK IN YOUR HOME
    THE TIME-LIFE BOOK OF THE FAMILY CAR
    THE TIME-LIFE FAMILY LEGAL GUIDE
    THE TIME-LIFE BOOK OF FAMILY FINANCE

This volume is part of a series offering homeowners
detailed instructions on repairs, construction
and improvements they can undertake themselves.

HOME REPAIR
AND IMPROVEMENT

REPAIRING APPLIANCES

BY THE EDITORS OF
TIME-LIFE BOOKS

TIME-LIFE BOOKS
ALEXANDRIA, VIRGINIA

Time-Life Books Inc.
is a wholly owned subsidiary of
TIME INCORPORATED

Founder Henry R. Luce 1898-1967

Editor-in-Chief Henry Anatole Grunwald
President J. Richard Munro
Chairman of the Board Ralph P. Davidson
Executive Vice President Clifford J. Grum
Chairman, Executive Committee James R. Shepley
Editorial Director Ralph Graves
Group Vice President, Books Joan D. Manley
Vice Chairman Arthur Temple

TIME-LIFE BOOKS INC.

Editor George Constable
Text Editor George Daniels
Director of Design Louis Klein
Board of Editors Dale M. Brown, Thomas H. Flaherty Jr., William Frankel,
Thomas A. Lewis, Martin Mann, John Paul Porter,
Gerry Schremp, Gerald Simons, Kit van Tulleken
Director of Administration David L. Harrison
Director of Research Carolyn L. Sackett
Director of Photography Dolores Allen Littles

President Carl G. Jaeger
Executive Vice Presidents John Steven Maxwell, David J. Walsh
Vice Presidents George Artandi, Stephen L. Bair, Peter G. Barnes,
Nicholas Benton, John L. Canova, Beatrice T. Dobie,
James L. Mercer

HOME REPAIR AND IMPROVEMENT

Editor Robert M. Jones
Senior Editor Betsy Frankel
Designer Edward Frank

Editorial Staff for Repairing Appliances
Picture Editor Adrian Allen
Text Editors Steven J. Forbis, Brooke Stoddard (principals),
Lynn R. Addison, Robert A. Doyle, William Worsley
Writers Patricia C. Bangs, Carol J. Corner, Rachel Cox,
Kathleen M. Kiely, Victoria W. Monks, Ania Savage,
Kirk Young Saunders, Mary-Sherman Willis
Researcher Marilyn Murphy
Copy Coordinator Diane Ullius
Art Assistants George Bell, Fred Holz, Lorraine D. Rivard,
Peter C. Simmons
Picture Coordinator Betsy Donahue
Editorial Assistant Cathy A. Sharpe

Editorial Operations

Production Director Feliciano Madrid
Assistant Peter A. Inchauteguiz
Copy Processing Gordon E. Buck
Quality Control Director Robert L. Young
Assistant James J. Cox
Associates Daniel J. McSweeney, Michael G. Wight
Art Coordinator Anne B. Landry
Copy Room Director Susan Galloway Goldberg
Assistants Celia Beattie, Ricki Tarlow

Correspondents: Elisabeth Kraemer (Bonn); Margot
Hapgood, Dorothy Bacon, Lesley Coleman (London);
Susan Jonas, Lucy T. Voulgaris (New York); Maria
Vincenza Aloisi, Josephine du Brusle (Paris); Ann
Natanson (Rome). Valuable assistance was also
provided by: Judy Aspinall (London); Carolyn T.
Chubet, Miriam Hsia, Christina Lieberman (New
York); Mimi Murphy (Rome).

THE CONSULTANTS: Roswell W. Ard is a consulting
structural engineer and a professional home inspector in
northern Michigan. Trained as a mechanical and electrical engineer, he has worked as a design consultant spe-
cializing in automatic controls for industrial machinery
and is experienced in the repair of small appliances.

I. N. Miller is the owner of a home-appliance store in
Arlington, Virginia. He specializes in appliance repairs
and consulting services, in cooperation with appliance
manufacturers.

John and Jeff Lefever are operators of Alco Appliance
Inc. in Beltsville, Maryland. The Lefever brothers have
worked for many years repairing appliances and manag-
ing appliance-repair companies.

Harris Mitchell, special consultant for Canada, has
worked in the field of home repair and improvement for
more than two decades. He is Homes editor of *Today*
magazine, writes a syndicated newspaper column, "You
Wanted to Know," and is the author of a number of books
on home improvement.

For information about any Time-Life book, please write:
Reader Information
Time-Life Books
541 North Fairbanks Court
Chicago, Illinois 60611

Library of Congress Cataloguing in Publication Data
Time-Life Books.
Repairing appliances.
   (Home repair and improvement; 29)
   Includes index.
   1. Household appliances, Electric—Maintenance and
repair—Amateurs' manuals. I. Time-Life Books.   II. Series.
TK9901.R44   643'.6   81-9279
ISBN 0-8094-3484-9   AACR2
ISBN 0-8094-3483-0 (lib. bdg.)
ISBN 0-8094-3482-2 (retail ed.)

Contents

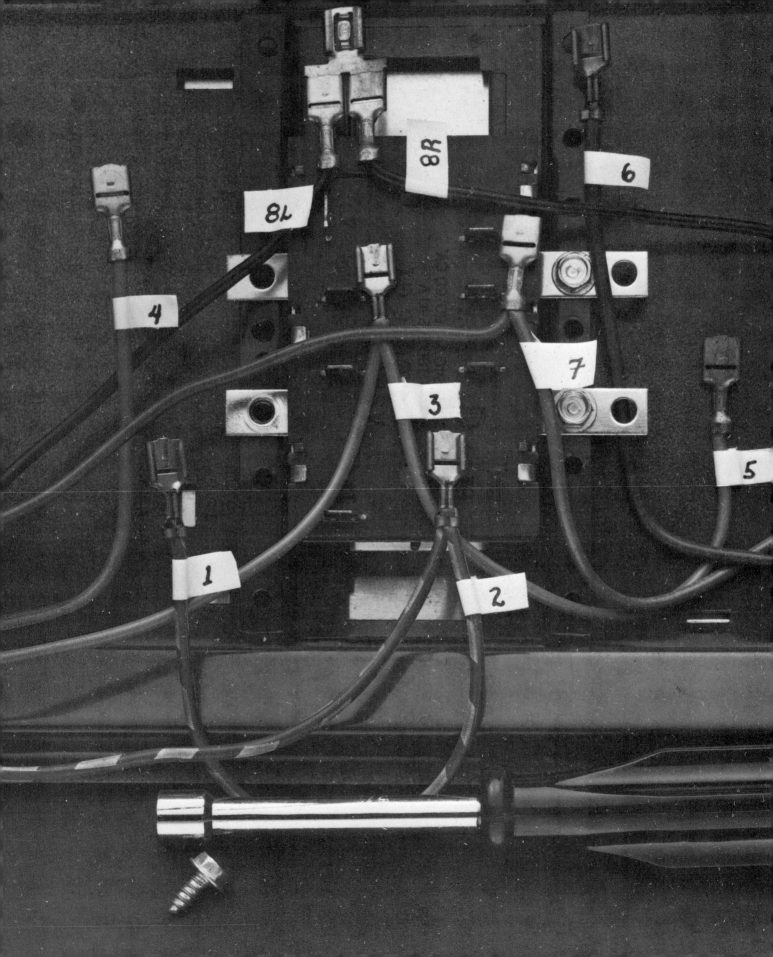

1

The Key: An Orderly Approach

A return address for each terminal. Removing an electrical part for replacement—in this case, the temperature-selector switch of a clothes washer—requires that the wires connecting it to the rest of an appliance be disconnected. To impose order on what could become chaos, the wire that leads to each terminal should be tagged with a numbered strip of masking tape. The numbers correspond to the numbers printed next to the terminals on the switch panel. The switch may now be removed. This requires unfastening its hex screws with an appropriate tool, such as the nut driver shown, and removing the selector knob on the front of the machine.

Household appliances help their owners stay well fed and comfortable in tidy surroundings and in spotlessly clean clothes. Each is taken so much for granted that only when a device fails is its real value appreciated—as anyone knows who has tried to make toast in a broiler when the toaster is broken. Furthermore, not only is a broken appliance of no use in solving everyday problems; it has become a problem itself.

Although it is tempting to toss out a small appliance or call in a professional to fix a large one, there often are good reasons for making repairs yourself. Doing it yourself can save the time it takes to ferret out a reputable repair shop, and save the money that such repairs or replacements cost. Also, you can often put the appliance back into service sooner, get it doing the job it is supposed to do instead of letting it sit around waiting to be fixed. Furthermore, each repair you do yourself gives you that much more familiarity with the machine and makes subsequent repairs easier.

Your new-found capability will tend to transfer from one device to another since all appliances are assemblies of a limited number of basic parts, many of which are illustrated in this chapter. Familiarity with these parts makes the unknown territory within a toaster or a washer less puzzling. If you take the time to look carefully at the device and make some deductions about the roles the various parts are playing, you can form a pretty clear idea of how the device works and make quick strides to an effective repair. Keep in mind what the machine is supposed to do in normal operation, then look for the parts that fulfill these functions.

Your theory of the appliance's operation must account for all of the parts; appliance manufacturers simply do not include any extra, nonfunctioning parts. Furthermore, by observing telltale scratches in metal, the positions of arms and levers, and the placement of springs and hinges, you can usually discover how the parts are supposed to move with relation to one another.

Once you know which part performs what function, you will know which part is the most likely to be out of phase when the machine does not work. When an appliance breaks down, chances are most of it is still in working order; in most cases you need to find only one broken part in order to correct the damage and start the machinery working again. However, there is one caveat. The failure of one part can cause a chain reaction. It often pays to check parts that relate to an obviously damaged one, to see if any of the related parts have become damaged too—or, alternatively, to find out whether the obvious damage of one part was not caused by some previous, and less visible, damage in another part.

Electricity, the Machine's Mind and Muscle

Most household appliances rely on electricity to perform tasks that would otherwise be monotonous, time-consuming, sometimes even dangerous handwork. Electricity powers motors, generates heat and coordinates interaction of mechanical parts. It can also protect an appliance from self-destructing—by shutting it off if it begins to malfunction.

As baffling as the internal workings of an electric appliance may seem, there is always an inherent logic to the arrangement of its parts. An electrical system can be likened to a plumbing system, in which water flows through pipes under pressure. In the electrical system it is current, measured in amperes, or amps, that flows through the "pipes" of wire. The pressure that drives the current is called voltage and is measured in volts. The product of the two (the volts multiplied by the amps) is called wattage, or watts.

All electricity consists of current and voltage, but the current can flow in two different patterns. How it flows depends on its source. The current supplied by the outlets in most homes is called alternating current, normally abbreviated AC. Alternating current pulsates forward and backward about 60 times per second, a characteristic that permits it to travel great distances.

Current can also flow continuously through a circuit without reversing its path. Called direct current (DC), this type is most commonly found in cordless, battery-run appliances because direct current, until recently, could not be transmitted easily by power companies over distances greater than a few miles. (Laser beams and solid-state circuitry are now circumventing this handicap.)

Regardless of the type of current passing through it, every material exposed to an electrical charge exhibits certain characteristics. The most important is the material's resistance or conductivity—its ability either to stop the charge or to carry it along. Metals are the best conductors—silver and copper head the list—so metals are used to make electric wires. Paper, wood and even air will resist the flow of current, and plastic and rubber are such good resistors that they are used to insulate metal wires.

Resistance, which is measured in ohms, can be useful in other ways too. Even the best copper wire presents a certain amount of resistance, and this property can be exploited. Just as water in a pipe of narrow diameter will build up a great deal of friction, so current passing through an undersized wire will be resisted sufficiently to cause the wire to heat. On some appliances wires are deliberately overloaded to become red-hot, and the resultant heat is used as a source of energy. But accidental overheating, which can cause wires to melt, is a major source of breakdowns in appliances.

Wire carrying electrical current displays one other important characteristic: It develops a temporary magnetic field. This electromagnetism can be used to make parts move and is essential to the functioning of electric motors and various other devices found in appliances.

Electricity creates other useful effects in passing through conductive and nonconductive materials. For instance, if two conductors are separated by a nonconductive insulator, current applied to one conductor will be stored there until the build-up reaches the conductor's electrical capacity. Then the first conductor will discharge the current to the second conductor. This ability to store and then release a current is the principle behind the capacitor, a boosting device used with an electric motor to help it start.

A similar effect is produced when alternating current is run through one of two adjacent but unconnected conductive materials. The current passing through the first conductor creates, or induces, current in the second conductor. This effect, induction, powers the most common and efficient type of motor found in household appliances.

One or more of these effects operate every electrical component in an appliance, and each component is linked in an electric circuit. When one component malfunctions, the effects are likely to extend to the performance of others in the circuit. In diagnosing the cause of an electrical failure, it is therefore necessary to know how the electricity is supposed to move through the circuit (page 9).

Two tools for troubleshooting problems in the circuitry are a continuity tester and a multitester, both battery-powered. A continuity tester drives a small amount of current into one end of a circuit and indicates—usually by lighting a small bulb—whether the current emerges at the opposite end. Since appliances depend on complete circuits to perform their tasks, this test allows you to check out an entire electric system to see if the malfunction is indeed an electrical problem. A multitester—also called a volt-ohm meter—allows you not only to test individual components for continuity, but also to measure the specific amount of voltage or resistance present at the component.

Whenever you disconnect a component for such a test, carefully mark its wire connections with a wax pencil or with a taped label so that there will be no question later about where to reconnect the wires. Before getting involved in such disassembly, however, look for more obvious solutions. Very often an appliance's problem can be traced to its plug and electric cord; you can check these for continuity without taking the rest of the appliance apart. Equally fundamental is a blown fuse or a tripped circuit breaker at the house service panel.

A less obvious source of trouble, but one that can also be spotted without taking the appliance apart, is a temporary drop in voltage from the power company—during the summer, for example, when the demand for electricity is high. When the voltage drops more than 10 per cent below normal, an induction-type motor will draw more current in an effort to maintain power; the excess current may overheat the motor and burn it out.

The test for the amount of voltage being supplied is made at the outlet where the appliance is plugged in. In fact, this test is a standard trouble shooting procedure. Remember, however, that even though the outlet is considered to supply 120 or 240 volts, the actual amount of voltage may vary from 108 to 135 volts, or from 208 to 260 volts, depending on the power company. The motors in appliances, which are powered by 120-volt circuits, and the heating elements in large appliances such as ranges and dryers, which require 240-volt circuits, are made to work efficiently despite these variations from the nominal voltage.

Tracking a Current through Its Circuit

The wiring in an appliance carries current to each electrical component, supplying it with power either to do work or to make decisions by turning switches on and off. The path of the current is a loop, or circuit, that links the components, starting and ending at the power source.

Tracking the current's path is an important technique in appliance repair. Professionals decipher the organization of a wiring system by referring to a symbolic drawing called the schematic diagram. On large appliances, this diagram is likely to be glued to a panel cover, but for any appliance it can always be obtained from the manufacturer. By following a wiring diagram, you can systematically test the components in sequence and thus locate the point at which a circuit has broken down.

Despite their dissimilar appearances, both the pictorial representation of the heater *(top right)* and its schematic diagram *(bottom right)* contain basic elements found in a typical electrical circuit: the entrance and exit points of the current and the electrical components it services. In general usage, a zigzag line represents a resistor or a heating element; an oval or circle respresents a large device such as a motor, and the shapes within the oval or circle represent the motor's components; a broken line with an arrowhead angled to one side of the circuit indicates the presence of a switch.

The first element to look for on any wiring diagram is the source of electrical power. Whether it comes from a wall outlet or a battery, the power enters an appliance and each component at terminals—thin metal plates that touch the source of their electrical current. On a wiring diagram a terminal is represented by a small dot or circle.

The current is carried between the terminals by wires, represented on the diagram by lines. The lines turn at right angles at the corners of the circuit, and very often will split off in more than one direction, to indicate current carried to separate circuits within the main circuit. In the actual appliance, these various circuits create a maze of wires.

To help identify the circuits, the wires often are color-coded, and the colors are then labeled in abbreviated form on the wiring diagram.

One important wire found in all appliances is a black wire leading to the first component and marked L, for "line," in the wiring diagram. This is a hot wire—the incoming power line, which supplies the current. Another wire is colored white and labeled N, for "neutral." This wire completes the circuit by carrying current from the last component back to the power source. The neutral terminal often is indicated not with the usual dot or circle, but with stacked horizontal lines in the shape of an arrow. The neutral wire is sometimes called the power ground, because it is connected to a power line that carries the current directly into the earth.

Within the circuit, a ground wire can also serve a different purpose. If a defective component leaks current to the metal body of the appliance, it poses the risk of a dangerous shock. To guard against this hazard, a ground wire, usually colored green, is attached to the body of the appliance and connected to a separate ground terminal. The appliance has a three-prong plug; the third prong is connected to the third wire in the power cord, which serves to carry the leaking current from this safety terminal directly to a pipe that is buried in the earth. Hence the circuit is quite literally grounded.

The last two elements found in a typical circuit are the controls that start and stop the flow of electricity and the components that actually perform the work. In the diagram a switch is the means of control; it acts like a drawbridge in the circuit. When it is down, current flows across to the working components, in this case a heating element and a motor. The circuit is then said to be closed, or continuous. When the switch is open, the current cannot cross and the circuit is said to be open, or not continuous.

Wiring diagrams. Two types of diagrams, pictorial *(top)* and schematic *(bottom)*, map the wiring and identify the components in an appliance—in this example, a heater that is equipped with a blower fan *(page 123)*.

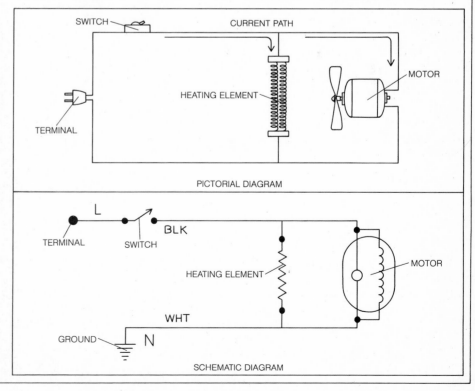

PICTORIAL DIAGRAM

SCHEMATIC DIAGRAM

A Simple Tool to Test the Flow of Current

Checking the current in an electric cord. Unplug the cord, detach it from its terminals on the appliance, and fasten the clip of a continuity tester to one of the exposed wires at the end of the cord. Touch the tip of the tester's probe in turn to each of the prongs on the plug. If there is continuity in the cord, the bulb on the tester should light up against one prong but not the other. If the bulb lights up on both prongs, there is a short circuit in either the plug or the cord. Check the other wire in the cord by moving the clip and repeating this procedure.

To check the cord for internal shorts, clip the tester to one wire and touch the probe to the prong that does not light the bulb. Twist and bend the cord along its length. If the bulb lights, replace the cord. If the bulb does not light, clip the lead to the other wire and repeat the test.

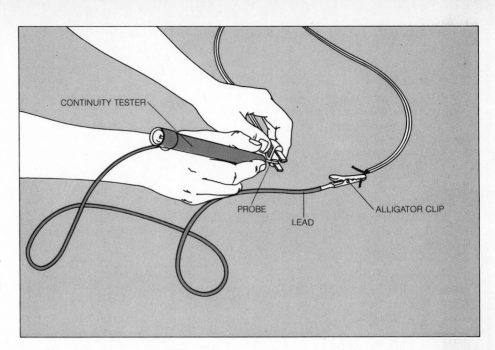

A Meter That Performs Multiple Electrical Tests

Anatomy of a multitester. A multitester will measure the exact amount of voltage or resistance in an electric circuit, and by means of the ohms scale, it can also be employed to check continuity.

The selector switch on this typical multitester is divided into four zones to test ohms, DC volts, AC volts or DC amps. To use the tester, set the selector switch for the test desired and read the appropriate scale on the meter.

To connect the multitester to a circuit or component, turn off the power to the appliance and place the two metal probes on the terminals of the circuit or component. Then plug the leads to these probes into jacks on the multitester— the red lead into the jack marked with a plus sign, the black lead into the jack with a minus sign. As a safety precaution, when making voltage tests with the appliance power turned on, use a set of leads with insulated alligator clips instead of the metal probes *(inset),* to protect yourself against shocks *(box).*

Before using the multitester to check resistance or continuity, adjust the calibration on the meter to register 0 on the ohms scale; set the selector switch at RX1, touch the probes together and turn the small knob marked OHMS ADJUST until the needle stands at 0 on the ohms scale.

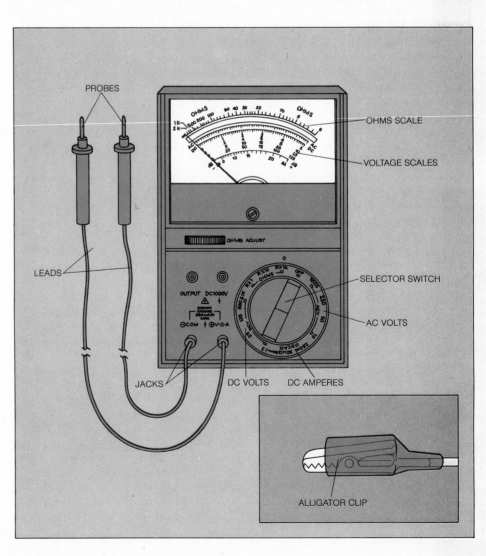

Reading the multitester scale. To measure either resistance or continuity, make sure the power is off, turn the selector switch to an ohms setting and read the uppermost scale. For resistance readings up to 500 ohms, set the selector switch at RX1 (resistance times 1) and read the amount directly off the meter. For resistance readings up to 5,000 ohms, set the selector switch at RX10 and multiply the reading on the meter by 10. For resistance readings greater than 5,000, set the selector switch at RX1K (resistance times 1 kilo ohms, or 1,000 ohms) and multiply the meter reading by 1,000.

For a continuity test, set the switch at RX1, turn off the power and touch the probes to the circuit terminals. If the needle swings to the right, the circuit has continuity, if the needle stays on the infinity reading, the circuit is open, i.e., there is maximum resistance to the current.

For a voltage test, turn the selector switch to the AC or DC voltage setting just above the voltage you expect from the circuit. Then, with the power on, take the reading from the appropriate voltage scale—AC or DC. For example, appliances that are plugged into a standard wall outlet with 120 or 240 volts would be tested at the 250-volt AC (250 ACV) setting and be read from the AC scale. There are four bands of numbers under these voltage scales. If the selector switch is set at 5, 25 or 125 on the DC voltage scale or at 10 on the AC scale, use the band ending in that number for your reading. If the selector switch is set at 50, 250 or 1000 on the AC scale, or at 500 or 1K on the DC scale, divide the setting number by either 10 or 100 and use the band that ends with the resulting figure. For example, if you set the selector switch at 250 volts AC, divide 250 by 10 and use the band ending with 25 for your reading. In such instances you must multiply the reading by either 10 or 100, whichever number you divided by.

For greater accuracy, close one eye and move your head until the needle and its mirror reflection are perfectly in line. Then note the needle's position in relation to the numbers.

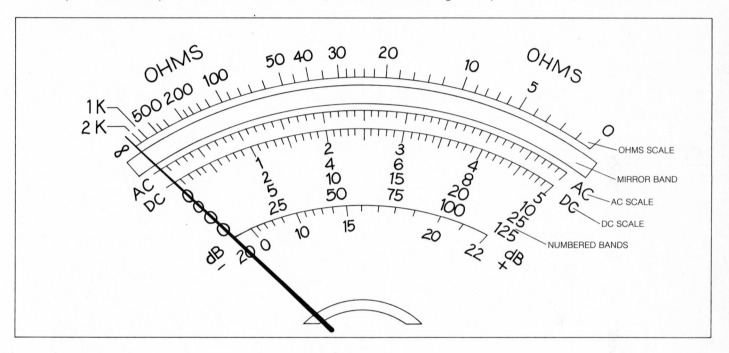

A Checklist for Working Safely with Electricity

A standard 120-volt wall outlet carries up to 30 amperes of current (15 amperes in Canada)—more than 100 times the amount it would take to stop a person's breathing and immobilize the heart. But repairing an electric appliance, despite this danger, can be a safe operation if you routinely take some precautions.

First of all, disconnect the appliance each time you make a repair or an electrical test. If the appliance is wired directly to the house electric system, remove the fuse or flip off the circuit breaker at the main service panel. Mark the fuse or breaker with tape to warn other members of the household that they should not reconnect the power.

When you must perform a test with the power on, as in testing a component for voltage, protect yourself from contact with the live terminal by routinely following a four-step procedure. Turn off the power. Connect the testing probes to the component's terminals with alligator clips—special connectors that look like small metal clothespins covered with insulating plastic shields. Then restore the power and observe the test results visually. Turn off the power again before disconnecting the clips.

In rare instances when it is not feasible to use alligator clips, use probes instead. Since you must hand-hold the probes against the live terminals, hold the probes by their long, insulated handles; take very great care not to let your fingers touch the probes' metal tips or the live terminals. And when testing a component that stores a charge, such as a capacitor, be sure to discharge it (page 19) before touching its terminals.

Finally, when you replace a defective part, make sure that the new part matches the old one identically and that it is of top quality. Mismatched or carelessly made components may cause the appliance to malfunction or may create a fire or shock hazard.

Using a Multitester to Discover Short Circuits

Testing for a current leak. With the appliance unplugged, set the multitester's selector switch to RX1K on the ohms scale, and touch one probe to a prong on the appliance plug; touch the other probe to the metal body of the appliance. The needle should not move; even a slight jump to the right indicates a current leak from the circuit to the appliance body great enough to cause a shock. Repeat the test on the other prong.

If your appliance has a three-prong plug *(inset),* touch one probe to the cylindrical ground prong and the other probe to the body of the appliance. The needle should show 0 ohms; if it does not, the appliance is not properly grounded. Check for a loose green wire inside the wall of the appliance and reconnect it to its terminal.

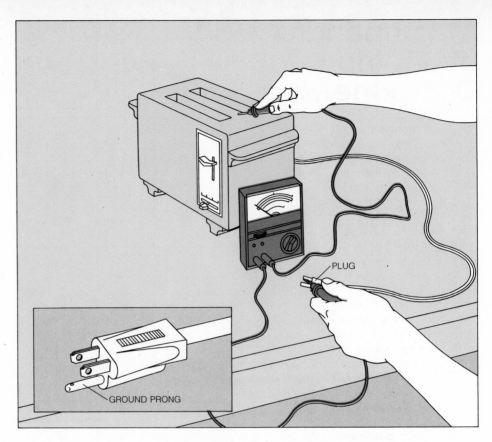

PLUG

GROUND PRONG

Checking the Incoming Power at a Wall Outlet

Testing the voltage at a wall outlet. With the power turned on and the multitester set for 250 volts AC, hold the probes by their insulated handles and insert them in the outlet slots. Be extremely careful not to touch the metal part of the probes. The multitester should register within 10 per cent of the minimum voltage specified by the manufacturer of the appliance.

To test the functioning of the round opening that is found on some outlets, designed to accept the ground prong on a three-prong plug, keep the same setting on the multitester. Insert one probe in the round opening and the other in the smaller of the two oblong openings—the hot wire of the receptacle. The multitester reading ought to show full voltage.

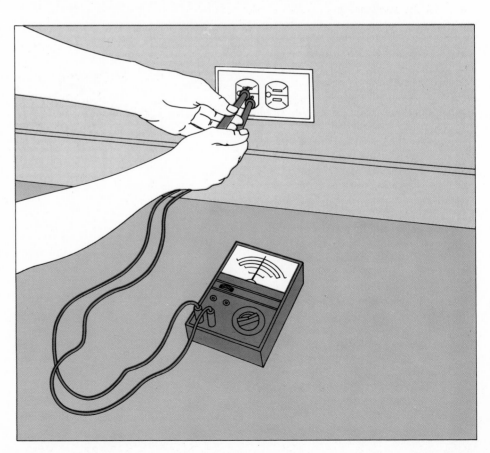

A Compendium of Electrical Components

The tangle of wires and other electrical parts that confronts anyone who opens an appliance may seem bewildering at first glance. But with the help of this glossary, even a novice should quickly learn to recognize the components and diagnose their malfunctions.

In general, electrical parts fall into two groups—those that perform tasks and those that make decisions. The "workers" include heating elements, which convert electrical energy into heat; solenoids, which use electromagnetism to move parts; and motors, which develop electromagnetism to spin a shaft.

The decision-making parts include the many switches that govern the flow of current. These can be activated in a number of ways—manually, mechanically, by heat, by pressure, or by magnetism.

The first step in diagnosing an electrical malfunction is to interpret the sensory clues that the appliance provides. A non-heating wire that is hot to the touch, a switch terminal that is charred, a burning odor, a screeching, chattering motor all are certain signs of trouble. Disconnect the appliance from its power source at once and make an orderly exploration with a continuity tester or a mulititester before you use the machine again.

Once you have located the defective part, replace it with a new one made for exactly the same wattage, voltage or amperage. These ratings are usually stamped on the body of the component. If you have any doubts, take along the old part when you go to buy its replacement.

Replacing electrical components is normally a straightforward job. Most wires can be coupled with the fasteners discussed on page 14. If you choose to solder the connections—a procedure still favored by many professionals—you will need a 25- to 50-watt soldering iron, a spool of rosin-core 60-40 solder, and a long-nosed soldering clamp to keep your hands free for the job.

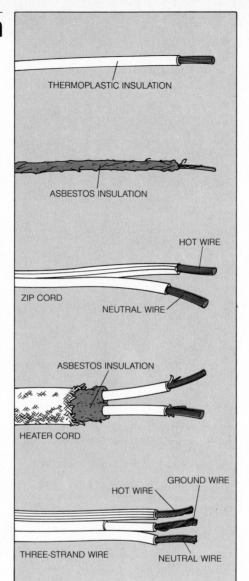

THERMOPLASTIC INSULATION

ASBESTOS INSULATION

HOT WIRE

ZIP CORD

NEUTRAL WIRE

ASBESTOS INSULATION

HEATER CORD

GROUND WIRE

HOT WIRE

THREE-STRAND WIRE

NEUTRAL WIRE

Wires Tailored to the Tasks

Wires and power cords. The wires used in appliances come in a range of diameters—referred to as gauges—numbered from 10 to 20 in order of decreasing thickness. They almost always consist of thin copper filaments combined into a single strand and insulated with a sheathing of thermoplastic or heat-resistant vinyl. The combined filaments make the wire flexible and tough. In high-heat applications, such as the connections to a heating element, the sheathing may be asbestos and the copper wire may be nickel-plated to prevent corrosion and to resist melting.

For internal connections in most appliances, single small-gauge wires are used. Such wires come in a variety of colors, sometimes striped, to make them easier to trace along a circuit. To bring power into appliances, wires are combined into three kinds of power cords. For light-duty applications lamp cord, or zip cord, is used; this is a double strand of No. 18 or No. 16 wire. On newer zip cords the insulation of one line may be ridged or textured to identify the hot wire carrying current to the appliance. Heater cord, used to carry power to heating appliances, is a double-strand cord insulated with asbestos or heavy rubber. The third type of cord, used on appliances that are individually grounded for safety—such as electric clothes dryers and ovens—is a heavy-duty three-strand cord of No. 12 to No. 10 wire. The hot wire is ridged or black, the neutral is white; the green wire is connected to the machine's ground terminal.

Any single-strand wire can be tested for continuity with a continuity tester connected to the two ends of the wire. Multiple-strand cords are tested as on page 10. Visual signs of trouble are burns or broken insulation at the ends of a wire or cord. Or you may be able to smell the burning insulation of a defective wire.

Quick Connections for Sections of Wire

Splicing wires. Three common fasteners used to splice wire ends are the crimp connector, the wire cap and the locking-terminal connector. A wire cap is a cone-shaped insulating cap of hard plastic with a spiral of copper or molded threads inside; it is used to make connections that may need to be disconnected. To make a splice with a wire cap, twist the stripped ends of the wires together, then screw the cap onto the wire ends. To undo the splice, twist the cap off. A special type of wire cap, made of soft plastic, cannot be removed; it is sometimes used in appliances that are subjected to vibration.

A crimp connector is an insulated metal tube that is crushed around the ends of two wires to fasten them together permanently. It comes in three color-coded sizes: red for No. 20 to No. 18 wires, blue for No. 16 to No. 14, yellow for No. 12 to No. 10. To use a crimp connector, strip ½ inch of insulation from the end of each wire with the wire-stripping cutters of an electrician's multipurpose tool *(inset)*. Insert one wire into each end of the connector and pinch the tube near each end, using the tool's crimping jaws.

Locking-terminal connectors are common in appliances with components whose terminals are short lengths of wire, called leads, built into the component. The connectors consist of two clips—a male plate and a female receptacle. The male functions as a terminal and is attached to the lead from the component. The joined clips are covered by an insulating sleeve. To disconnect them, reach inside the sleeve with long-nose pliers to grasp the stem of the male clip, then pull off the female clip with your other hand.

Joining Wire to a Terminal

Soldering a connection. To fasten a wire to a prong-type plate terminal, clamp the wire in place, then melt rosin-core solder over the wire end, after stripping off ½ inch of insulation and twisting the wire filaments tight. Heat the wire for several seconds with the soldering iron; then touch the solder to the wire, allowing it to melt into the filaments, a process called tinning. Then clamp the wire against the terminal and heat it again; fasten it securely with more solder.

Alternatively, you can use a detachable connector *(inset)* that can be crimped to the wire end. These connectors have color-coded insulation to show what gauge wires they fit; the heads are shaped for different types of terminals. Most common is the spade connector *(below)*; it slides into a plate terminal. The round and U-shaped clips attach to screw-type terminals.

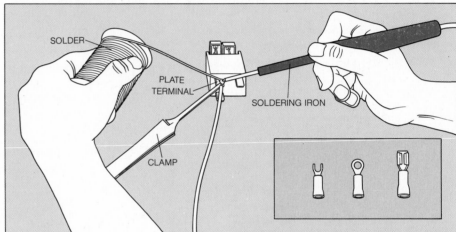

SOLDER
PLATE TERMINAL
SOLDERING IRON
CLAMP

Clustered connectors. Both the terminal block and the quick-disconnect plug are designed to organize complex systems of wires and terminals. A terminal block is a panel of insulating material—plastic in this example—with rows of plate- and screw-type terminals. On some appliances the terminal block is the point where electricity enters the machine, so voltage checks are often made on the terminals that connect the power cord to this block.

Quick-disconnect plugs contain as many as 12 cylindrical prongs and receptacles to connect up to 24 wires. The male and female parts of the plug are grooved on one side so that they fit together only in the proper direction. This type of plug is used to organize the wiring of a complicated component, such as a timer.

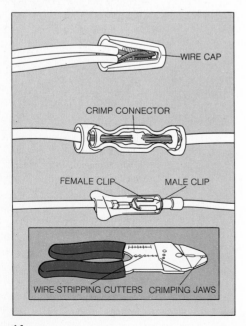

WIRE CAP
CRIMP CONNECTOR
FEMALE CLIP
MALE CLIP
WIRE-STRIPPING CUTTERS   CRIMPING JAWS

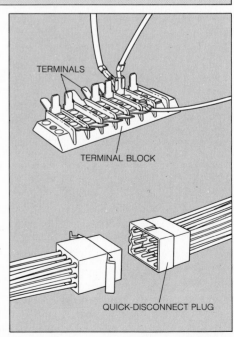

TERMINALS
TERMINAL BLOCK
QUICK-DISCONNECT PLUG

Reluctant Conductors That Radiate Heat

Heating elements. Most heating elements are made of nichrome, an alloy of nickel and chromium, which offers a slight amount of resistance to the flow of current, thus causing the element to heat. Heating elements fall into two groups—those made of bare wires and those covered with a protective sheath. The uncovered elements consist either of thin metal strips called ribbons or of wire coils. The ribbons or coils are held in place by being wrapped around a sheet of mica or threaded through ceramic insulators.

Sheathed heating elements are covered with ceramic-lined steel, glass or fiberglass. They are usually either plugged into receptacles in the appliance or connected with asbestos-insulated wires. Sometimes they are welded in place.

Visual signs of a defective element are broken wires or corroded sheathing. Usually, either the element is working or it is not, and it needs only to be tested for continuity. Unplug the appliance and disconnect the element, set the mul-

titester at RX1K, and touch the probes to the heating-element terminals. The needle will swing to the right and stop near 0 ohms if the element has continuity. To test resistance, disconnect the element, set the multitester at RX1, and connect the probes to the element's terminals. The resistance reading of a working element will range from a few ohms for a thick element to several thousand ohms for a thin one. If the element must show a specific amount of resistance, the owner's manual will say so.

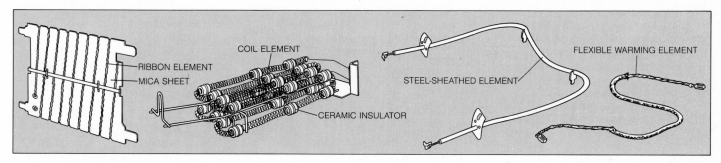

RIBBON ELEMENT
MICA SHEET
COIL ELEMENT
CERAMIC INSULATOR
STEEL-SHEATHED ELEMENT
FLEXIBLE WARMING ELEMENT

Switches That Govern the Current's Flow

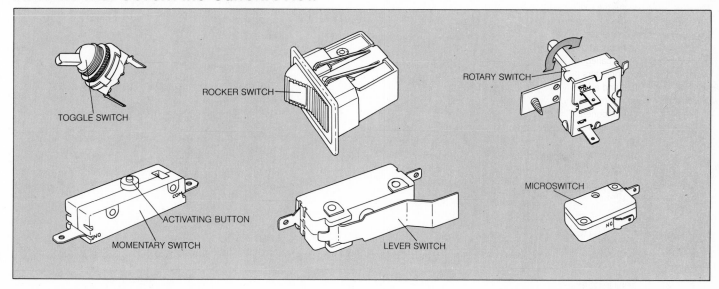

TOGGLE SWITCH
ROCKER SWITCH
ROTARY SWITCH
MOMENTARY SWITCH
ACTIVATING BUTTON
LEVER SWITCH
MICROSWITCH

Manual and mechanical switches. All of these switches are activated by hand or by a moving part inside the appliance to make or break contact between two legs of an electric circuit. The toggle, rocker and rotary switches move electrical contacts together to start or apart to stop the flow of current through their terminals. A momentary switch also moves contacts, but it returns automatically to its set position once its activating button is released. If such a switch is normally open (off), it has a terminal labeled NO, for "normally open"; a switch that is normally closed (on) will have a terminal labeled NC, for "normally closed." Some momentary switches have an added lever that enables

them to be mechanically activated by a closing door or a turning cam. A very small momentary switch, called a microswitch, is used where space is limited.

Some switches control more than one circuit; they have extra terminals and contacts. This type of switch has one common terminal, labeled COM, that works with each of the other terminals—called poles—at various switch settings. The switch settings are called throws. Hence the rotary switch in the drawing, for example, is a double-pole, triple-throw switch: It has one common terminal with two poles and can be set in three positions. Switches are tested for continuity

(page 16), but you will not be able to determine when the terminals of a multithrow switch should show continuity and when they should not, without a special wiring diagram for that particular switch. However, before you test any switch for continuity, unplug the appliance and examine the switch for signs of wear. Look for burn marks near the terminals; these indicate a short circuit. If you can open the casing of the switch, check the contacts for corrosion or pitting. Use emery cloth to smooth the surface of the contacts if they are rough. And make certain that there are no broken or bent parts around the contacts. Then disconnect the leads from the switch terminals for testing.

Testing a single-throw switch. After removing a switch from an appliance, test it for continuity with a multitester *(page 11)* set at RX1. Touch the probes to the switch terminals and note the resistance reading. Then move the activating button and check the reading again. The switch should register continuity in only one position. If it shows continuity in both positions, it is defective. A momentary switch with a terminal labeled NO should show continuity only when you are depressing its activating button. A switch with a terminal labeled NC should show continuity only when the button is released.

Instead of plate terminals, some switches have self-locking terminals *(inset)*—openings into which you push the end of a stripped wire, stiffened by being tinned with solder *(page 14)*. To test the terminals of a self-locking switch, unplug the machine and release the wires by inserting a straightened paper clip into each of the terminal holes, then pulling out clip and wire. For the test, put a paper clip into each hole and touch the multitester probes to the paper clips.

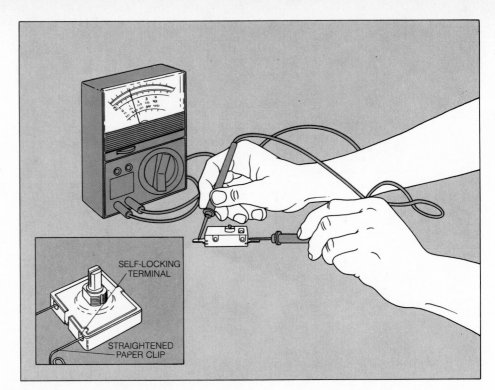

SELF-LOCKING
TERMINAL

STRAIGHTENED
PAPER CLIP

Thermostats: Temperature-Controlled Switches

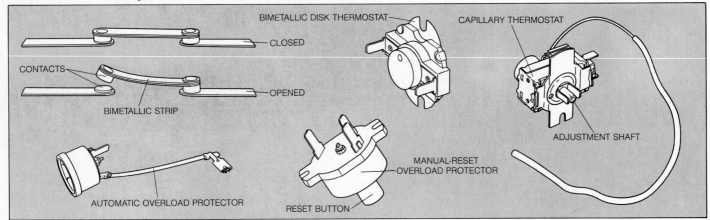

CLOSED

CONTACTS

OPENED

BIMETALLIC STRIP

BIMETALLIC DISK THERMOSTAT

CAPILLARY THERMOSTAT

ADJUSTMENT SHAFT

MANUAL-RESET
OVERLOAD PROTECTOR

AUTOMATIC OVERLOAD PROTECTOR

RESET BUTTON

An assortment of thermostats. All thermostats operate on the principle that most substances expand when heated. The simplest thermostat is a strip of metal with an electrical contact at one end. The metal strip flexes when heated, thus making or breaking the continuity of a circuit. The strip is made of bonded sheets of two metals that expand at differing rates when heated, causing the strip to curve. When the spacing between the contacts is adjusted or the thickness of the metals is varied, this bimetallic thermostat can be made to activate a circuit at a specific temperature. A disk thermostat uses a bimetallic disk instead of a strip. At a set temperature, the disk flexes, moving a plunger with an electrical contact and either making or breaking electrical contact. Disk thermostats are used as overload protectors, which

monitor the temperature of a motor and open the circuit if the motor overheats. As the motor cools, the disk pops back in most protectors, automatically closing the circuit and allowing the motor to restart. Some overload protectors have a manual reset button that must be pushed in to restart power to the circuit.

A second type of thermostat is called a capillary, or hydraulic, thermostat. It has a long sensing tube filled with gas, mercury or oil at one end and a spring-loaded flexible metal bellows at the other end. The gas or liquid expands when it is heated, working its way up the tube and compressing the bellows, which then close electrical contacts. A capillary thermostat has an adjustment shaft that controls the spacing of the thermostat's electrical contacts and thus determines the distance the bellows must move to bring the contacts together.

Before testing a thermostat, inspect its contacts if they are exposed. Corrosion can build up to the point where the contacts are fused together, or dust and debris such as bread crumbs or lint can accumulate to keep the contacts apart. Like other switches, a thermostat can be tested for continuity with a multitester or a continuity tester. Depending on its use, however, the thermostat may or may not have continuity at room temperature. To test a thermostat that is activated only at a high temperature, for example, place it in a heated oven with a cooking thermometer. Allow the thermometer to reach the temperature specified in the owner's manual, then test the thermostat.

Relays: Magnetically Controlled Switches

Magnets created by electricity. A relay is an electromagnet that, when activated, attracts an armature otherwise held open by the tension of a spring. This magnetic pull instantly closes the contacts to one or more circuits *(below, left)* or depresses an activating button *(below, right)*. The magnet consists of tightly bundled windings of thin wire, coiled around an iron core to concentrate the magnetism that develops when a current flows through the wire. The action

of a relay is faster and more precise than that of a mechanically activated switch and is used to control circuits by electrical impulse.

If you suspect that a relay is malfunctioning, first inspect its contacts for corrosion or grime, and clean them if necessary. Then test the windings for continuity, using a multitester set at RX1K with its probes on the terminals that lead to the coil. The needle will swing toward 0

ohms if the relay has continuity. Because the coil's wire is so thin, it will probably register some resistance; the thinner the wire, the greater the resistance will be. On some appliances you may need to test a relay against a range of resistance values. In such a case, test with the multitester set at RX1. Too low a reading will indicate a short circuit in the windings; too high a reading means that part of the coil is broken or melted. In either case, replace the relay.

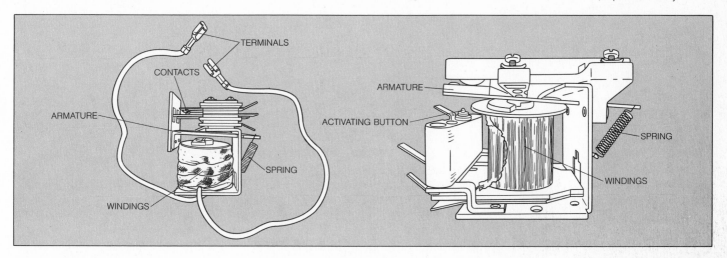

Solenoids: Electromagnets That Perform Varied Tasks

Actions induced by current. Like a relay, the most common type of solenoid consists of tightly coiled wire windings around an iron core. But instead of being stationary, the core of the solenoid is a shaft that usually is held outside of the windings by a spring, and when the solenoid is energized the shaft is instantly pulled into the coil by magnetism. The solenoid shaft performs a task as it moves. This kind of solenoid is used, for example, as a door latch or as a water valve. Another type does not have a moving shaft; instead, the energized electromagnet pulls on an armature—such as a pop-up toaster's catch release—to move a mechanical part.

You can test a solenoid for continuity or resistance across its windings terminal as you would test a relay *(above)*. Although a solenoid has no contacts to become corroded and prevent the device from operating, its shaft will sometimes stick inside the sleeve. It can be worked free with long-nose pliers.

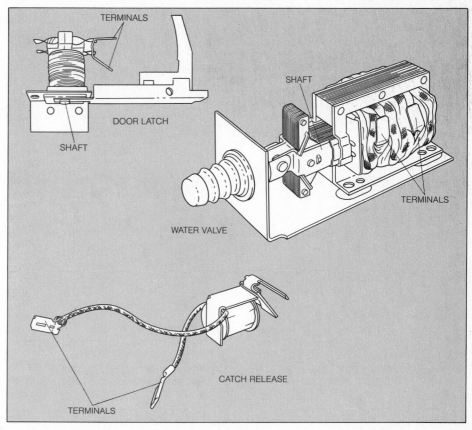

Motors: Electromagnets That Produce Motion

Electric appliance motors vary greatly in size and appearance, ranging from the 8-inch motor in a clothes washer to the inch-wide motor of a timer. But their inner workings are similar: Two electromagnets—one a movable magnet called the rotor or armature, one a stationary magnet called the stator or field—interact to spin a shaft.

The motor most often found in an appliance is the all-purpose universal motor, so called because it operates on either alternating or direct current—AC or DC. Because it is so versatile, the universal motor is also the most mechanically intricate and thus is vulnerable to minor breakdowns. Consequently, universal motors are made to be quickly disassembled for maintainance, testing and repair, and most of their parts are replaceable.

The universal motor is used where a small, fast, medium-strength motor is needed—in a hand mixer or a vacuum cleaner, for example. To vary its speed, a universal motor is connected to a multiple-pole switch *(page 49)*, which taps selected sections of the motor's windings, sending current only to certain parts of the electromagnet and thus varying the strength of the magnetism produced.

A second type of electric motor relies on induction as its operating principle *(page 8)*; this type includes both the most powerful and the smallest of the motors commonly found in appliances—the split-phase motor and the shaded-pole

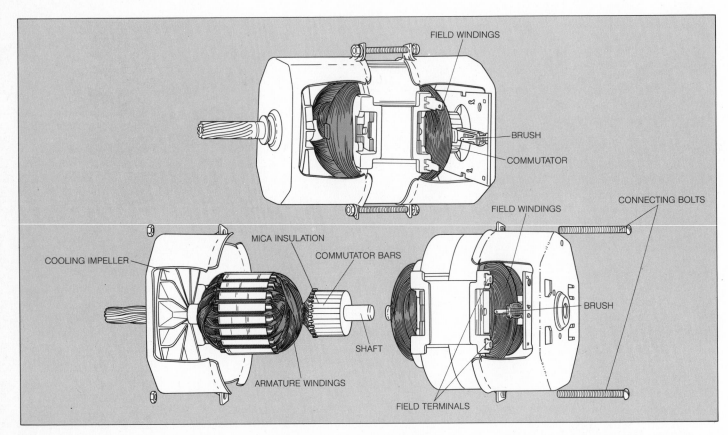

Anatomy of a universal motor. Exposed copper windings and two spring-held brushes immediately identify a universal motor. The brushes, actually small bars of carbon, press against opposite sides of the commutator, a movable cylinder of brass bars insulated from each other by strips of mica. If the connecting bolts are removed, the motor can be separated into two sections. The outer section consists of a bundle of copper windings with a hollow core; this is the stationary field, or stator, of the motor. To it are attached the two brushes. The inner section, a second bundle of windings, is the rotating armature; it contains the motor shaft, a cooling impeller and the commutator. The armature windings are magnetized by current flowing through the brushes to the commutator; the field windings are magnetized by current flowing directly from the power source. The interaction of the two magnetized groups of windings makes the motor shaft spin.

The most common problem in a universal motor is worn brushes, which fail to deliver current to the armature. When a brush has worn to such a point that it is shorter than it is wide, it should be replaced *(page 103)*. Also, the brass bars in the commutator may become pitted or corroded. A light sanding with fine-grit sandpaper will correct this problem.

To test the condition of the field windings, set a multitester at RX1K and touch the probes to the field terminals. If the field windings are good, the multitester will read near 0 ohms; if they are defective, the multitester will register near infinity ohms. To test the connection between the armature windings and the commutator bars, touch the probes to pairs of adjacent bars, working around the entire cylinder. A good connection will show as 0 ohms; an infinity reading indicates a broken connection. Finally, check for a short circuit between the shaft and the armature windings: Touch one probe to the shaft and the other to one of the commutator bars; the meter should show no continuity.

motor. Induction motors run on alternating current. Consequently, they are mechanically simple and virtually indestructible; there is little you can do either to test or to repair the motor itself, though you can often test and replace certain of the starting components.

The split-phase motor is found in clothes washers, dryers, and the compressors of refrigerators and air conditioners. Split-phase motors are so named because they incorporate a separate electromagnet; it contains the start windings, which provide starting torque—an initial twist that turns the motor over.

This extra push is usually augmented by a capacitor—a battery-like device that stores electricity, then releases it in a surge to start the motor. Capacitors can be tested and replaced. They are rated in microfarads (MFD); a new one should match or exceed the original rating.

After a split-phase motor has reached 80 per cent of its full speed, the start windings—and their capacitor—must be disengaged; otherwise the motor will run less efficiently. Two kinds of switches are used. One is a centrifugal switch, activated by the spinning of the motor shaft; the other is a relay that senses the drop in

the amount of current being drawn as the motor reaches full speed.

Speed, in a split-phase motor, is also governed by a multipole switch; but the switch activates sets of paired windings, one set at a time.

The shaded-pole motor, a much smaller induction motor, is a simple, dependable motor that needs no special starting mechanisms. It is adequate only for light duty, such as powering small fans, and is usually a one-speed device. A shaded-pole motor is easy to test for continuity or resistance in its coils and is inexpensive to replace.

A split-phase induction motor. The components of a split-phase motor are almost entirely enclosed in its housing. In many cases, an oblong dome fastened to the side of the barrel housing encases the capacitor. Located on the end of the housing opposite the motor shaft are at least three, and often as many as seven, terminals for the sets of windings within the motor.

Disassembled, this motor resembles a universal motor. But the armature—here called the rotor—consists only of an iron cylinder and is not connected to the source of electricity. Instead, current is induced in the rotor by the current in the field windings. In addition, there is a second layer of heavier-gauge windings surrounding the field windings that serves as the start windings for the motor.

The centrifugal switch that on some motors disconnects the start windings consists of two parts. One part is a weighted actuator connected to the motor shaft in front of the rotor. When the motor is off or is just starting, the actuator presses against the other part of the switch—a pair of contact arms fastened to the rear wall of the motor housing; the actual contacts are located in the back of the arms. As the rotor starts to spin, centrifugal force swings the weights of the actuator outward, releasing the contact arms and disconnecting the start-windings circuit. If the switch contacts become corroded, clean them with an emery cloth. In some cases the centrifugal switch is enclosed in a box outside the motor housing; test it as shown on page 87. An internal switch must be tested by someone familiar with wiring diagrams. On some split-phase motors, a relay (inset) rather than a centrifugal switch disconnects the start windings. Test the relay for continuity (page 17). To test a start capacitor, remove its housing and discharge the capacitor of stored current by touching the shaft of an insulated screwdriver across its two terminals. Then set a multitester at RX10, and connect it to the capacitor terminals; the meter should momentarily register 0 ohms and then read infinity resistance.

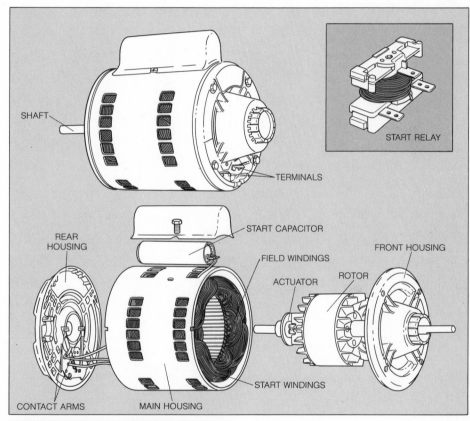

SHAFT

START RELAY

TERMINALS

REAR HOUSING

START CAPACITOR

FIELD WINDINGS

FRONT HOUSING

ACTUATOR

ROTOR

START WINDINGS

CONTACT ARMS

MAIN HOUSING

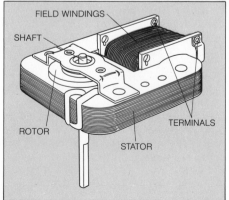

FIELD WINDINGS

SHAFT

ROTOR

TERMINALS

STATOR

A shaded-pole motor. Although shaded-pole motors take a number of shapes, they are usually recognizable by the presence of two pairs of diagonally placed heavy copper wires, called shades, which loop over a block of laminated-iron plates, called a stator. The shades provide the torque needed to start the motor. The stator is indented on one side for the field windings and has a hole to accommodate the rotor and shaft.

Test the field windings of a shaded-pole motor for continuity or resistance just as you would test a relay or a solenoid (page 17). For both tests, touch the multitester's two probes to the terminals, one on each side of the field windings.

Diagnosing What Goes On inside an Appliance

When an appliance stops doing what it is supposed to do and its familiar noises give way to new sounds or peculiar vibrations, chances are that some moving part needs replacement or repair. Interpreting these distress signals is an important part of fixing appliances. But to diagnose the signals correctly you will need to know the functions of the various moving parts. You may also need to understand the basic mechanical principles involved in translating the rotation of a motor shaft into some usable form of working power.

Begin your diagnosis by listening to the sounds the broken appliance makes. A loose bearing in a motor or pump will rattle rhythmically. Unlubricated bearings will produce a high-pitched scream. If water is seeping into the pump of a clothes washer or dishwasher, dampening its bearings, the pump will make a roaring, rumbling sound. A broken drive belt will leave an electric motor humming—and turning—fruitlessly, while all other moving parts remain at a standstill. At times you may have to call upon your other senses: A loose drive belt will produce the bitter smell of burning rubber.

Bearings can be a source of trouble in an appliance motor. There are several types of bearings, but all of them collar the motor shaft, allowing it to spin smoothly while holding the shaft in alignment. Subject to wear from the friction between bearing and shaft, they need constant lubrication.

The bearings in some machines must be lubricated at regular intervals with a lightweight non-detergent oil, such as sewing machine oil. Lubrication can be a temporary remedy for worn bearings that must eventually be replaced, before they seize or score the motor shaft. And some ball-bearing race assemblies *(page 21)* are fully encased and cannot be lubricated; when flawed, they must be replaced.

Gears, another source of trouble, pass along a motor's power, change the direction of rotation between motor shaft and drive shaft, or increase the torque (turning force) produced by the motor shaft. On some appliances a reduction gear *(page 22)* is responsible for increased torque; it transfers the force of a rapidly revolving motor shaft to a drive shaft that moves more slowly but has greater power. Gears, like bearings, need lubrication. Metal gears are lubricated with a general-purpose grease, which clings to the gear teeth better than oil does. If the gears are plastic, either grease or a silicone spray can be used.

Drive belts and pulleys also pass along the driving power of a motor or increase the motor's torque. On some large appliances, the drive belt can also serve as a clutch, thus protecting the motor—if the working parts jam, the moving pulley will slip under the belt, so that the motor is not placed under too much stress. When this kind of stress is unlikely to occur and the work load is heavy, a chain-and-sprocket assembly sometimes replaces the drive belt and pulleys.

To forestall problems with a drive belt, check its adjustment. There should be about ½ inch of play in the belt of a clothes washer, less on a smaller appliance. The owner's manual usually specifies the precise adjustment. Also inspect the belt for abrasions, deep cuts, burn spots or excessive stretching—all signs that the belt needs to be replaced. But never improvise. Replace the belt only with one designed for the appliance. On a chain-and-sprocket assembly, lubricate the chain with lightweight oil.

When you disassemble an appliance, inspect its rubber seals and gaskets. These are another source of trouble; they tend to become badly compressed or cracked with age. Silicone spray is sometimes useful in adding moisture resistance to these parts, but usually a worn seal or gasket should be replaced.

Last but not least, the springs in an appliance will squeak if they are not lubricated occasionally with oil or a silicone spray. Because tension springs stretch and compression springs are compressed with years of use, they may have to be replaced.

The Bearings That Make a Motor Shaft Run Smoothly

A sleeve bearing. This bearing has a deep, adjustable collar that holds a motor shaft in alignment even under the lateral tension of a belt and pulley. Sleeve bearings are often used on universal motors *(page 18)*, in the gear box of clothes washers and in dishwasher pumps.

A sleeve bearing is aligned around the motor shaft by the screws that attach the bearing to the motor housing. When a sleeve bearing works loose from the housing, the shaft can become misaligned, causing the housing to vibrate or the shaft to wobble. Such movement can cause friction, which can damage the moving parts of a machine. Sometimes you can adjust the bearing to compensate for a bent shaft by inserting a brass shim under one of the screws to lift that side of the bearing slightly.

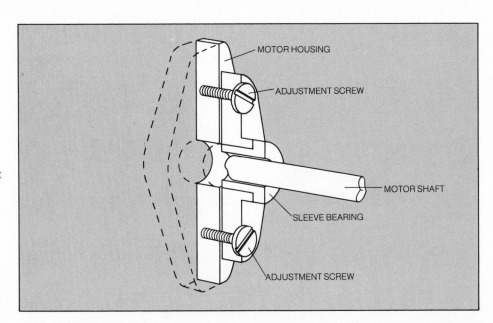

MOTOR HOUSING

ADJUSTMENT SCREW

MOTOR SHAFT

SLEEVE BEARING

ADJUSTMENT SCREW

A clip-held bearing. The heart of a clip-held bearing is a bushing of copper alloy permeated with oil that in effect supports the motor shaft while allowing it great freedom of motion. Metal clips hold the bushing against the bearing housing but at the same time permit the bushing to shift its position slightly should the motor shaft be jarred out of alignment. To that extent the clip-held bearing is self-aligning. An oil port in the housing of the bearing provides access for lubrication.

Clip-held bearings are normally used in pairs—there is one bearing at each end of the motor shaft. Bearings of this kind are frequently found in small appliances and in the fans of larger appliances; their floating motion helps maintain bearing and shaft alignment.

A ball-bearing race assembly. This kind of bearing is made up of a pair of steel collars flanking a ring of steel ball bearings. There are side walls that hold the balls between the collars, and protrusions in the side walls that keep the balls apart, reducing friction as they turn. The inner collar is made to fit snugly on the shaft of a motor, and this collar turns freely along with the shaft. The outer collar is held stationary either by the motor housing or by some other part of the machine. Ball-bearing race assemblies are designed to hold a motor shaft in precise alignment at very high speeds and are extremely durable. They are typically found in the motors of dishwashers and small appliances.

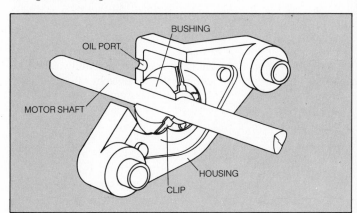

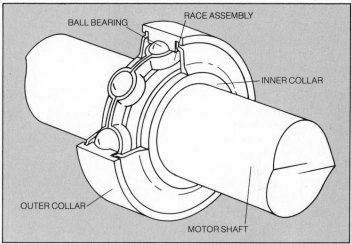

The Connections That Tie the Motor Shaft to the Work

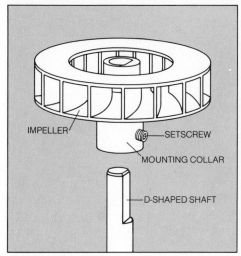

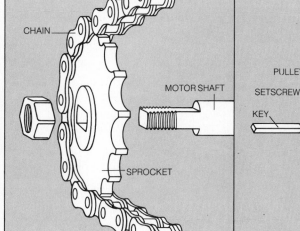

Pulling power directly from the shaft. To transfer the driving power of a motor shaft directly to a working part, the shaft is cast with a flattened D shape that fits inside a correspondingly shaped slot in the mounting collar of the working part—in the example shown here, the impeller of a pump. To secure the joint, a setscrew on the mounting collar is tightened against the flat side of the D-shaped shaft.

Conveying the shaft's power. A metal or plastic disk called a pulley and a toothed disk called a sprocket are frequently attached to the motor shaft to transfer power elsewhere.

On a sprocket are teeth that interlock with the links of a chain *(above, left)* to drive such heavy-duty mechanisms as the ram of a trash compactor. The end of the motor shaft is threaded and flattened on two sides and fits into a

matching slot in the sprocket's mounting collar. The sprocket is held by a nut that threads onto the shaft in the direction opposite to its rotation. The pulley *(above, right)* often has a V-shaped rim to accommodate and turn a V-shaped drive belt. Here the pulley is attached to the motor shaft by a square metal pin, called a key, that fits notches in the motor shaft and the mounting collar of the pulley, called a keyway. This connection is often bolstered by a setscrew.

Devices That Increase Power by Reducing the Speed

Reduction gears and pulleys. In the belt-and-pulley system *(below, left)* a small drive pulley, attached to the motor shaft, turns a much larger reduction pulley; the reduction pulley in turn is attached to the drive shaft, which moves a working part. The drive shaft turns more slowly than the motor shaft, but it turns with greater force. If the circumference of the reduction pulley is three times greater than that of the drive pulley, it will make only one rotation for every three made by the drive pulley; but its power, the torque, will be increased proportionately. Reduction pulleys are often used in appliances.

Reduction gears, such as those employed on an electric can opener *(below, right)*, rely on the same principle. A rapidly revolving motor shaft with helical-cut threads drives a matching helical-cut reduction gear. This gear turns a small pinion gear, which rides beside it on an intermediate shaft. The pinion gear's straight-cut teeth mesh with the straight teeth of a second large reduction gear, which turns the drive shaft of the working part, giving it a slow, powerful rotation.

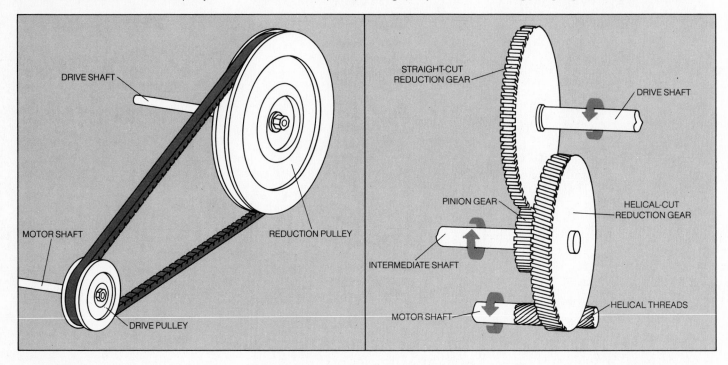

A Screw That Alters a Motor's Direction of Force

Worm and beater gears. When the spiraling threads of a worm gear at the tip of a motor shaft mesh with the angled teeth of a beater gear lying parallel to it, the motor shaft and drive shaft turn at right angles to each other. Such a gear system is common on a food mixer, where there are two beater gears turning two drive shafts in opposite directions, as in this example. Worm-gear threads are deeper than helical-cut threads *(above, right)*, giving the worm gear a more positive grip but also making it noisier. To minimize noise and protect the motor, beater gears are usually made of soft plastic. If the drive shafts become jammed, the gear teeth strip off to protect the motor from an overload.

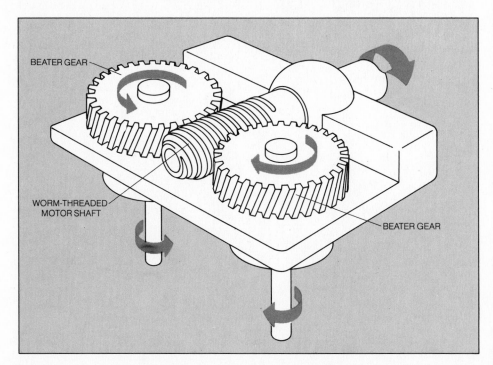

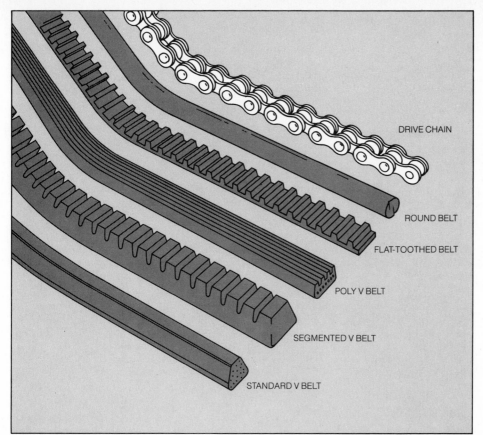

DRIVE CHAIN

ROUND BELT

FLAT-TOOTHED BELT

POLY V BELT

SEGMENTED V BELT

STANDARD V BELT

Parts That Most Often Need Replacing

Drive belts and chains. The drive belts most commonly found in appliances are shaped to fit pulleys with a V-shaped rim. These V belts are composed of rubber reinforced with nylon, rayon or cotton; the fabric inhibits the rubber's tendency to stretch. Either a standard V belt or a segmented version, which allows a tighter turning radius, will be found on most clothes washers. A poly V belt, which is grooved to mesh with a similarly grooved pulley, is commonly used to drive the drum on a clothes dryer. A flat-toothed rubber belt reinforced with fabric is used in some food processors. A round, all-rubber belt is used to drive the beater brush in an upright vacuum cleaner. A sturdy metal chain is made of the only material strong enough to drive the ram on a trash compactor.

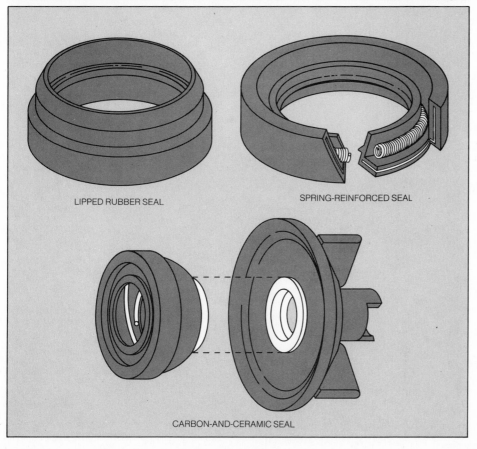

LIPPED RUBBER SEAL

SPRING-REINFORCED SEAL

CARBON-AND-CERAMIC SEAL

Motor-shaft seals. A simple lipped seal is used in the pumps of dishwashers and clothes washers to separate the oil-lubricated motor, at one end of the shaft, from the water that surrounds the shaft's working end. The rubber lip of the seal stretches tight around the shaft; the steel base is coated with rubber or plastic and serves to seat the seal firmly in place against the motor housing. Another type of lipped seal is held tight around the shaft by a steel spring. Such a seal may be made of rubber, neoprene, or even leather, but it is usually reinforced inside by an L-shaped flange of thin metal.

Still a third waterproof seal, made of carbon and ceramic, relies on its perfectly smooth surface to create a molecular bond. In this case a stationary graphite ring, seated in a spring-reinforced rubber fitting, clings to a ceramic ring embedded in the base of a fitting that turns with the motor shaft. These seals are common in the drain pumps of washing machines.

Gaskets in appliances. Gaskets, like seals, close the seams between adjoining parts, but in the case of gaskets, the parts always are stationary. In appliances, gaskets are commonly found between sections of housing or between the housing and a lid or door. When the sections are assembled or the door is closed, the gasket is compressed, ensuring a tight fit. A lipped rubber gasket is shaped to simply perch along the edge of a housing section; mounting gaskets have holes to accommodate the screws used in assembling adjoining parts. Mounting gaskets can be made of metal, cork, heavy paper or rubber. O-ring gaskets are small, rigid rings of molded rubber; they fit into grooves cut for them in the housing.

The intricate moldings of a magnetic door gasket *(inset)* commonly seal refrigerator and freezer doors. The sheet-metal screws that hold such a gasket in place are concealed by a rubber lip that can be folded out of the way when the gasket must be removed. This gasket contains a magnetic strip that creates an airtight seal with the metal doorframe when the door is closed and the gasket is compressed.

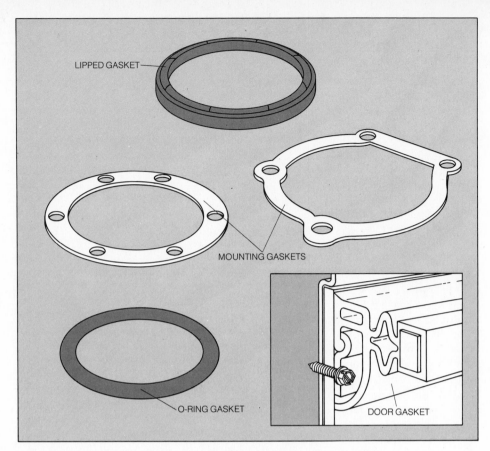

LIPPED GASKET

MOUNTING GASKETS

O-RING GASKET

DOOR GASKET

Springs That Smooth the Motion of Moving Parts

Two kinds of springs. Compression springs are found in the dash pot of a toaster *(page 46),* the light switch on a refrigerator or freezer door, and water-inlet valves. The metal coils of a compression spring are spaced apart when at rest. As the coils are compressed, the spring offers progressively stronger resistance. When this resistance is equal to or greater than the compressive force, the coils thrust outward to their resting position.

For a compression spring to work efficiently, it must be held straight. The spring can be enclosed in a cylinder *(near right),* or a shaft can be inserted through the length of the spring.

Tension springs *(far right)* are often used to support the weight of heavy, bottom-hinged dishwasher and oven doors as they are opened and closed. One end of the spring is attached to the door hinge, the other to the appliance body. When the door is closed, the spring's coils are tightly wound and at rest. As the door is opened, the coils are pulled apart, creating a counterbalancing tension.

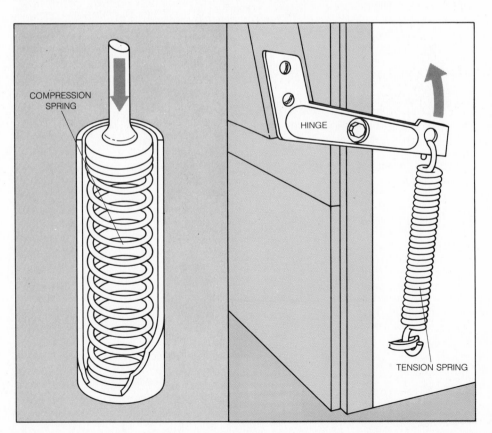

COMPRESSION SPRING

HINGE

TENSION SPRING

Gaining Access to the Insides

Dismantling a damaged appliance to mend it calls for the right disassembly tools and a logical approach. Otherwise you will be in danger of compounding the damage or losing critical parts. On many appliances the fasteners are deliberately concealed for the sake of appearance. Recesses, plugs and nameplates often hide the heads of screws *(page 27)*. Seams may conceal interlocking parts that hold the halves of the housing together *(page 27)*. Sometimes control knobs must be removed before you can take off other parts *(page 28)*.

Even when you locate the fasteners, you may have to use specialized tools or techniques to take them off. Fortunately, the tools are common enough to be found in hardware stores. A more irksome problem is attempting to free frozen fasteners, but the procedures shown on pages 31-32 should help. When things do begin to come apart, note the order in which they separate—or make sketches or snapshots of complex assemblies while they are still in one piece. Generally parts go back together in reverse order. Be sure to store the disassembled parts where they will stay clean, safe and organized. Small easy-to-lose items, such as fasteners, clamps and clips, are best kept in marked containers.

Finally, no matter what kind of fasteners you find, the specialized tools shown on page 26 may be helpful. In addition, your appliance-repair kit should include various sizes of flat-tipped and Phillips screwdrivers with insulated handles for electrical work, slip-joint pliers and long-nose pliers with insulated handles, and a set of open-end wrenches or, in its place, an adjustable wrench.

An array of appliance attachments. The screw is the most common of appliance fasteners. The screw with the strongest grasp is the blunt-end machine screw, which fits directly into threads on the appliance or into a washer and nut. Machine screws come with slotted or hexagonal heads or with a combination of the two. One variant, the headless setscrew, is used where pressure on the screw base contributes to its holding action. A sheet-metal screw holds sheet-metal panels together by gripping them around predrilled holes; self-tapping screws join sheet metal by the grip of their threads in the metal.

The most common appliance nut is the hexagonal nut, which threads onto a machine screw and is always used with a washer. Its next of kin is the nut-washer, which combines washer and nut. The easily removed wing nut is used where appliance parts may need adjustment; it is almost always used with a washer. When sheet-metal screws join parts under light stress, stamped sheet-metal nuts provide extra stability. A nylon nut mount does the same for a machine screw; it snaps into an opening in an appliance and can be pried out with a screwdriver. Decorative chrome-plated ring nuts hold the shafts of knobs and switches against control panels.

The standard washer in appliances is a flat metal ring. Toothed and spring-shaped lock washers add more gripping power.

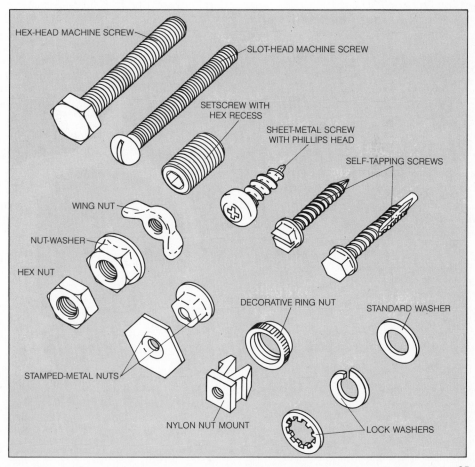

Tools That Make it Easy to Take Appliances Apart

Tools for hexagonal fasteners. Hex wrenches, which are often referred to as Allen wrenches *(below, left)* are simply L-shaped hexagonal shafts designed to fit into the hexagonal recesses of setscrews. Each wrench is bent so that it

has a short and a long arm. The terms "long arm" and "short arm" are also used to identify the two series of hex wrenches. These wrenches are available with shaft diameters ranging from 5/64 to 1/4 inch.

A set of detachable sockets *(below, right)* can be mounted on a nut driver to turn hexagonal-headed screws or hexagonal nuts. The most useful socket sizes for the home workshop are 1/4, 9/32, 5/16, 11/32, 3/8, 7/16, and 1/2 inch.

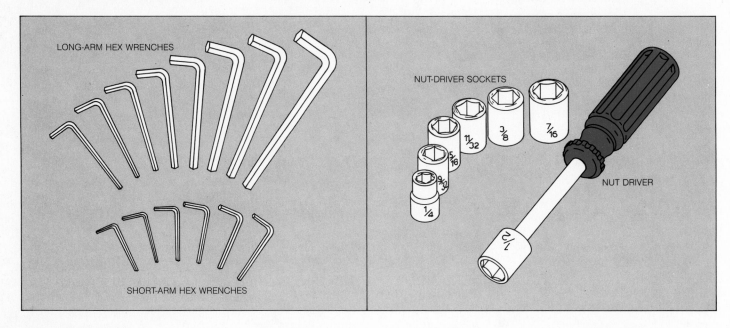

LONG-ARM HEX WRENCHES

SHORT-ARM HEX WRENCHES

NUT-DRIVER SOCKETS

11/32 3/8 7/16

5/16

9/32

1/4

1/2

NUT DRIVER

Hidden Places for Assembly Screws

Sunken screws. Screws that hold the parts of a plastic housing together are often hidden in deep recesses molded into the appliance's underside. The recesses themselves may be concealed by soft plastic or rubber plugs *(inset)*, set flush with the surface of the appliance housing and sometimes camouflaged with a color matching that of the housing. To remove a plug, pry it out with a large needle, a screwdriver, an awl or some similar instrument.

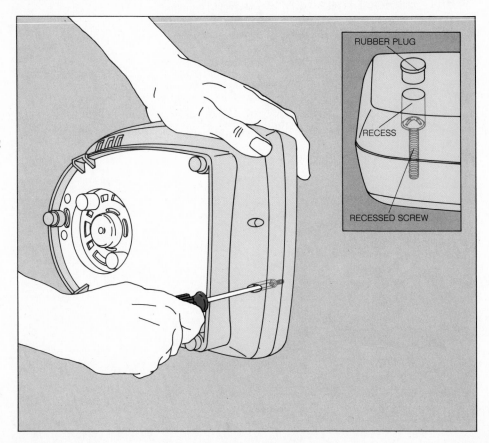

RUBBER PLUG

RECESS

RECESSED SCREW

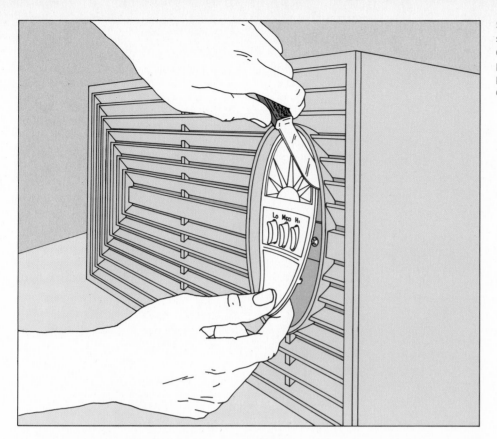

Secret Screws. After searching all other possible locations on the appliance, look for screws concealed under the manufacturer's nameplate. Use a dull knife to peel or pry off the nameplate, taking care not to crack or tear it if it contains operating instructions.

Parts That Hold Themselves Together

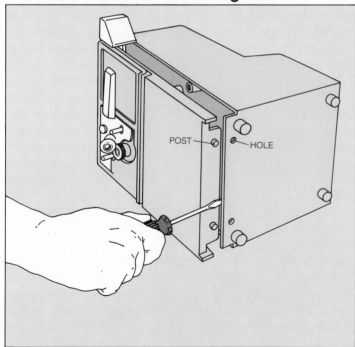

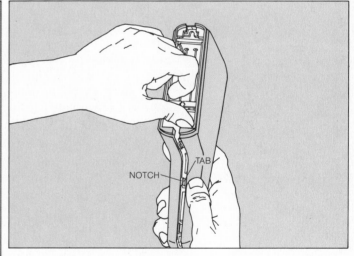

A molded post and hole. Examine the appliance housing for plastic posts that protrude from one part into another. Look for a seam near these posts and pry the seam open with a screwdriver, snapping the posts out of their holes.

A concealed tab and notch. Look for a seam around an appliance housing, which would indicate that the housing halves are held together by tabs and notches beneath the seam. To see which half of the housing has the tab and which the notch, try to peer inside the appliance through a vent or opening. If you cannot, press down along the seam with your thumb. The housing half with the tabs will give slightly. Press down gently but firmly at a tab location and pull the two halves apart. As the seam opens, work your way around it, pressing and pulling it apart.

Removing Control Knobs: the Final Key to Disassembly

A knob pinned by a setscrew. The last barrier to unsheathing an appliance from its housing may be a control knob. Examine the knob collar for a setscrew holding the collar on. Loosen the setscrew with a hex wrench, or with a screwdriver if it has a slot. Then pull the knob off the shaft.

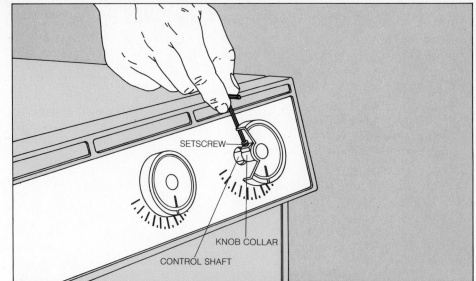

An interlocking knob and shaft. If no setscrew is visible on the knob collar, chances are that the knob and shaft are held together by matching notches on the collar and shaft. With a screwdriver, carefully pry up the knob, a small section at a time, working gradually around the knob until it is free of the shaft.

To reattach the knob, line up the flat side of the D-shaped collar with the flat side of the D-shaped shaft, and press the knob onto the shaft.

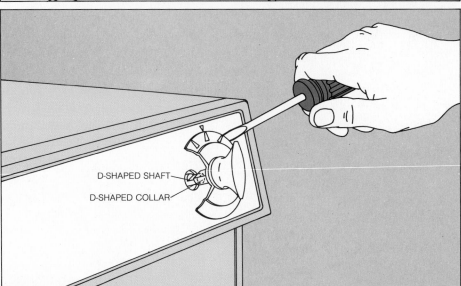

A two-part knob. Disassemble a two-part knob one part at a time from its separate shafts. First unscrew the outer knob from the threaded shaft, and then pry or pull the inner knob off the D-shaped inner shaft.

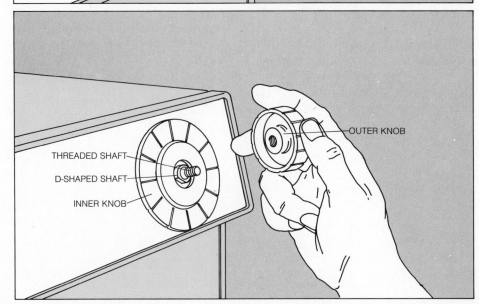

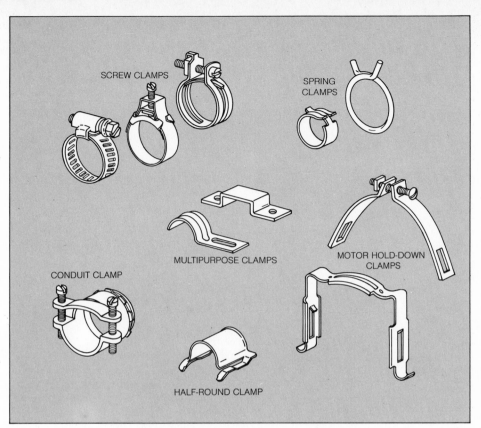

SCREW CLAMPS

SPRING CLAMPS

CONDUIT CLAMP

MULTIPURPOSE CLAMPS

MOTOR HOLD-DOWN CLAMPS

HALF-ROUND CLAMP

An Assortment of Holders for Wires and Hoses

Clamping an appliance's life line. Clamps keep water hoses, air hoses and electrical wires from being jostled or struck by an appliance's moving parts, and even hold in place such major elements as the motor. Multipurpose clamps hold wires and hoses against the side of an appliance cabinet. The deep cuff of a conduit clamp anchors and supports the main electrical cord of a large appliance at the point where the cord enters the appliance. Spring clamps and screw clamps connect hot- and cold-water hoses to valves and pipes. A half-round clamp clips into slots on an appliance cabinet to secure either wires or hoses. Of the two types of motor hold-down clamps, one locks onto its mount with screws, the other holds with two hooks and spring tension.

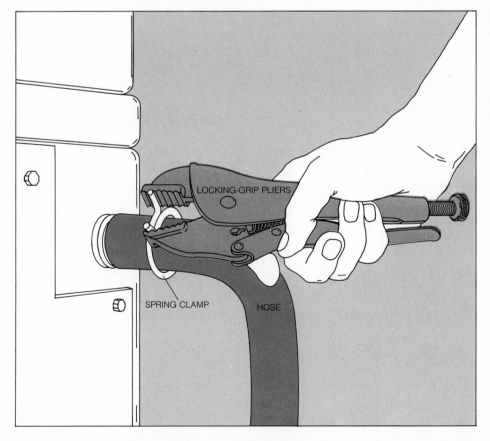

LOCKING-GRIP PLIERS

SPRING CLAMP

HOSE

Positioning a Spring Clamp to Hold a Flexible Hose

Clamping a hose. Open the spring clamp by pressing the clamp ends together with locking-grip or channel-joint pliers. Slip the clamp over the end of the hose, and slide the hose onto its connection. Slide the clamp to within ¼ inch of the end of the hose, and then let the clamp tighten by releasing the pliers.

Ingenious Clips and Pins That Tie It All Together

Keeping parts in their places. Various pins, clips, rings and supports make the parts of an appliance stay put. A cotter pin slips through a hole in a stationary shaft to prevent moving parts from sliding off the shaft. The cotter pin is held in the hole by its round head and its two arms, which are spread apart with pliers after the pin is inserted. Semicircular snap rings hold pulleys and gears on a revolving shaft by snapping into a groove cut in the shaft; they can be pried off with pliers. A special circular snap ring, sold under the trade name Truarc, is a more secure retainer, but it can be removed only with special dual-jointed pliers *(below)*.

A wire hold-down clip, made of steel, holds clusters of wires against the side of an appliance cabinet. A panel clip holds the front or top panel of a clothes washer or dryer against the main cabinet frame. Plastic shelf and drawer supports are snapped into the side walls of a refrigerator or freezer to hold the shelves and drawers, and door-shelf retainers support shelves on refrigerator and freezer doors.

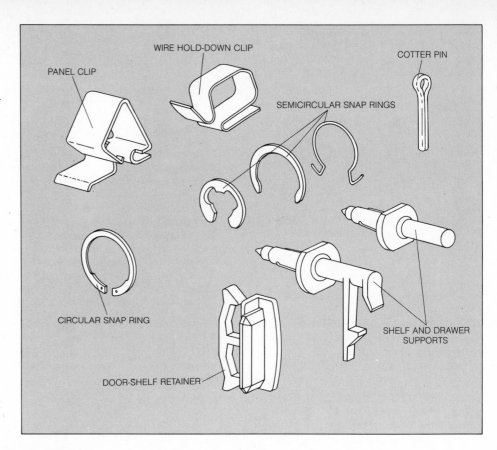

Reversible Pliers for a Special Snap Ring

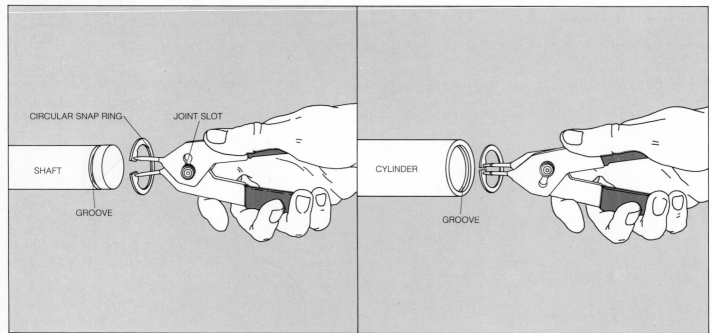

Working with circular snap rings. To remove a circular snap ring from a shaft *(above, left)*, position the legs of special dual-jointed pliers so that they pivot around the left side of the joint slot. Insert the tips of the pliers in the snap-ring holes, and squeeze to open the snap ring. Slip the ring out of the groove on the shaft, remove the ring, and release the pliers. Replace a circular snap ring on a shaft in the same way.

In order to remove or replace a circular snap ring that is located inside a cylindrical part *(below, right)*, position the legs of the pliers so that they are on the right side of the joint slot. Then insert the tips of the pliers in the holes of the snap ring and squeeze the pliers, compressing the ring. Finally, slip the snap ring into or out of the groove in the cylinder.

Freeing Stuck Fasteners

Efforts to get inside an appliance may be thwarted by threaded fasteners that refuse to budge. But most fasteners will eventually yield to the proper means of persuasion. First, it is important to use tools that provide good leverage—screwdrivers with large handles and wrenches whose jaws are not worn, for example. Sometimes the fastener heads can be filed for better purchase.

Fasteners gripped by corrosion call for treatment with penetrating oil. The oil should be carefully applied so that it lubricates only the threads of the fastener, not the head; otherwise it will be impossible to grip the head securely. Allow the oil 30 seconds to seep into the corroded metal, and tap the fastener a few times to help the oil penetrate more threads.

Sometimes setscrews are coated with adhesive at the factory before they are positioned in the appliance. Releasing such fasteners may require the application of heat from a propane torch to weaken the grip of the adhesive. Flame is also effective on aluminum nuts fastened to steel bolts. The general rule for loosening fasteners with heat is to work from the outside in, using the heat to expand the nut or metal housing into which the screw or bolt fits.

However, flame should not be used on any part covered with penetrating oil, which is flammable. Nor should flame be used near rubber or plastic. In the vicinity of these two materials, the most appropriate form of heat may be boiling water—but water must be used with care if there are electrical components nearby.

Filing a fastener head. If hex heads of bolts or screws are rounded with wear, file two parallel sides to flatten them. Use a wrench to test for fit as you file, choosing a size slightly smaller than the one intended for the head. When the wrench grips the newly shaped head firmly (inset), loosen the fastener.

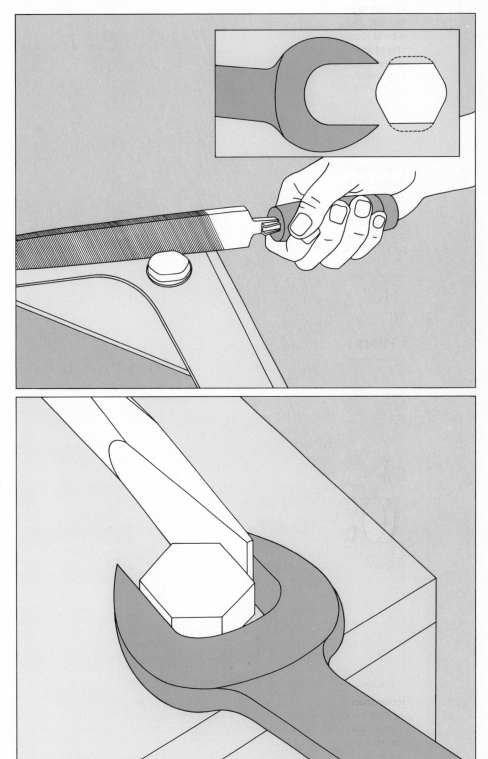

Using a screwdriver as a wedge. To grip a worn hex head or one of an odd size for which you do not have a wrench, wedge the blade of a screwdriver between the head and one jaw of an oversized wrench. When the head is firmly gripped, turn the wrench and screwdriver simultaneously to loosen the fastener.

Using a screwdriver and wrench. To remove a setscrew that has a damaged hex recess, force the blade of an old screwdriver into the recess, then turn the screwdriver with a wrench clamped over the screwdriver shank *(below, left)*.

The same combination of screwdriver and wrench can be used on slotted or Phillips-head screws. The screwdriver needs a square shank for gripping—or you can flatten a round-shanked one by filing two opposite sides *(below, right)*.

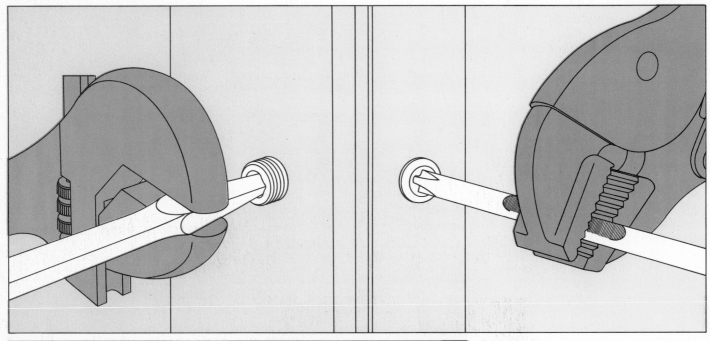

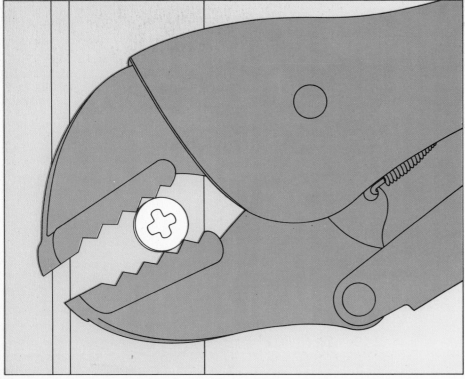

Using locking-grip pliers. Lock the jaws of locking-grip pliers around the head of a stuck screw or bolt, and waggle the pliers back and forth to loosen the fastener. This method is especially useful when an appliance has both left- and right-threaded fasteners: The waggling motion usually discloses the direction in which the fastener should be turned to be loosened.

Where to Look for Parts and Information

When you need a replacement for an appliance's broken part, look first at the local retail outlet for the appliance. You can often find its address listed under the appliance's brand name in the telephone book, or in a classified directory under such categories as "Electric Appliances" and "Gas Appliances." Call first to see if the part is in stock. The dealer will need to know the model number of the appliance and the serial number of the part, along with any other identifying symbols. Usually these are found on the casing or in the service manual or the "Use and Care" booklet that came with the appliance.

When you go to the store, take the broken part with you for comparison. Be sure the replacement is rated for exactly the same voltage, amperage, wattage, horsepower or capacitance as the old part. The new part should also match the old in appearance. Do not purchase the part unless you are satisfied that it matches. Most dealers have a no-return policy on parts and do not give refunds or exchanges.

In addition to supplying parts, the dealer is a good source of repair information. Many sell repair manuals for specific appliances, containing trouble-shooting procedures, electrical and mechanical diagrams, lists of parts and their identifying numbers. A dealer familiar with your appliance can also be a fund of diagnostic advice, especially for portable appliances that can be examined on the spot.

When the part is from an odd or old appliance, the dealer may not have it in stock but will sometimes order it for you. Or you can continue the search yourself by consulting the same categories in the classified directory for the name of the manufacturer's nearest parts distributor.

The parts distributor operates a kind of warehouse for the manufacturer, selling parts not only to dealers and repair shops but to the public as well. Like the dealer, distributors can be reached by phone, but they usually will also respond to written requests. You can even send in the broken part. Depending on the availability of the new part, most parts distributors will mail the replacement to you the same day they receive the order. Be sure to ask the price before ordering, however, for such distributors, like dealers, do not make exchanges or refunds. Distributors are also a good source of service manuals and of information on hard-to-find parts. If they do not have an obscure part, they can often tell you who does.

If neither the dealer nor the distributor can fill your request, contact the manufacturer directly. Manufacturers prefer not to sell parts to the public, but they will tell you whether the parts are available and where to get them.

Certain manufacturers have set up "hot line"—toll-free telephone numbers that handle customers' questions. You can find out if a manufacturer has a toll-free line by dialing (800) 555-1212. To get the manufacturer's address and regular phone number, ask the dealer or distributor. Or look in the Thomas Register, available at most public libraries. The register is a multivolume catalogue published yearly, listing industrial products and services, along with company addresses and phone numbers. You can also get the manufacturer's address by writing or calling the Association of Home Appliance Manufacturers, 20 North Wacker Drive, Chicago, Illinois 60606; or telephone (312) 984-5800.

In Canada, the equivalent to the Thomas Register is the Canadian Trade Index; or you can contact the Canadian Manufacturers' Association, 1 Yonge Street, Toronto, Ontario, M5E 1 J9.

Before you embark on this search for parts and information, check your appliance's warranty. Perhaps the work you are contemplating is still covered by the warranty and will be done free at an authorized service center. You may void the warranty if you attempt to do the repair yourself and fail.

In addition, some or all parts may be warranted for a longer period than the period for the entire appliance. Parts under warranty will be supplied free by a distributor but only a dealer or service center can tell you whether the service warranty on a specific part is still valid; you must present your appliance warranty to get this information. If you have lost your warranty but still have your sales slip, you can write the manufacturer for a copy of the warranty, enclosing a facsimile of the sales slip as proof of the date of purchase.

Finally, if you want to learn about electrical repairs in general, the Institute of Electrical and Electronics Engineers (IEEE) publishes a glossary of electrical symbols to help you interpret wiring diagrams, and the Whirlpool Corporation offers a manual explaining how to read the wiring diagram of a home appliance. For the glossary, write IEEE, 345 East 47th Street, New York, New York 10017; ask for booklet number Std 315, *Graphic Symbols for Electrical and Electronics Diagrams*. For the manual, write to the Whirlpool Corporation, Consumer Affairs Training, 2000 Highway 33 North, Benton Harbor, Michigan 49022.

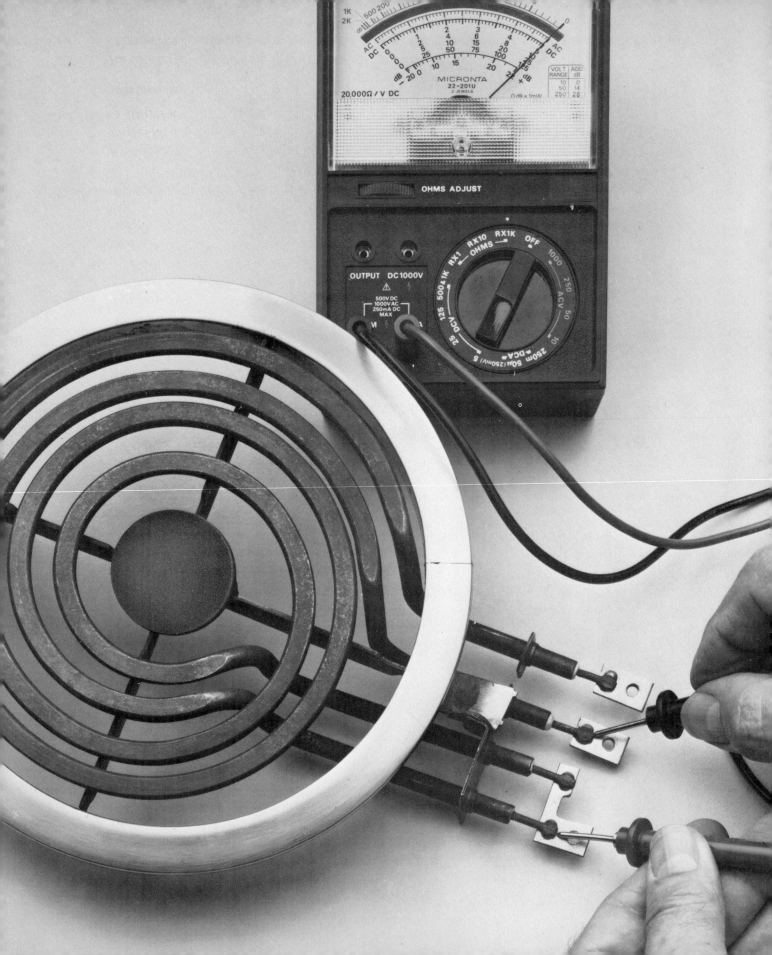

2

Keeping the Kitchen Humming

The process of detection. With the aid of a multitester, the chief tool in locating electrical problems, a range element that will not heat is being checked for continuity—the existence of a complete path for current through the coil. After the tester's selector knob is set on the RX1K scale, the probes are placed on the terminals of one of the two coils that form the element. The needle rests near 0 on the top scale, indicating that the circuit is complete. The reason for the element's failure to heat must be found elsewhere in the range's wiring system.

Kitchen appliances play a crucial role in the operation of a household, and two of them, the range and the refrigerator, share the distinction of being the most important of all appliances. While both function in extremes of temperature—a difficult challenge for any device—both, fortunately, are also unusual in their longevity. It is not uncommon for either of these kitchen workhorses to last 20 to 30 years or longer. Part of the secret of their reliability is that both have relatively few moving parts, and the parts that do move do not move much. One exception is the compressor of a refrigerator—in 30 years it can cycle more than 13.5 billion times. But it generally does so without incident, in spite of the precise fit its moving parts require. This is possible because of careful manufacture and because the compressor is a sealed system, with dirt kept out and lubrication kept in. As a result, this high-precision portion of the refrigerator often still works when the rest of the machine is ready to fall apart.

Despite the long-life potential of a range or a refrigerator, problems will occur that temporarily put it out of action—a switch fails, a thermostat stops working, a door jams or a heating element burns out. When parts like these do fail, the decision to repair the machine rather than replace it is usually an easy one. New refrigerators and ranges can cost a great deal, whereas the cost of a new part and the effort needed to replace or repair the old can be small.

Furthermore, because the refrigerator and range are needed every day, family routine is disturbed until the appliance is fixed. You can shorten the time considerably by making the repairs yourself, and the quickest way to start is to unplug the unit, pick up a screwdriver and an electrical tester, and look for the cause of the trouble. The problem may be as simple as a burnt-out heating element or dirty condenser coils. If you can diagnose the malfunction and buy your own replacement part, you will avoid waiting for a service call.

Small kitchen appliances are another matter. The failure of one of these is seldom a disaster, and the cost of a new one is often quite small. The decision to repair rather than replace is not automatic. In fact, a simple rule of thumb frequently spells doom for a balky appliance: If the replacement parts will cost more than half the price of a replacement appliance, it probably is better to buy a new appliance. Even so, the knowledge of how to fix a small appliance permits you to evaluate the merits of repair or replacement. Furthermore, you can be audacious while working on a small unit, treating the repair itself as a learning experience. Meanwhile, chances are that the problem will turn out to be something as simple as a screw that has worked loose—and one twist of a screwdriver will put the household helper back in working order for years to come.

Care for the Small Food-Preparation Helpers

The heart of every small kitchen appliance, whether it brews coffee or chops onions, is either a heating element or a motor. On devices with heating elements, such as toasters and percolators, the element is controlled by thermostats, fuses and other electrical parts. On machines with motors, such as food processors and electric knives, the speed and power of the motor are directed by gears and pulleys. In both cases, the devices are likely to be equipped with multisetting switches.

The simplicity and size of small kitchen appliances, few of which have more than three commonly fallible parts, may enable you to find the source of the trouble immediately, by sight or sound instead of with electrical tests. When a motorized appliance begins to make unaccustomed noises, a mechanical part is to blame. When a heating device does not heat, either the heating element is broken or the switch, thermostat or wires that send it current are defective. Thus, you can often confirm your suspicions by looking for a loose wire connection, burned terminals or a corroded element.

Inspect a motorized appliance also for burned motor windings, a broken gear or a leaky gasket. Then, if the defect is not visually apparent, use a multitester to check the electrical components for continuity *(page 10)*.

Repairing small appliances—especially the least expensive ones—may not be practical in all cases, as it was in the past when most appliances contained cheap interchangeable parts. Today parts are often combined into modular assemblies that must be replaced in their entirety when only one part has failed. Although a modular assembly may be easier to install than a single part—many simply snap into place—buying a new one may not be worthwhile. Before doing so, compare the cost of the replacement part or assembly with that of a new appliance.

If the appliance is still under warranty, do not attempt to repair it—you might void the warranty. Instead, take the appliance to an authorized repair shop.

Most breakdowns of small kitchen appliances are caused by a failure to clean food from them. Crumbs in a toaster or spills on the control panel of a blender can jam critical mechanical parts or gum up electrical contacts. Drip coffee makers in particular require a periodic cleaning process called deliming, which removes mineral deposits from the heating element. To delime a coffee maker, pour vinegar or a commercial deliming solution into it and turn it on. Clean the outer surfaces of all appliances, after unplugging them, with a moist cloth and mild detergent. And be sure never to immerse any appliance in water unless it is clearly labeled as immersible.

Machines That Brew Coffee

A drip coffee maker that uses gravity. A potful of water poured into the reservoir is held there temporarily by a heat-sensitive bimetallic strip that acts as a plug for the reservoir's drain hole. When the switch is turned on, the heating and warming elements heat up, and the bimetallic strip bends, unplugging the drain hole. Dripping over the heating element, the water heats to brewing temperature and seeps through the basket that holds the ground coffee. When all the water has dripped through, a thermostat shuts off the heating element, but the warming element stays on to keep the coffee warm.

All the parts of this type of coffee maker slide out of the housing. If the coffee maker does not work at all, test the terminals of the electric cord and the on/off switch for continuity *(page 10)*; if either one shows no continuity, replace it. If the cord and switch show continuity and the warming element works but the heating element does not, the problem is in the heating element or in its fuse or thermostat. All three must be replaced as a unit. First pull out the pin holding the element to the tray, and disconnect the spade connectors from their terminals. Install a new heating element in the same position. To replace the warming element, unscrew it from the base plate, disconnect its wires from their terminals in the tray and attach a new warming element in the same position.

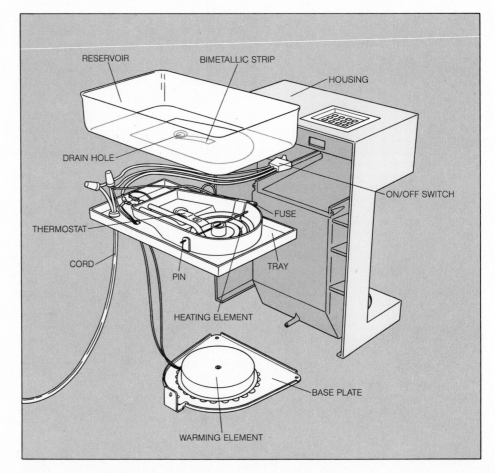

RESERVOIR · BIMETALLIC STRIP · HOUSING · DRAIN HOLE · ON/OFF SWITCH · THERMOSTAT · FUSE · CORD · PIN · TRAY · HEATING ELEMENT · BASE PLATE · WARMING ELEMENT

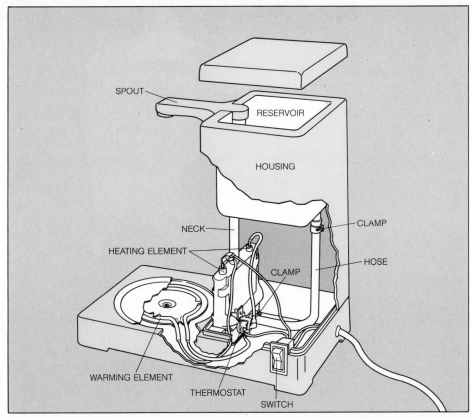

A drip coffee maker with a steam pump. In this type of coffee maker, the water in the reservoir flows down a hose to a pump. The heating element in the pump turns some of the water to steam, which pushes the heated water up the neck, through the spout and down into the ground coffee. After all of the water has passed through, a thermostat turns the heating element off, but the warming element stays on.

If the coffee maker's pumping action does not work, use a multitester *(page 10)* to test the terminals of the on/off switch, the thermostat, and the heating element for continuity; replace them if necessary.

If the warming element is faulty, remove the bracket that holds the element against the underside of the warming plate and slip a new warming element under the tabs on the bracket.

Mechanical problems can also keep coffee from brewing. Make sure the hose between the reservoir and the heating unit is not pinched. Flush the device periodically with a delimer to prevent mineral build-up. Mineral deposits on the bottom plate indicate a leak in the water line—replace or adjust the hose, its clamps or the pump gasket, as necessary.

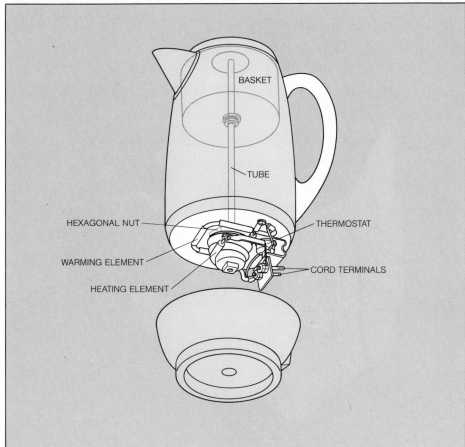

An electric percolator. Inside the well at the bottom of the percolator, water is boiled by the heating element until it squirts up through the tube and splashes off the lid onto the ground coffee in the basket. A thermostat monitors the brew; when it reaches a certain temperature—depending on the desired coffee strength—the thermostat turns off the heating element. The warming element, which remains on, keeps the coffee slightly warmer than the thermostat setting, to prevent the heating element from turning on again.

If the brewed coffee does not stay warm or if it re-perks, the warming element is not working and should be replaced. If the coffee boils, the thermostat is turning off the heating element at too high a temperature and must be replaced. If the coffee will not brew at all, use a multitester *(page 10)* to check the terminals of the electric cord, the thermostat and the heating element for continuity; replace the part that does not show continuity.

To remove the warming element, unscrew its terminals; the thermostat simply lifts out. To remove the heating element, loosen the hexagonal nut inside the pot with a socket wrench and an extension; or use a pair of wrenches, one to hold the nut, one to twist off the heating element.

The Toasters and Cookers

Putting a toaster through its paces. When a toaster's carriage-lowering lever is depressed, it closes a switch that turns on the heating elements. As the bread toasts, a heat-sensitive bimetallic arm bends and trips a solenoid switch, whose position is set by the light/dark lever *(below)*. The solenoid lets the carriage pop up, turning off the heating elements at the same time. To keep the toast from being thrown out, the dash pot—a spring-loaded cylinder with a vacuum action—slows the rise of the carriage.

If the toaster does not heat, check the cord for continuity *(page 10)* and the switch for dirty contacts. Replace the cord or clean the switch if necessary. If the carriage throws the toast out or rises too slowly, clean the dash pot with alcohol. If this remedy fails, replace the toaster. If the bread toasts but does not pop up, check the solenoid for continuity. If it is faulty, replace the toaster. If it is not faulty, the solenoid switch or the bimetallic arm may be defective. Check their performance by toasting a piece of bread with the toaster housing removed; do not touch any parts of the mechanism as the bread toasts. If the arm does not trip the switch and activate the solenoid, replace the toaster.

Adjusting the light/dark setting. To determine the length of time the bread stays in the toaster, the light/dark lever controls the distance between the solenoid switch and the bimetallic arm. The farther apart they are, the farther the arm must bend to reach the switch and pop up the carriage—and the darker the toast gets. A calibration knob on the toaster bottom can be used to adjust this distance.

To recalibrate the light/dark scale, move the lever to MEDIUM and toast a piece of bread. Then unplug the toaster, turn it over, and open the crumb tray. Observe the action of the bimetallic arm and the solenoid switch as you turn the knob a quarter turn each way. Move the switch farther from the arm if the toast was too light, closer if too dark. Test the adjustment by toasting another slice of bread, and continue readjusting the knob until the medium setting produces toast properly browned for your taste.

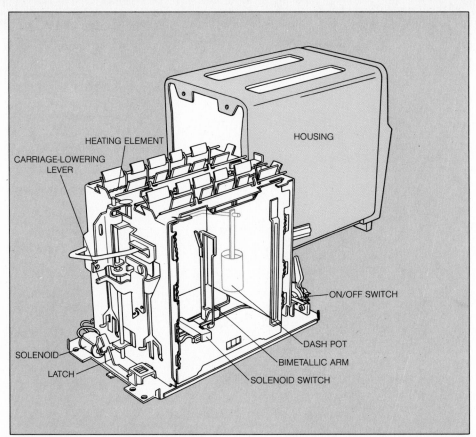

HEATING ELEMENT

CARRIAGE-LOWERING LEVER

HOUSING

ON/OFF SWITCH

DASH POT

BIMETALLIC ARM

SOLENOID SWITCH

SOLENOID

LATCH

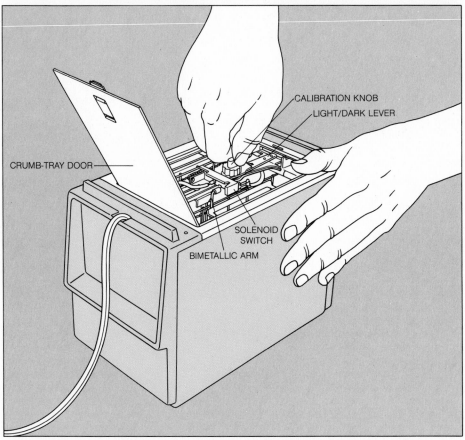

CALIBRATION KNOB

LIGHT/DARK LEVER

CRUMB-TRAY DOOR

SOLENOID SWITCH

BIMETALLIC ARM

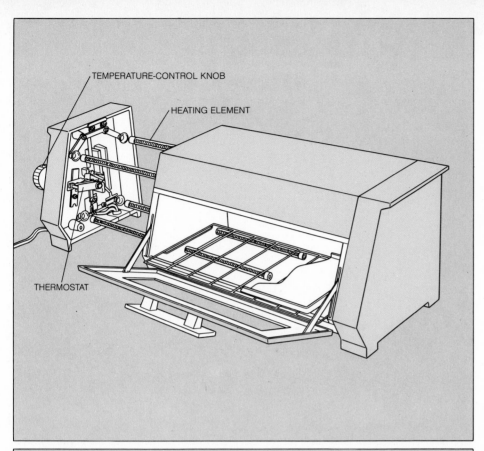

TEMPERATURE-CONTROL KNOB

HEATING ELEMENT

THERMOSTAT

Replacing the elements in a toaster-oven. The temperature-control lever of a toaster-oven operates a thermostat that regulates the heating elements for dual functions: baking and toasting. Recalibrating the thermostat is best left to a professional, but on some models you can replace heating elements that fail to heat. Unscrew one side panel of the oven, or unlatch the panel by sliding a lock bar sideways; slip the elements out of their sockets. Test the elements for continuity, using a multitester *(page 10)*. If there is continuity, the problem may be in the electric cord. If there is no continuity, replace the defective elements, making sure that the ends are seated firmly in their sockets.

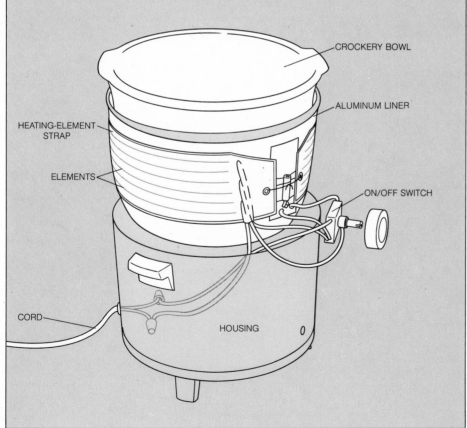

CROCKERY BOWL

ALUMINUM LINER

HEATING-ELEMENT STRAP

ELEMENTS

ON/OFF SWITCH

CORD

HOUSING

Restoring the heat to a slow cooker. A slow cooker contains a pair of wire heating elements sandwiched inside a single broad strap of fireproof paper that is tied around an aluminum liner. The liner fits between a crockery bowl and an exterior metal housing. A switch turned to LOW or to HIGH sends current to one or both heating elements, warming the crockery bowl.

Though a slow cooker that does not heat may have a faulty electric cord or on/off switch, the problem is more likely to be a burnt-out heating element. To test the terminals of all three, remove the aluminum liner from the housing by pulling off the knob of the on/off switch; then unfasten a screw or pull out a metal eyelet on the bottom of the housing. Check the cord, the switch and the heating element for continuity with a multitester *(page 10)*. To replace the element, untie the old element strap; pull the wires out of the switch's self-locking terminals as described on page 16, and disconnect the wires from the electric cord. Then install a new element strap, using the old one's wiring pattern.

The Cutters and Mixers

Restoring a food processor to service. The blades of a food processor fit onto a shaft that is turned by an assembly of pulleys, gears and a toothed belt. To protect the user from injury, a safety switch allows the blades to rotate only when the bowl is properly seated over the base and the bowl cover is locked in place.

To repair a food processor, take off the bottom of the housing and remove the motor cover. Test the electric cord, the safety switch and the on/off switch for continuity *(pages 10, 16)*; if they do not show continuity, replace them. Inspect the motor for damaged or burned windings; if you find any, replace the motor. If the motor runs but the shaft does not turn, look for a stripped reduction gear or a broken pulley belt. To replace the belt, slip a new one around the pulleys. Replace a stripped gear as shown below.

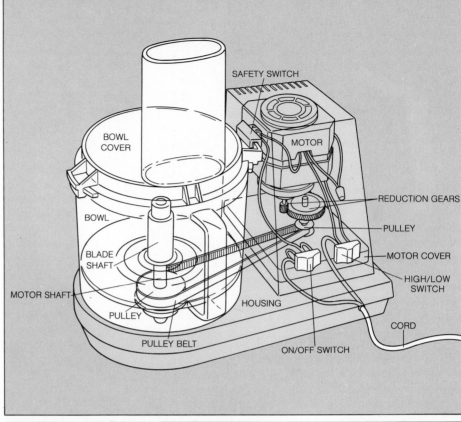

Replacing a food-processor gear. With the bottom of the housing and the motor cover removed, slip off the pulley belt. To replace the small reduction gear on the motor shaft, immobilize the shaft by inserting a screwdriver between two blades of the fan on the base of the motor; unscrew the gear with your fingers, and screw on a new gear. To replace the large reduction gear on the motor cover, slip the broken one off and replace it with the new one.

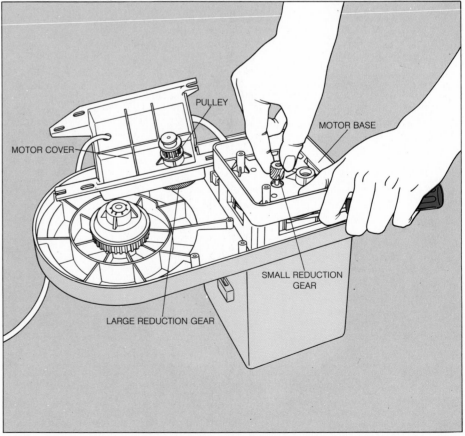

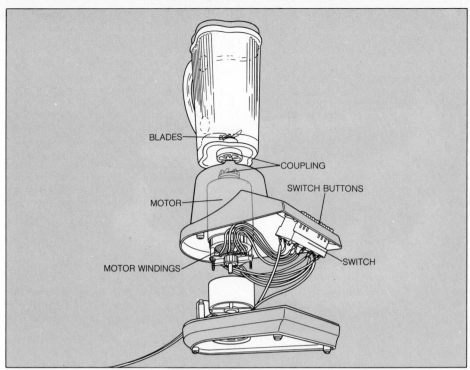

Fixing a sluggish blender. A blender's motor turns a coupling that drives mixing blades inside a food jar. The speed of the blades is governed by a switch. On some blenders there are as many as 14 switch buttons, each of which sends current to certain copper windings inside the motor; the more windings energized, the faster the motor shaft turns. On models with a high/low button, a simple electronic device called a diode reduces the current to the motor when the button is set on LOW.

Sticky liquids often find their way into the cracks and crevices around the buttons, jamming the switch. If you cannot loosen stuck buttons by tapping them, replace the switch, taking careful note of the wiring pattern.

If the motor seems to strain, check the mixing blades; they should move smoothly when spun by hand. If they are sluggish, replace the assembly to avoid damage to the motor. If the motor does not run, is especially noisy or smokes, examine the copper coil for burned or discolored windings; but burned wires at the ends of the coil are just the normal result of soldering.

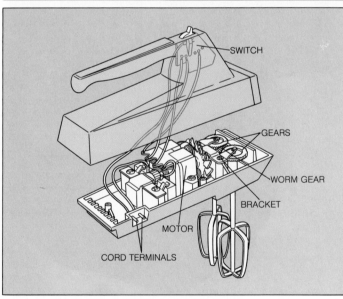

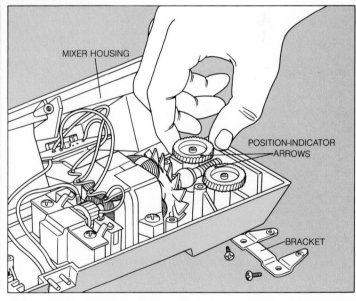

Upgrading a worn food mixer. The switch on a food mixer, like that on a blender *(above)*, often has multiple settings that control motor speed by activating certain windings of the motor. The motor shaft is a worm gear *(page 22)* that turns two gears, and they rotate the beaters.

If the switch does not turn the motor on, or if the motor operates only at certain speeds, remove the top of the mixer housing and inspect the terminals on the switch for bent or dirty contacts or loose wires. Test the switch for continuity *(page 16)*; if even one setting shows no continuity, you must replace the switch. Replace damaged gear wheels as shown at right.

Replacing a food mixer's gears. Remove the top of the mixer housing and unscrew the bracket that holds the gears in position. Lift out the gears and replace both of them, even if only one is broken. Install the new gears with the L arrow of the left gear facing the R arrow of the right gear, so that the blades of the beaters will mesh without striking each other. Lubricate the gear teeth with petroleum jelly before you put the bracket and housing back on the mixer.

Servicing an electric knife. The reciprocating motion of an electric knife's two blades is caused by a special gear that has an off-center cam on each side. As the gear is turned by the motor-driven worm gear, the two cams rotate out of alignment with each other, simultaneously pushing and pulling two drive arms that move the knife blades back and forth in a sawing motion.

If the knife does not run, the switch contacts may not be touching when the switch button is depressed. Remove the housing and bend up the end of the upper contact with pliers; if the contacts are dirty, clean them with fine sandpaper. If the knife vibrates or is noisy, run it with and without the blades attached to determine if the problem is that the blades are either worn or bent; replace the blades if necessary.

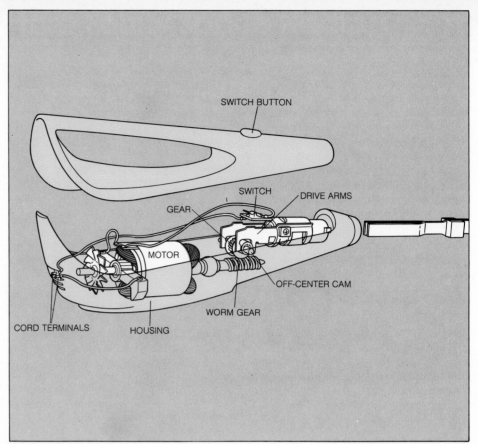

Replacing the knife's drive assembly. If the motor runs but the blades do not move, remove the housing and unscrew the drive-assembly cover, exposing the gear and the drive arms. Remove the gear by pushing out its retaining pin; install a new gear, greasing it well with petroleum jelly before you reattach the retaining pin.

If the blades fall out of the knife handle, either the drive assembly is cracked or the retaining clip that holds the blades is broken. Replace the entire assembly as a unit by first removing the gear, then lifting out the drive arms. Install a new assembly in the same position as the old.

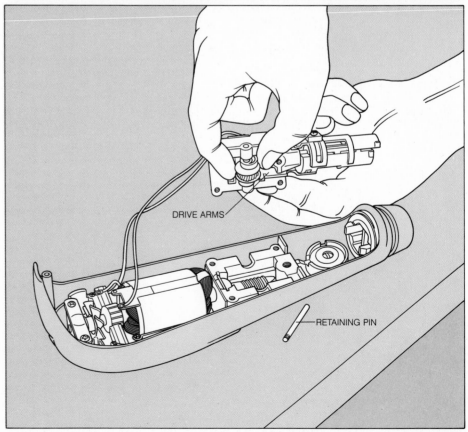

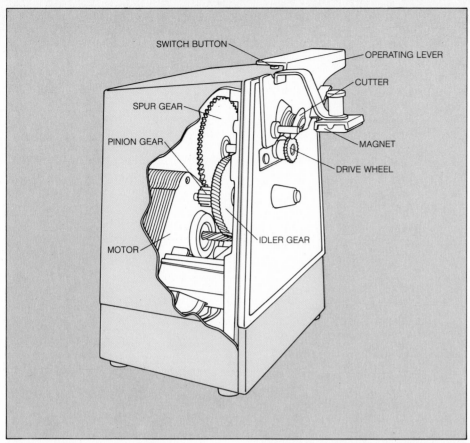

SWITCH BUTTON

OPERATING LEVER

CUTTER

SPUR GEAR

PINION GEAR

MAGNET

DRIVE WHEEL

IDLER GEAR

MOTOR

Getting At the Innards of a Can Opener

Changing gears on a can opener. When the rim of a can is hooked over the opener's serrated drive wheel, the operating lever pushes the cutter into the lid and simultaneously turns on the motor by pressing a switch. A high-speed motor is slowed by reduction gears to increase the turning power of the drive wheel, which spins the can. On some can openers the same motor, used without reduction gears, drives a high-speed grinding wheel for sharpening knives.

If the drive wheel does not turn, examine the reduction gears; to expose them, take off the housing and unscrew the motor from its mount. If the gears are stripped, remove them by holding the spur gear with one hand while you twist off the drive wheel with pliers; pad the wheel with cloth to keep its teeth from being damaged by the pliers. With the spur gear removed, the idler and pinion gears will slip out. Install identical new gears in the same configuration.

If the cutter is dull, replace it by unscrewing the single screw that holds it to the face of the can opener. Clean the cutting mechanism regularly with hot water and detergent.

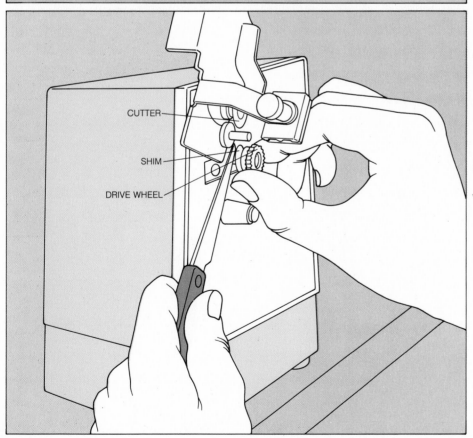

CUTTER

SHIM

DRIVE WHEEL

Adjusting the drive wheel. If the operating lever fails to hold cans securely, the gap between the cutter and drive wheel may be too wide; it should be no wider than the thickness of a sheet of paper. To narrow the gap, unscrew the drive wheel and insert a washer behind it, which will serve as a shim. Washers of varying thicknesses are available at repair shops; choose one that produces exactly the needed gap. Unscrew the drive wheel from its shaft, while holding a knife edge against the threads of the shaft to prevent it from falling inside the housing; then slide the washer on the shaft, and screw the drive wheel back on until it is hand-tight. To unscrew the drive wheel you may need to use pliers; if so, pad the wheel with a piece of cloth to prevent the pliers from damaging its teeth.

Salvaging Old Stand-bys

A favorite old appliance with a damaged electric cord or a broken heating element can almost always be salvaged. Unlike many other appliance ailments, these two can be cured with standardized off-the-shelf parts. If the cord is still good but the plug is defective, cut off the plug close to the end of the cord and replace it with a new plug *(near right)*. To replace a defective cord attached to an appliance, you should buy both a new cord and a new plug—and for any appliance that heats, the cord should be heavy-duty, marked 15 AMP or 16 GAUGE.

Some older appliances—waffle irons and percolators, for instance—have separate cord sets with a female plug that fits over terminals on the appliance. New female plugs are seldom available, but if the original is still good, you can attach it to a new cord *(far right)*.

To detach an old cord from some appliances, you may first have to remove a strain-relief grommet, designed to prevent wires from being pulled off their terminals through repeated use. The two halves of the grommet *(right, bottom)* fit around the electric cord where it enters the appliance housing.

Before attaching a cord to any plug, first prepare the cord wires. With standard zip cord, pull the two wires apart for 1½ inches and strip ½ inch of insulation from each end, using wire strippers. Then twist the strands together on each wire and shape them into hooks. With other types of cord, first strip away 1 inch of the rubber or cloth insulation to expose the rubber-covered wires inside, then strip, twist and shape the wires as above.

In addition to cord problems, some cooking appliances such as waffle irons and popcorn poppers are subject to another easily cured ailment. The heating element in these devices—typically a nichrome (nickel-chromium) coil supported by ceramic insulators—may break. The coil can be replaced *(opposite)* with a new coil of the same diameter and with the same wattage rating as that stamped on the appliance. Do not use a coil with a higher rating—it will overheat.

New Life for a Worn-out Electric Cord

Uniting cords with plugs. To attach a new male plug to a new or an old cord *(below, left)*, pry out the center cap of the plug with a small screwdriver and remove the prong-shaped terminals. Pass the end of the cord through the plug, prepare the wires as described at left, and screw a new terminal to each hooked wire. Slide the plug back over the terminals, and push the terminals back into the plug. Then reinsert the center cap *(inset)*.

To attach a female plug *(below, right)*, separate the two plug halves by removing the screws or drilling out the rivets. Lift out the terminals and the strain-relief spring. Pass the end of the cord through the spring, prepare the wires as described at left, and screw a terminal to each wire. Position the terminals and the strain-relief spring in the appropriate slots in one plug half, and screw the other half on *(inset)*. If the halves were joined with rivets, use tiny bolts.

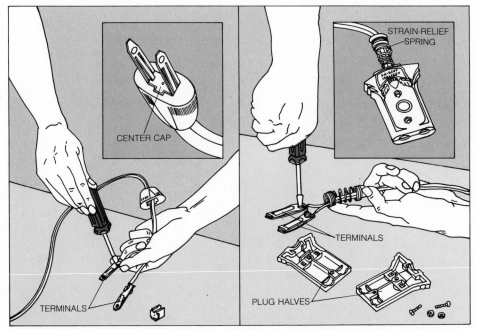

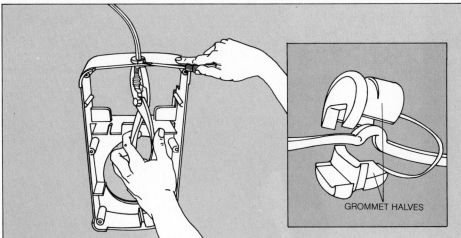

Removing a strain-relief grommet. Disassemble the appliance housing, exposing the inner part of the grommet. Force the grommet up and out of the housing by squeezing together the two halves of the grommet's inner part with pliers, simultaneously wedging the tip of a screwdriver under the lip of the outer part. If the inner part of the grommet is inaccessible, use pliers to compress the two halves of the outer part of the grommet, working it back and forth to unseat it.

Before attaching the new cord to the terminals on the appliance, secure the grommet to the cord *(inset)*. When the wires are securely in place, snap the grommet back into the housing, if necessary squeezing it with pliers.

Replacing a Coiled-Wire Heating Element

1 **Stretching a nichrome coil.** Remove the appliance housing and unscrew the old heating coil from its terminals. Lift it gently out of the appliance and straighten it without stretching it beyond its original length. Measure its length. (If it is broken, measure the length of the pieces.) Stretch the new coil to this length by securing one end in a vise and slowly pulling the other end with pliers; hold a folding rule or a steel tape against the coil as a guide. Do not overstretch it; the coil is designed to carry a certain wattage, and cutting off any part of it will increase the remaining coil's wattage, causing it to burn out.

2 **Installing the new element.** Bend ½ inch at each end of the coil into a hook shape. Fasten one end between the washers of a terminal screw, then carefully loop the coil around the ceramic insulators in the same pattern as was formed by the old coil, fastening the other end of the coil to the second terminal screw. Keep the tension on the coil even—neither taut nor slack. If necessary, adjust the coil slightly at each insulator to equalize the tension, but do not stretch the coil.

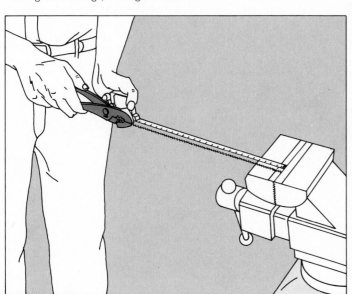

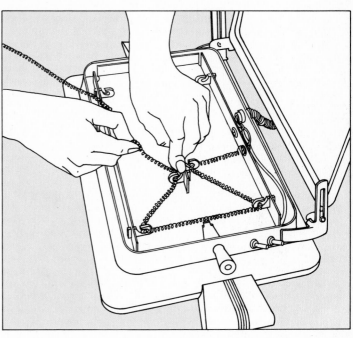

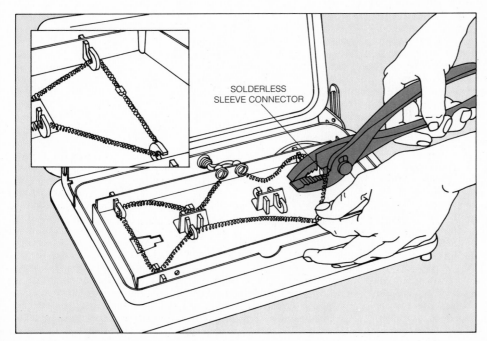

SOLDERLESS
SLEEVE CONNECTOR

A Splice That Saves a Broken Heating Coil

Applying a solderless sleeve connector. Loosen the coil from the ceramic insulators nearest the break and, using needle-nose pliers, carefully straighten ¼ inch of each broken end. Slip the straightened ends into a solderless sleeve connector, a tiny nichrome tube used to mend heating elements. Use the pincer tips of a pair of slip-joint pliers to squeeze the sleeve flat, then crimp the flattened sleeve with the pliers' cutting jaws. Return the patched coil to its ceramic insulators, making sure the sleeve connector does not touch the appliance housing *(inset)*.

Where to Look for Trouble on a Kitchen Range

Whether a kitchen range is used to boil water or to cook a five-course meal, it is indispensable in any home. When a range stops working properly, the flow of daily life is dramatically interrupted.

With few exceptions, repair procedures differ for gas ranges and electric ranges. And totally different techniques are needed for microwave ovens *(page 54)*.

An electric range will have its own 120/240-volt circuit from the house service panel—120 volts for the light and clock and 240 volts for the heating elements. For some ranges, the wires of this circuit run directly out of the wall to the back of the appliance; other ranges are plugged into a wall outlet with a heavy-duty cord. In either case three lines, two live and one grounded, are connected to the main terminal block on the back of the range. If you are getting insufficient heat in either the surface elements or the oven, check these connections. If one of the live lines is disconnected, the heating elements may operate on low settings but not on high settings.

Most range repairs begin with a series of visual checks. When a heating element on the top or in the oven does not work, inspect it for breaks or bubbles in the sheathing. Also look for burned wires, broken connections or charred insulation near the wire terminals, and check to see if there is pitting or corrosion on the terminals at the ends of the top heating coils. The latter are a prime cause of intermittent heating.

If no damage is visible, the next step is a sequence of electrical checks with a multitester, working back from the defective heating element's terminals to its receptacle, its control switch and finally its connection with the main terminal block. The first of these tests is for continuity; it is conducted with the power turned off and the wires disconnected. The other three are for voltage, and they are done with the power turned on and the wires connected. But note that in testing voltage, it is safest to keep the power to the range turned off until the multitester probes are securely in place—insulated alligator clips add safety here.

Testing procedures for the top heating elements differ slightly from range to range, depending on the unit's age. Older models have heating elements consisting of two coils operated by a control switch that clicks into progressively higher heat settings. This type of switch applies either 120 or 240 volts to either or both of the coils, depending on the heat setting. Newer ranges have single-coil elements operated by thermostatically controlled infinite switches that turn smoothly from LOW to HIGH and can be set at any point between.

When testing two-coil elements, you must test the ends of both coils. The click-type switches for such elements also require two sets of tests for power. Single-coil elements and infinite switches, with just two terminals, require only one test for power.

On many newer ranges the terminals of the control switches are marked H_1 and H_2 for wires leading to a heating element, and L_1 and L_2 for wires leading to the main power line. Some ranges, however, have switch terminals that are merely numbered, making identification more difficult. You can usually determine which terminals hold the wires from a heating element by noting the color of the wires at the element receptacle and finding where wires of those same colors terminate on the switch. You can then deduce that the remaining lines are connected to the power source.

If your range has an indicator light on the backsplash to tell you when a heating element is on, the control switch will have an additional terminal, usually marked P (for "pilot"). Terminals for this light are easy to recognize because the wires for it leap from one switch to another, in parallel.

Simple adjustments and replacements can correct many oven problems. Loss of heat, for example, may be caused by a cracked or torn oven-door gasket. Sometimes the gasket is held in place with stainless-steel clips; a replacement can simply be snapped in. On other models you must loosen the oven liner, held in place with screws at the sides and rear. Pull the liner forward and insert the new gasket. If the gasket is fixed to the door, you must loosen screws and remove a door panel in order to replace the gasket.

If the oven seems to be overheating, make sure that the oven vent is not blocked. (It usually has its exit under one of the rear surface burners.) Also be sure that the thermostat's sensing bulb, located near the top of the oven, is not touching the oven wall and is not coated with oven cleaner. Overheating can also be caused by hampered circulation; do not cover the openings in the oven bottom or line the shelves with aluminum foil.

If the oven timer is not working, suspect a bad fuse or a tripped circuit breaker. Look for the fuse or circuit breaker near one of the back burners; consult the owner's manual for its exact location. Replace the fuse with one of the same amperage rating as the old one. The same fuse may also be at fault if a convenience outlet or a light is not functioning.

One of the most frequent complaints about ovens is that they do not hold the temperature at which they are set. To test the thermostat control, place an oven thermometer in the center of the oven and set the oven dial for 350°F. Let the oven heat, and allow it to cycle on and off for about 25 minutes. Then monitor the temperature two or three times over the next 20 to 30 minutes. If you have to open the oven door to do this, be sure to let the door remain closed at least 10 minutes before taking the next reading. As the oven cycles on and off, the temperature will rise and fall as much as 20 degrees from the dial setting, but it should average 350°.

If the oven temperature is less than 100° off, you can adjust it by turning a small screw in the thermostat control, usually located in the knob shaft. You will need a tiny screwdriver, such as the kind used to adjust eyeglasses. If the temperature is off by more than 100°, the thermostat should be replaced. It should also be replaced if the difference between the on-cycle temperature and the off-cycle temperature is greater than 75°.

Self-cleaning ovens are subject to the same electrical breakdowns as regular ovens, but you may need professional help to repair them. These ovens have a special cleaning cycle during which the temperature is raised above 900°. Also, they have additional wiring to control a door-locking mechanism that keeps the door latched until the oven cools to baking temperature.

Anatomy of an electric range. Power for the range enters at a main terminal, located on the back of the range near the floor. The power is distributed by wires that fan out to the controls for the oven and the top heating elements and to such optional features as a clock, a timer, a convenience outlet or an oven light. When a top element is turned on, current is metered through a calibrated control to a receptacle at the selected rate. The coiled heating elements that plug into these receptacles are supported by trivets that rest in porcelain or stainless-steel drip pans.

The two heating elements inside the oven are shaped in large loops to heat the oven evenly. On some ranges the heating elements plug into a receptacle; on others they are held in place by retaining plates. The top element is used for broiling, the bottom element for baking. Both are connected to a thermostat and to a selector switch that controls the cooking mode: baking or broiling. A rodlike sensing bulb attached to the back wall, the side or the roof of the oven is connected by a tube to the thermostat. When the liquid or gas in the bulb expands or contracts, it travels through the tube and activates a bellows in the thermostat, which opens or closes the electric circuit that supplies the oven's heat. The oven is vented through the top, underneath one of the rear heating elements.

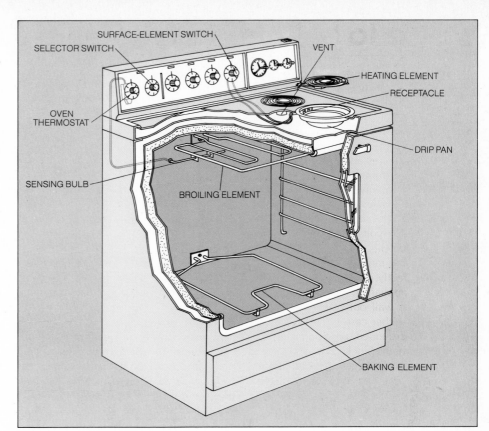

SURFACE-ELEMENT SWITCH
SELECTOR SWITCH
VENT
HEATING ELEMENT
RECEPTACLE
OVEN THERMOSTAT
DRIP PAN
SENSING BULB
BROILING ELEMENT
BAKING ELEMENT

Checking Incoming Power

Testing the terminal block. If neither the oven nor the top elements are heating properly, check for power at the main terminal block. After shutting off the power to the range at the main service panel, pull the range away from the wall and remove the back sheet-metal cover. Set the multitester *(page 10)* for 250 volts and clip the probes to the two terminals on the block for the power line. Usualy these are marked L_1 and L_2, and they are located on the lower outside surface of the block. Restore power to the range. The meter should register double the voltage measured at a standard wall outlet *(page 12)*. If not, check the range fuses or circuit breaker at the main service panel.

Next, shut off the power and move one probe to the lower center screw on the terminal block—the ground-wire connection. Restore power and check the multitester reading, which should be half the prevailing voltage of the house. If it is not, call an electrician.

If power comes into the terminal block but does not reach the heating elements, turn off the power and look for burned or broken wires or terminals; replace them. If the terminal block is burned, label and disconnect the wires, take out the retaining screws and install a new block.

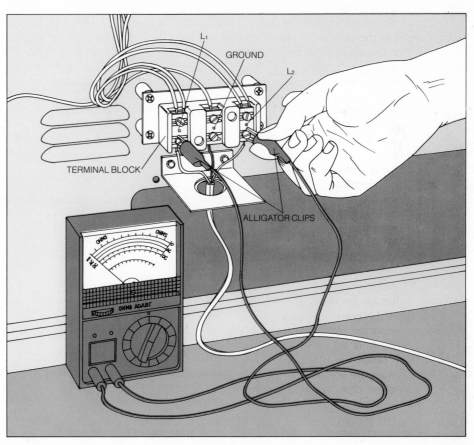

L_1
GROUND
L_2
TERMINAL BLOCK
ALLIGATOR CLIPS

Clues That Lead to the Flaw in a Faulty Cooking Coil

1 **Testing the heating element.** With the power to the range turned off, detach the faulty element. On a single-coil element, touch the probes of the multitester, set on RX1K, to the terminals at each end of the coil. If the test shows continuity *(page 15),* check for a short circuit; Place one probe on a terminal and the other probe on the sheathing. If the test still shows continuity, the heating element is shorted and must be replaced.

If the heating element has two separate coils *(inset),* you will have to test each coil for continuity separately. First trace the path of one coil and touch the probes to the terminals at the two ends of that coil; then repeat the test on the second coil. Usually such two-coil elements have a common terminal connecting one end of each of the coils, so there are in effect three terminals rather than four.

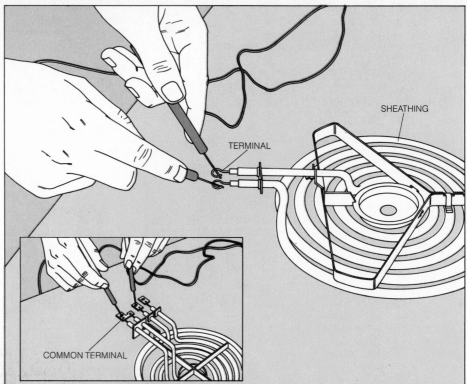

SHEATHING

TERMINAL

COMMON TERMINAL

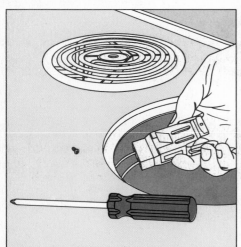

2 **Inspecting the receptacle.** With the power to the range turned off, unscrew the receptacle and pull it away from underneath the top. (On some models you must lift the top first.) Snap off the metal bracket and inspect the slots, where the element makes contact with the wires leading to the switch. If these slots are charred or broken, replace the receptacle; if they are just dirty, clean them with a fingernail file.

Then examine the wire connections inside the receptacle slots; make sure the wires are firmly anchored to their clips and have not burned out. If either wire is damaged or its connector clip is broken, push the wire out of its slot and cut off the damaged end. Strip the new end and attach a new clip, then insert the wire in the receptacle. If there is not enough slack in the wire for such a repair, use a wire cap to splice on additional heater wire *(page 14).* Place the splice at least 6 inches away from the receptacle.

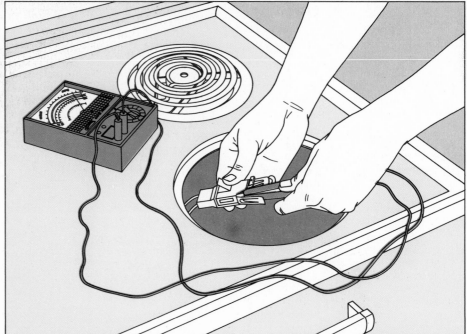

3 **Testing the voltage.** If there is no visible damage to the receptacle, test to see if it is getting power from the control switch. With the power off, insert the multitester probes in both slots, touching the metal clips inside. Set the multitester for 250 volts, restore power to the range, and turn the control switch to HIGH. The multitester should show double the voltage measured at a standard outlet in the house.

To test the voltage on a heating element that is wired directly to the control switch, reattach the element to the wires, then clip the multitester leads to the screws.

If the voltage test produces no reading, lift the top and trace the wires back to the control switch. To gain access to the switch, remove the cover plate from the back of the backsplash.

4 **Testing the control switch.** With the power to the range turned off, clip the multitester probes to the switch terminals that hold the wires carrying power from the main terminal block; usually these terminals are marked L_1 and L_2. Set the multitester for 250 volts and restore power. The meter should register double the voltage measured at a standard wall outlet.

Turn off the power and move the clips to the terminals that hold the wires from the heating-element receptacle (usually marked H_1 and H_2). Restore the power, then turn the switch on HIGH and check the voltage again; it should register double the voltage measured at a standard wall outlet. On a two-coil heating element, the switch has three terminals for the heating-element wires—one wire for the common terminal, two for the separate terminals—plus two line terminals and a ground terminal *(inset)*. Test for voltage on such a switch by clipping the probes to the line terminals. Then move the clips to the terminal for the common wire and, in sequence, to each of the separate wires. To locate these terminals, trace the wires from the heating element to the switch.

If you get power at the line terminals but not at the element terminals, the trouble is in the switch. Inspect the switch for loose wire connections and loose or burned terminals; if the terminals are defective, replace the switch. If you get power at the element terminals on the switch but not at the receptacle, the wiring to the receptacle probably is defective. If you get no power reading at the line terminals, trace the wires to where they connect to the terminal block, and look for broken or burned connections.

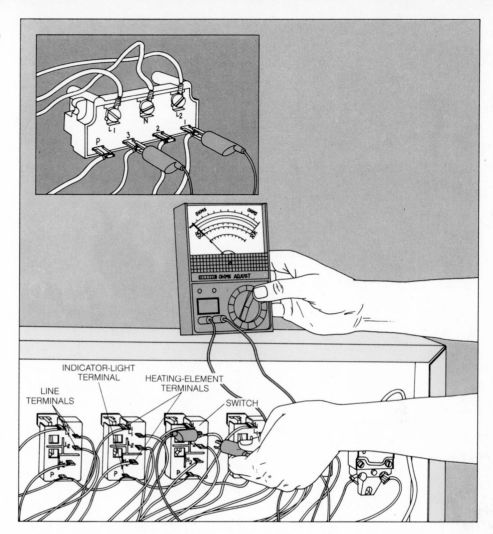

LINE TERMINALS

INDICATOR-LIGHT TERMINAL

HEATING-ELEMENT TERMINALS

SWITCH

Adjusting the Oven's Temperature Control

Adjusting the oven control. After testing the oven temperature *(page 46)*, pull off the thermostat knob and locate the calibration screw inside the shaft for the knob. Turn the screw in the direction specified by the owner's manual to adjust for a higher or lower setting; turn the screw very slightly—about one-eighth of a full turn. Test the oven at this new setting.

On some models, the calibration is adjusted by means of a movable disk on the back of the knob *(inset)*. Loosen the setscrews and move the disk according to the instructions printed on the knob. A third type of thermostat has a calibration screw located beside the knob shaft; adjust it as you would the internal shaft screw.

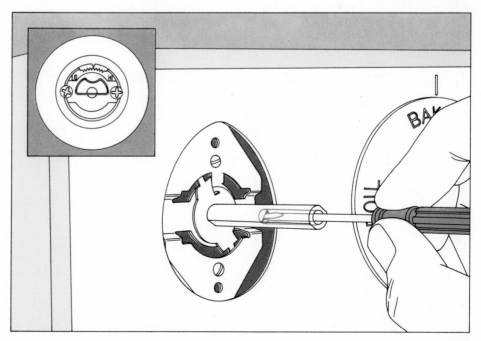

In-Line Tests for an
Oven That Does Not Heat

1 **Checking an oven element.** With the power to the range turned off, remove the screw that holds the oven element's retaining plate against the rear oven wall, and pull the element away from the wall; disconnect the leads to the element. If the element simply plugs in, pull the terminals out of the receptacle. Examine the leads and the terminals for pits or burns, and inspect the sheathing of the element for burns or cracks.

Use a multitester, set on RX1K, to test the element both for continuity and for short circuits (*page 48, Step 1*). If the element has continuity and is not shorted, reconnect the leads to the terminals, but do not reattach the element. Leave a plug-in element out of its receptacle.

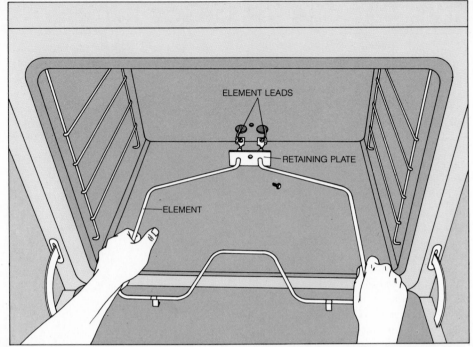

ELEMENT LEADS

RETAINING PLATE

ELEMENT

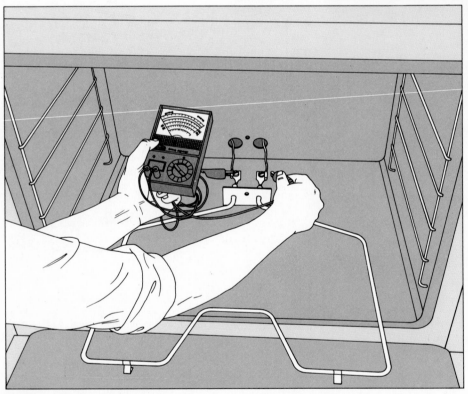

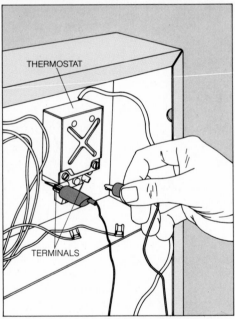

THERMOSTAT

TERMINALS

2 **Testing for power to the element.** With the power turned off, clip the multitester leads onto the two screws where they connect to the element terminals. Set the multitester for 250 volts, then restore power to the range and turn the oven thermostat to 300°. The meter should register double the voltage measured at a standard wall outlet. Turn off the power to the range before disconnecting the multitester. On a

plug-in oven heating element, test for power by inserting the multitester probes into the receptacle slots. If the tester indicates that power is present, the problem is in the heating element.

If no power reaches the leads, inspect the wires to the selector switch and the thermostat. Look for loose wires; if terminals on the switch or thermostat are burned, replace the mechanism.

3 **Checking the thermostat.** With the power to the range turned off, disconnect the two leads on the back of the thermostat and clip the multitester probes to the terminals. Turn the thermostat to 300° and test it for continuity (*page 16*). If the thermostat does not have continuity, it is defective and must be replaced. (If the thermostat has more than two terminals, it should be checked by a professional.) Also check the thermostat's sensing bulb for breaks. If the bulb is damaged, you must replace the entire thermostat assembly.

Safe Repairs for a Gas Range

Most repairs of a gas range are simple mechanical adjustments or maintenance tasks, such as adjusting the mixture of gas and air or clearing clogged holes in a burner. However, some gas ranges have electrical components such as timers, clocks and ignition systems that can malfunction and thus require electrical tests.

When a burner will not light, make a few preliminary checks. See if the burner is tilted or has come loose from the manifold—the pipe that runs just beneath the range top along the front, carrying fuel to the burners and oven. The burner may not light because the pilot flame has gone out or the small portholes that carry gas from the burner to the pilot flame are clogged with food or grease.

If a pilot lights but does not stay lit, it may need cleaning and adjustment. If it continues to go out after you adjust it, call the gas company for assistance.

The burners on a gas range require a balanced mixture of gas and air in order to burn efficiently. When a stove-top burner is set on HIGH the flame should be bright blue and steady. If the burner is not getting enough air, the flame will be colored blue, yellow and white; it will rise above the burner like a candle flame and leave soot on pots and pans. If the burner is getting too much air, the flame will be jumpy and unsteady, making abnormal noise. Either problem can be solved by adjusting the air shutter to regulate the air supply. The oven burner's air shutter can be adjusted in the same way.

Though most oven adjustments are relatively simple, any repair that entails interrupting the gas line, such as replacing a faulty safety valve, should be left to a professional repair service or to the gas company. The parts are not difficult to install, but the consequences of a gas leak can be extremely grave.

Though the thermostat on a gas oven is not an electrical device, its mechanical components can be tested and adjusted in the same way as those on an electric-range thermostat (pages 46 and 49). If a gas range has electrical accessories, such as a timer, a clock or an oven light, the range will have a plug-in—under the stove top or behind the oven—to provide current for them. If all the accessories fail, test the plug-in for voltage with the power on and the probes in the socket.

Several electrical components have become common features on modern gas ranges. Some ranges use a spark to ignite the gas in the burners. On others, the thermostat employs a switch that prevents gas from flowing to the oven burner unless the pilot flame is lit. Other ranges have electric coils that heat when the oven is turned on, igniting the gas. All of these electrical assemblies are easy to replace without interrupting the gas line.

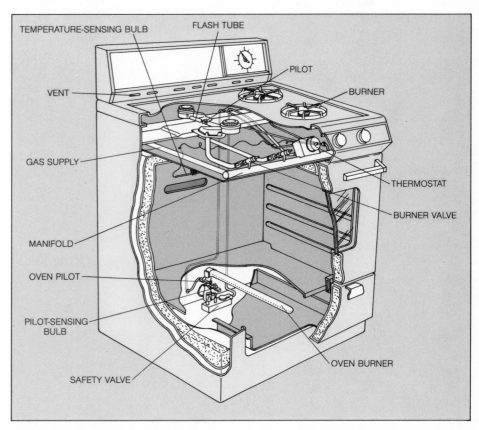

TEMPERATURE-SENSING BULB — FLASH TUBE — PILOT — BURNER — VENT — GAS SUPPLY — MANIFOLD — OVEN PILOT — PILOT-SENSING BULB — SAFETY VALVE — THERMOSTAT — BURNER VALVE — OVEN BURNER

Anatomy of a gas range. A supply pipe carrying either natural gas or liquefied petroleum enters the back of the range near the top and is connected to the manifold. There are valves that control the flow of gas from the manifold to the feeder lines for the surface burners and for the pilot lights. When a range-top burner is turned on, a small orifice in the burner valve opens to allow gas to rush into the feeder line. Air is drawn into this gas flow through an air shutter, whose aperture can be adjusted to control the amount of air in the mixture. To the side of each burner is an open-ended flash tube. The flash tube has one end aimed at the pilot flame between the burners, and the other end aimed at the portholes in the burner. Gas that enters the burner is ignited through the flash tube.

The gas line to the oven burner is connected to the manifold through the thermostat. A temperature-sensing bulb and a gas line to the oven pilot light also are connected to the back of the thermostat. A second, smaller sensing bulb next to the pilot light is connected to a safety valve on the oven burner's gas line. When the thermostat is turned on, the pilot flame enlarges, heating mercury inside the smaller sensing bulb. This signals the safety valve to open a flow of gas to the burner. Once the oven is lit, the main sensing bulb monitors the oven temperature.

First Aid for Ailing Gas Surface Burners

Clearing the portholes. If the pilot flame is lit but the burner does not ignite, clear the portholes in the base of the burner. To gain access to the portholes, raise the range top and lift out the burner assembly. Then push a piece of fine wire through each porthole and wash the burner heads in warm, soapy water. Replace the burner assembly, making sure that the portholes line up with the flash tube leading to the pilot.

If a pilot does not light, check the tiny orifice at the end of the pilot gas line. To remove the corrosive film that sometimes forms over the opening, rub across it with a pencil eraser. If the interior of the orifice is clogged, clear it by gently inserting a fine needle into it, taking care not to deform or enlarge the delicate opening.

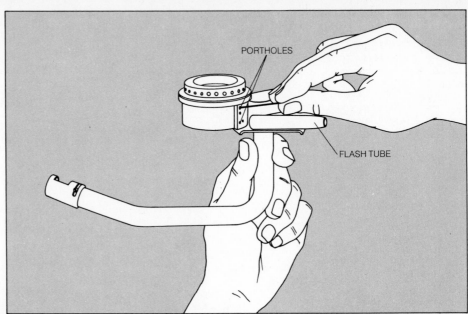

Adjusting the pilot. To raise or lower a pilot flame, lift the range top and follow the thin pilot gas lines from the burner area to the manifold. The lines are connected to the manifold through a single filter valve, which can be adjusted by means of a screw. Locate this screw and turn it until the flame is a compact blue cone with little or no yellow at the tip.

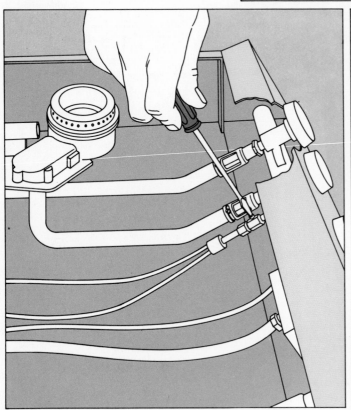

Regulating a burner. To vary the amount of air in the gas mixture reaching a burner, open or close the air shutter on the line running to that burner. The shutter, which may be fan-shaped or cylindrical, is located at the end of the line near the manifold, the pipe that distributes gas to all burners. Loosen the shutter screw and, with the burner turned on HIGH, twist or slide the shutter to change the size of the air-intake opening. When the flame is the correct size and color (*page 51*), tighten the screw.

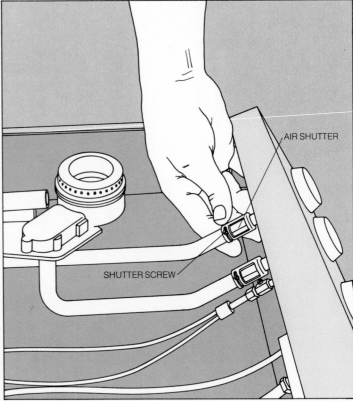

Tests for a Nonfunctioning Automatic Pilot

A spark ignition system. In a gas range that has spark ignition, rather than a pilot flame, look for a faulty ignition system when a burner fails to light. The system is activated when the burner's control switch is turned to LITE; simultaneously gas is released to the burner and a signal is sent to the ignition module (*inset*), on the lower back of the range or below the broiler compartment. The module sends current to the igniter,

and the current jumps from an electrode on the igniter to a cap above it. The resulting spark lights the gas in the flash tube.

If there is no spark, first make sure the electrode is not dirty; if it is, clean it with a soft cloth. Then, with power to the range turned off, check for loose or burned wires leading from the igniter to the module and from the module to the

control switch. At the control switch, pull off the two wires running to the module and, with the switch set to LITE, check for continuity across its terminals (*page 16*). Restore power, then test the matching terminals on the module for a 120-volt reading (*page 11*); these terminals leading to the control switch are usually marked N and L. If you get power at the module but the igniter does not spark, replace the module.

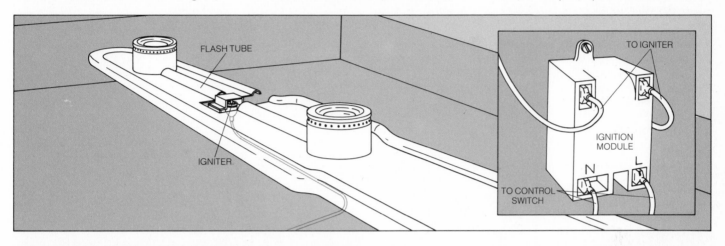

Checking a Gas Oven's Temperature Controls

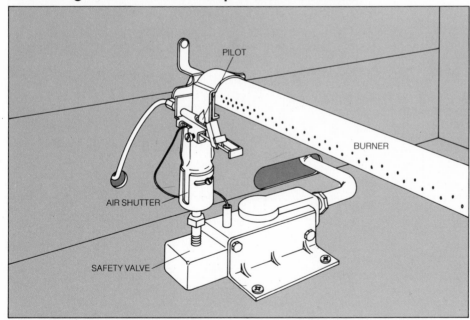

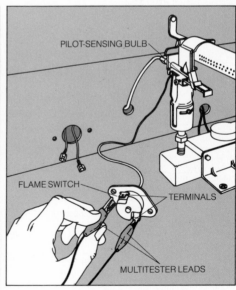

Checking the pilot and the safety valve. To gain access to the oven-burner controls, remove the oven floor and pull out the broiler drawer. If the pilot flame is burning but the oven burner fails to light, the pilot may be set too low. To increase its size, turn the pilot-adjustment screw on the back of the thermostat. Then observe the behavior of the flame when you turn on the thermostat; if the flame does not grow larger, the thermostat probably is faulty and should be re-

placed. If the pilot perks up but the burner does not light, the safety valve must be replaced. In either case, call a professional.

If the burner does light but the flames show signs of too much or too little air (*page 51*), adjust the air shutter just as on the top burners (*opposite*); the oven burner's air shutter is just above the safety valve. If the burner lights incompletely, unclog the burner holes with a wire.

Testing a flame switch. If the pilot flame is burning but the oven burner will not light on a gas oven that has an electrically controlled thermostat, test the thermostat's flame switch. With the power off, take out the screws that fasten the switch to the oven wall, and disconnect the two wires from the flame-switch terminals, but do not disconnect the wire that leads to the sensing bulb next to the pilot. Set the multitester at RX1, and test the flame-switch terminals for continuity (*page 16*). If the reading shows no continuity, replace the switch.

Microwave Ovens: The Accessible Problems

Microwave ovens, although quite common, are still a source of mystery to many of their owners—partly because repairs to the components that produce the microwaves are complex and best left to a professional. However, there are a number of useful steps that you can take to solve the simple problems that usually cause a microwave oven to fail. These include testing and replacing the switches and motors that operate the timer, the oven-door latches and the fan that stirs the microwaves for even cooking.

When a microwave oven simply will not operate, it may be that the fuse in the unit has blown—a problem that is easily remedied. But a blown fuse very often indicates other problems. The door-latching system is designed to blow the fuse if any of the system's switches is defective. A series of continuity tests (page 10) will reveal the defective switch.

When the oven runs but the food does not cook, the problem may lie in the magnetron—the component that produces microwaves. This needs professional servicing. But a common complaint is that food does not cook evenly. A defective stirrer in the ceiling of the oven is usually the cause of this problem, and the stirrer motor can be replaced.

For any repair that is more complicated than replacing the light bulb, you must remove the cabinet that covers the oven. Like many appliances, however, microwave ovens carry a warning that the warranty will be voided if the cover is removed by anyone other than authorized service personnel. If your oven is still under warranty, have the repairs done at the manufacturer's service center.

If you undertake the repair yourself, you must discharge the capacitor as soon as you remove the oven cover. The capacitor stores a high voltage charge when the oven is operating, and it holds some of this electricity even after the machine is unplugged. You can discharge this electricity with a screwdriver (opposite). To avoid shock, remember that the capacitor must be discharged after each test that requires the power to be turned on. During any test in which you turn the power on, keep a mug of water inside the oven to absorb the microwaves. Running the oven with nothing inside to absorb

them will make the magnetron overheat.

Much of the damage done to microwave ovens can be prevented if the oven is kept clean. Accumulated grease heats up when the oven is operating and can melt the plastic lining on the oven ceiling. Keeping the area around the door clean can also help prevent microwave leaks. Wipe out the inside of the oven periodically with mild soap and water; avoid oven cleaners and abrasives.

In spite of the electrical safety precautions built into the oven, you should occasionally inspect the seal around the door for a loose latch or a damaged gasket. If you suspect that the door is not closing perfectly, you should have it tested for leakage. There are inexpensive testing devices available at electronics

stores, but the equipment used by a repair service will yield more reliable results. Leave any mechanical repairs of the door or latches to a professional, although you can perform continuity tests on the door's electrical switches.

To prevent damage to the oven caused by overheating during normal operation, be sure that the vents on the bottom, back or top of the oven are not blocked. One vent is an air intake for cooling, the other is for exhaust.

As with an electric range, some breakdowns in a microwave oven can be repaired during a general inspection for loose or burned electrical connectors. Replace defective wires and connectors only with new ones that are the same size and quality as those removed.

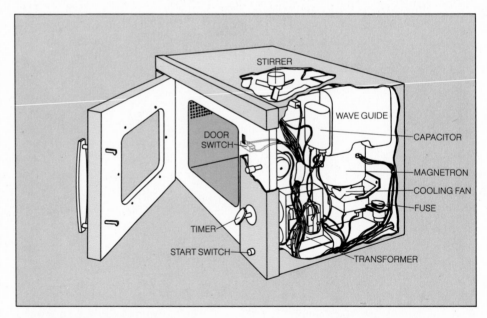

Anatomy of a microwave oven. The oven is powered by standard 120-volt house current, which is transformed into the high voltage required to generate microwaves. A transformer boosts the incoming current to about 4,000 volts AC, and a diode converts this high voltage to direct current for brief storage in the capacitor. When the current enters the electron tube called the magnetron, magnets act on the current's electrons to produce high-frequency electromagnetic waves. An antenna on top of the magnetron sends the waves up into the wave guide—a rectangular metal conduit that channels them to the oven. All of this activity is triggered by a series of interlock switches

that are activated when the door is closed and the timer and start switch are turned.

At the top of the oven, a metal blade called the stirrer bounces the waves around the oven chamber, where they are absorbed by the food. The energy in the waves agitates the molecules in the food, creating friction that causes them to heat. A fan below the magnetron keeps the magnetron cool. A fuse, located at the rear of the oven in this example, protects the unit from sudden surges of current and is also linked to the switches on the door, serving as an added precaution to keep the oven from operating when it is not securely latched.

Getting Inside the Microwave Cabinet

Removing the cover panels. To replace a burned-out light bulb on most ovens, remove the small lamp-access plate on the back or side panel of the oven *(below, left)*. To do this, unplug the oven, pull it away from the wall and locate the plate—usually it is on the upper right corner of the oven back. Remove the screws holding the plate in place, and either swing it out of the way or lift it off completely to reveal the bulb. Replace it with one of the same wattage. To obtain access to any other component, remove the metal cover that wraps over the top and sides. With the oven unplugged, unfasten the screws that hold the cover, slide it off *(below, right)* and immediately discharge the capacitor.

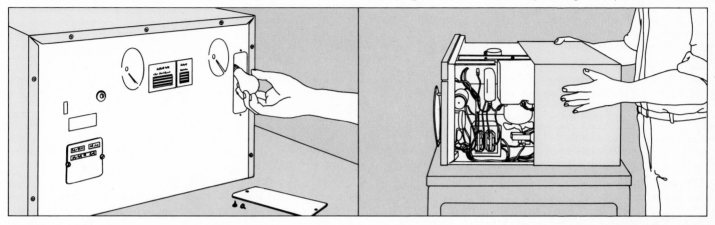

How to Empty an Electrical Storage Tank

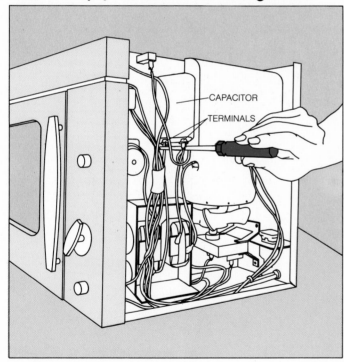

CAPACITOR
TERMINALS

Discharging the capacitor. Before touching any oven components, use a screwdriver with an insulated handle to drain electricity from the capacitor. With the unit unplugged, touch the screwdriver shaft simultaneously to the metal sleeves on the two terminal clusters. Do not let the shaft touch anything else, and keep your hands away from it and any part of the oven. The capacitor may spark as it discharges. It might have a resistor that discharges it automatically, so you may not see a spark, but discharge it anyway.

Trouble Spots: A Trio of Start-up Switches

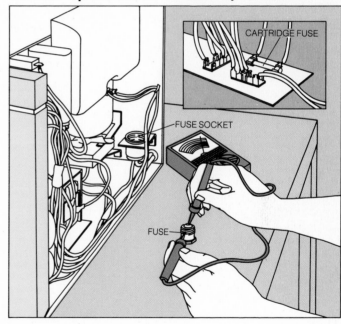

CARTRIDGE FUSE

FUSE SOCKET

FUSE

1 Checking the fuse. With the oven disconnected and the capacitor discharged, unscrew the fuse and test it for continuity with a multitester *(page 11)*. Place one probe on the bottom contact of the fuse and the other on the screw contact. If the fuse does not show continuity, replace it. Then continue checking for malfunctions that may have caused the fuse to blow.

The oven may have a cartridge fuse *(inset)* instead of the screw-type fuse, located on the junction board or near the oven back. To test a cartridge fuse for continuity, apply the probes to both ends of the cartridge.

2 **Testing the timer switch.** With the oven still unplugged and its cover removed, pull the timer assembly from the inside front panel. Uncouple the two wires attached to the terminals on the switch—a small box on the back of the timer next to its motor. Set the multitester to RX1, then turn the timer dial to ON and touch the tester probes to the switch terminals. If the terminals do not show continuity, replace the switch. On some of the models the timer switch cannot be obtained separately, and you will have to replace the entire timer assembly.

3 **Checking the start switch.** With the oven still unplugged and its cover removed, disconnect the wires from the terminals on the switch behind the start button on the control panel. Apply the probes of the multitester to the switch terminals, and have a helper push the button to ON. The switch should show no continuity before the button is pushed, and it should show continuity while it is pushed. If it fails one of these tests, replace the switch.

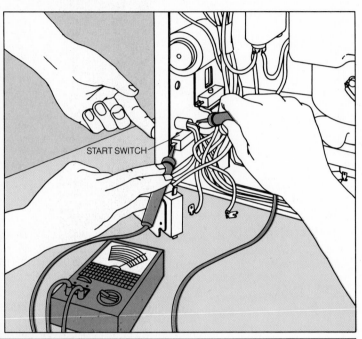
START SWITCH

TIMER MOTOR

TERMINALS

SWITCH

4 **Testing the door switches.** With the oven unplugged and the capacitor discharged, check for continuity on the switches activated by the door. On most units there will be three such switches—one behind every door latch—and on some models there is a button switch on the inner door frame. Remove the wires from one switch and place the multitester probes on its terminals; check for continuity first with the door open, then with it closed. The switch should show continuity in one case but not in the other. If the switch has continuity in both positions or no continuity in either, it must be replaced. Check the other two switches in the same way.

On some models one door switch may have three terminals (*inset*). To test such a switch for continuity, disconnect all three wires. Touch one probe to the single terminal marked COMMON, on one side of the switch, and the other probe to the terminal marked OPEN or NO. The test should show continuity with the door closed and no continuity with the door open. Then repeat the test with one probe on the common terminal and the other on the terminal marked CLOSED or NC. This time, the test should show continuity with the door open and no continuity with it closed. If the switch fails either test, replace it.

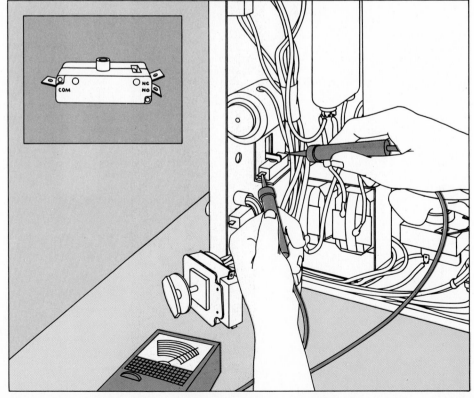

COM   NC
       NO

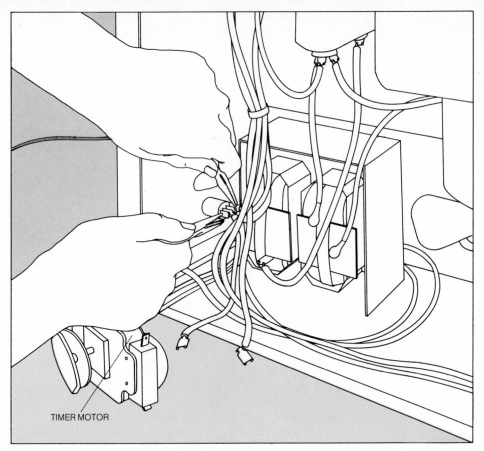

TIMER MOTOR

When a Timer Does Not Time

Checking the timer motor. If the timer switch is operative *(opposite, Step 2)* but the timer does not advance, test the timer motor to make sure it is receiving power. In performing this voltage check, be especially careful to discharge the capacitor each time the current is cut off. Unplug the oven, remove the cover and, if necessary for testing, pull the timer assembly from the inside front panel. If the terminals on the timer motor are exposed, clip a multitester lead to each terminal; if the terminals are concealed beneath the motor cover, trace the motor wires back to where they connect to a power source or plug into a junction board, and clip the multitester leads to those connections. Set the multitester for 250 volts, then plug in the oven and turn on the timer. The multitester should register 120 volts. If it does not, unplug the oven and look for defective connections between the timer and the power source. If the motor is getting power but the timer is not advancing, you should replace the timer assembly.

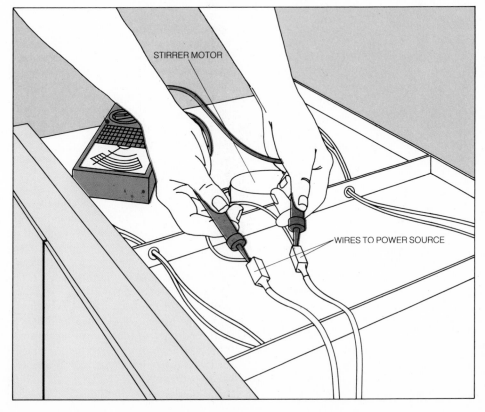

STIRRER MOTOR

WIRES TO POWER SOURCE

Curing an Oven That Cooks Unevenly

Checking the stirrer motor. With the oven plugged in, close the door and turn on the timer. Look through the window to see if the stirrer blades, above the plastic ceiling, are turning. If the blades are not visible, turn off the oven and remove the ceiling; then repeat the test.

If the blades do not move, unplug the oven, remove its cover and discharge the capacitor *(page 55)*. Locate the stirrer motor, just above the blades, and trace the motor wires back to their connection with wires from the power source. If these connections are completely insulated, separate the connector slightly to expose a bit of their metal. Close the door, plug in the oven and turn on the timer. Then, with the multitester set for 250 volts, touch the probes to the exposed metal. (Be sure to keep your fingers on the probes' insulated handles.) The multitester should register 120 volts. If you get the proper reading, showing the motor is receiving power, look for bent blades or for one hitting the cover. If there are no obstructions, replace the motor. On some models, the stirrer is driven by a belt attached to the motor. If the stirrer blades do not turn, check the belt before testing the motor.

How to Keep a Refrigerator Cool but Frost-Free

Between the old-fashioned icebox and the modern electric refrigerator stretch what seem to be light-years of mechanical and electrical advancement. Where once blocks of ice provided the chilling effect, today foodstuffs are cooled by refrigerant chemicals circulating through the connecting coils of an evaporator and a condenser. The refrigerant alternately absorbs heat and evaporates, becoming a gas, then cools and condenses, reverting to liquid form.

During the phase when the refrigerant is absorbing heat, water vapor inside the refrigerator collects as frost on the surfaces of the evaporator. For the refrigerator to function efficiently, this frost must be removed, and the three basic types of refrigerator are categorized by the manner in which this problem of frost removal is handled.

Of the three, the standard refrigerator, recognizable by its single exterior door and small, sometimes doorless freezer compartment, defrosts only when you turn the unit off and allow the frost to melt. The cycle-defrost type, generally a two-door model, has a small heater that keeps the refrigerator compartment free of frost automatically. The freezer section requires manual defrosting, but because the freezer is separated from the refrigerator, the frost build-up is much slower than in a standard refrigerator. The freezer of a cycle-defrost unit needs defrosting only two or three times a year.

Frost-free refrigerators are designed to remove the frost from both compartments almost as soon as it forms. A heater in the evaporator turns on and a drain carries the water to a pan beneath the refrigerator, where it evaporates.

Although refrigerators, especially standard and cycle-defrost types, can function smoothly for years, good maintenance can prolong their life and increase their efficiency. Vacuuming around the condenser coils, for example, allows air to circulate freely and cool the coils. Dirty coils can cause the unit to run continuously or to stop altogether.

Cleaning the drain system of a frost-free refrigerator is also important. Both the drain hole and the drain pan tend to collect debris. In addition, keeping the drain pan clean stops odors from developing and prevents bacteria from growing. When you replace the pan, be sure it clears the compressor, or it will rattle each time the refrigerator switches on.

If the rubber gaskets that seal the refrigerator and freezer doors are cleaned regularly with soapy water, they should last the life of the refrigerator. But if the gaskets become cracked or torn, or if gaps form in the seal, they should be replaced. To check the tightness of the gasket seal, close the door on a dollar bill at several points around the frame; if you feel resistance as you pull the bill out, the seal is good.

Replacing a gasket is a major job. The screws that anchor the gasket also hold the inner door panel against the outer door—along with the door's insulation. To avoid disturbing this assembly, the screws are simply loosened, not removed, and the old gasket is freed in sections. Each section is immediately replaced with a section of the new gasket, so that only a few of the screws are loose at any one time. New gaskets come molded to fit the dimensions of the door. They are packed in small boxes and should be soaked first in hot water to smooth out the crimps and to soften the stiff rubber.

Frost-free refrigerators are somewhat more prone to electrical malfunctions than standard or cycle-defrost models are, but some malfunctions are common to all three types. The button switch on the door, which turns on the interior light when the door opens, can wear out or break off, causing the light to stay on when the door is closed and increasing the interior temperature.

A refrigerator or freezer may not hold the temperature set by you on the control dial. If the cause is not dirt on the condenser coils or a deteriorated gasket, the thermostat probably is at fault. To check the temperature in a freezer, place a thermometer between two packages of frozen food; after 10 minutes the reading should be 0° to 10° F. To check the temperature in the refrigerator compartment, place a thermometer in a glass of water on the bottom shelf; after eight hours the reading should be 35° to 40°.

If the refrigerator runs constantly or cools poorly, the condensor fan may be at fault. Check first for dirty coils, then for an obstruction in the condenser fan—lost toys and other objects may become wedged between the blades and bring the cycle to a halt. If you find no obstruction, the fan motor itself should be tested for resistance (page 18).

Most electrical problems in frost-free refrigerators have to do with nonfunctioning phases in the frost-removal cycle. If frost accumulates on the walls of the freezer section, first check the door switch that activates the evaporator fan. If the fan switch is not the problem, inspect the fan blades for ice; melt the ice by aiming a hair dryer, set on low heat, at the fan. If no ice is found on the fan blades, test the fan motor for resistance.

If everything in the operation of the evaporator fan checks out, from door switch to motor, examine the type of ice collecting on the evaporator coils. If the fins projecting from the coils are clogged with hard ice near the bottom, the drain system is clogged; if the coils are covered with white, fluffy frost, the problem is in the defrost timer, the heater or the defrost-limit switch.

To identify which of these components is malfunctioning, start the defrost timer manually and observe what happens. If the timer is defective, advancing it by hand will bypass the problem: The heater will come on, defrost the ice, and then turn itself off in 20 to 30 minutes. A faulty timer must be replaced. If the heater does not come on when the timer is advanced, test the heater for resistance. If the heater shows proper resistance, it is the defrost-limit switch, by elimination, that is at fault and must be replaced.

Although refrigerators vary in design, their mechanical and electrical parts usually function identically. Replacement parts should always be an exact match of the original, identified by model number. Also, though most refrigerator repairs require standard tools, some need special tools and special precautions. Leaks in the tubing of the evaporator or compressor should be left to a trained technician. So should the replacement of a compressor. A faulty compressor, in fact, may signal the end for the refrigerator. It may be better economy to invest in a new refrigerator than in a new compressor.

Two Approaches to the Need for Removing Frost

A totally automatic system. In a frost-free refrigerator, the compressor pumps refrigerant through two sets of coils connected by a thin tube. The evaporator coils, inside the partition dividing the freezer from the refrigerator, cool the unit by absorbing heat. The condenser coils, at floor level, expel the heat into the room with the help of a condenser fan. An evaporator fan in the freezer compartment circulates chilled air from the evaporator coils through the freezer compartment and helps to prevent condensation on the freezer walls. Two door switches—one in the freezer compartment for the evaporator fan, the other in the refrigerator compartment for the interior light—turn the fan on when the door is closed, and the light on when the door is open. The thermostat, with its dial control, regulates the temperature in both the refrigerator and freezer compartments.

During the defrost cycle, which occurs two to three times a day for 20 to 30 minutes, the defrost heater mounted in the evaporator coils melts the frost that collects there. The heater is activated by a defrost timer and is turned off by a defrost-limit switch. The defrost water flows down the inside back wall of the refrigerator and out through a drain hole into a drain pan underneath, where it evaporates into the room.

A semiautomatic system. In a cycle-defrost refrigerator, evaporator plates are located in the top, bottom and back of the freezer and also in the back of the refrigerator compartment. Refrigerant is pumped through them by the compressor, and the heat is expelled by condenser coils, which cover the outside back of the refrigerator.

A defrost heater mounted on the evaporator plate of the refrigerator compartment melts frost that collects in that compartment. When the temperature on the evaporator plate drops below a point set on the thermostat control, the compressor turns off and the heater turns on. A drain hole in the bottom of the compartment carries off the defrost water. When the temperature in the compartment rises to 35°, the heater shuts off and the cooling cycle resumes.

The freezer is defrosted manually when the thermostat control is turned to OFF. In some models, the water drains out of the freezer into a pan placed in the refrigerator compartment. More commonly, it puddles on the bottom of the freezer compartment, to be mopped up by hand.

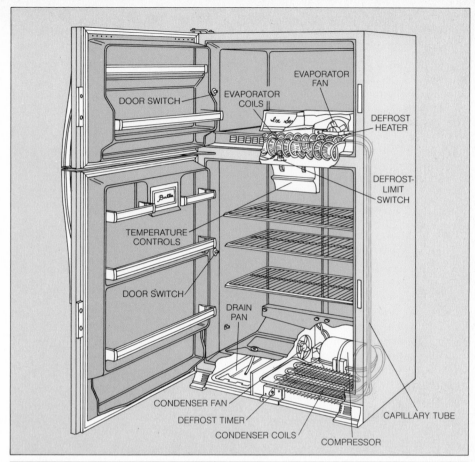

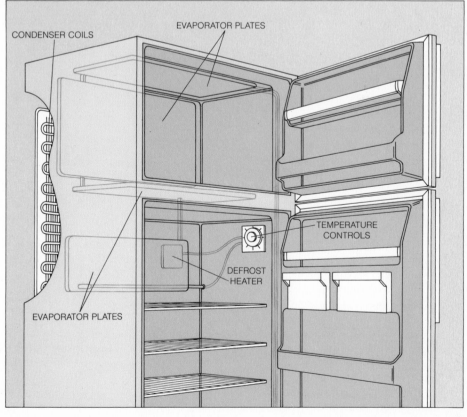

Superficial Repairs for Doors and Drains

Adjusting a sagging freezer door. Using a nut driver, loosen the two hex-headed bolts in the single hinge at the top of the freezer door. Reposition the door squarely over the opening of the freezer compartment by pulling upward on the door handle. Then, holding the door firmly in place, tighten the hinge bolts. Check the door by opening and closing it several times: It should clear the top of the refrigerator compartment door and should align with the top of the cabinet.

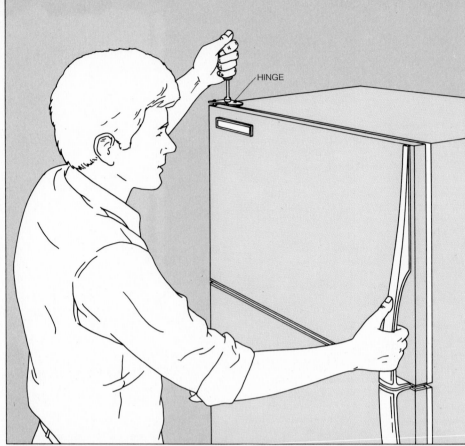

Unclogging the drain hole. Remove the storage bins at the bottom of the refrigerator compartment to locate the drain hole. Pry out the stopper plug, and clear the drain by inserting a length of flexible ¼-inch plastic tubing or a pipe cleaner into the hole and pushing it through the drain canal into the drain pan below. Flush the drain with a solution of soapy water and ammonia, forcing it through the canal with a basting syringe; rinse the syringe well after using it for this purpose. Empty and wash the drain pan.

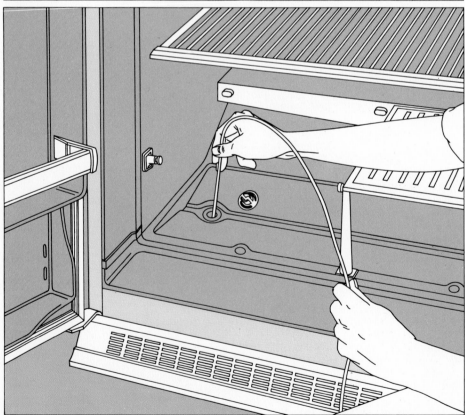

A New Seal for the Door

1 **Loosening the retaining screws.** Starting at the top outer corner of the door, roll back the rubber gasket with one hand, exposing the metal retaining strip beneath. Use a nut driver to loosen the retaining screws two turns each, working across the top of the door and to a point one third of the way down each side.

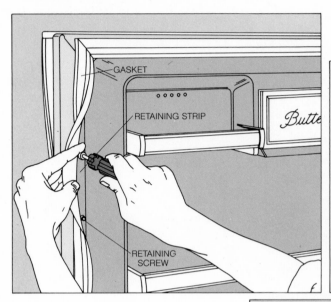

2 **Installing the new gasket.** Pull the old gasket straight up to free it from behind the loosened retaining strip. With the old gasket hanging out of the way, slide the new gasket behind the retaining strip, beginning along the top of the door and working down the two sides; tighten the retaining screws as you go. Continue loosening the retaining screws down the remaining length of the two sides, stripping off the old gasket and simultaneously inserting the new. At the bottom of the door, slip out the old gasket at one corner, replacing it with the new gasket before loosening the retaining screws at the final corner. Then complete the last few inches of the installation.

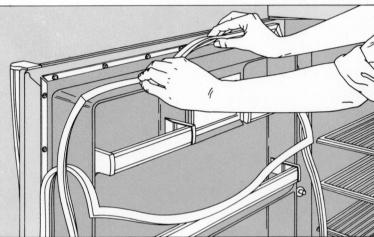

3 **Squaring the door.** When the entire gasket is in place, realign the door within its frame by adjusting the tension of the retaining screws. To determine if the door is skewed, close it and inspect the seal between the door and its frame for gaps. If the door is out of alignment, note the direction of the twist and, with the door open, exert pressure against the lower edge of the door to bring it into alignment. Adjust the tension of the retaining screws as necessary, tightening or loosening them until the twist is straightened. At the same time, make sure that the inner door is firmly secured to the outer door; otherwise the lightweight outer door will shimmy when it is opened and closed. To steady the lower door during these adjustments, brace it with your foot; to steady the upper door, have a helper hold the door square with the top of the cabinet.

Testing the Door Switches for the Light and Fan

1 **Removing the push button.** Unplug the refrigerator and, with the tip of a screwdriver, gently pry the push-button collar out of its hole in the door panel. Pull the push button out of the panel, along with its wires, by tipping the button down to free the right-angle terminals *(inset)*.

2 **Checking the circuit.** Pull the wires off the switch terminals and test the switch for continuity *(page 11)*. A light switch should show continuity when the push button is extended and no continuity when the button is depressed; a fan switch should show continuity when the button is depressed and no continuity when the button is extended. If the two switches are operated by a single button, test the four terminals in pairs until continuity between two of them is found. If you find that the switch is faulty, simply replace it with a new one, reattach the wires and snap the push button back into the door panel.

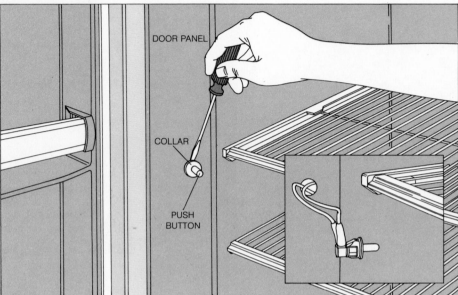

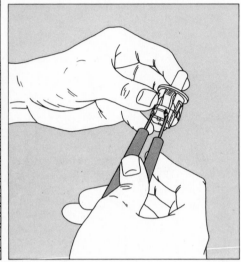

How to Examine the Temperature Control

1 **Getting at the thermostat.** Unplug the refrigerator and remove the control dial on the side or back wall of the refrigerator. On some models this dial is mounted on a console that unscrews from the wall; on others the dial is flush against the wall, and you can remove it by pulling it off or by unscrewing a setscrew. Pull the thermostat out of the wall and lower it gently onto the nearest shelf, taking care not to bend the slender tube of the thermostat's sensing bulb. Disconnect the wires from the thermostat terminals.

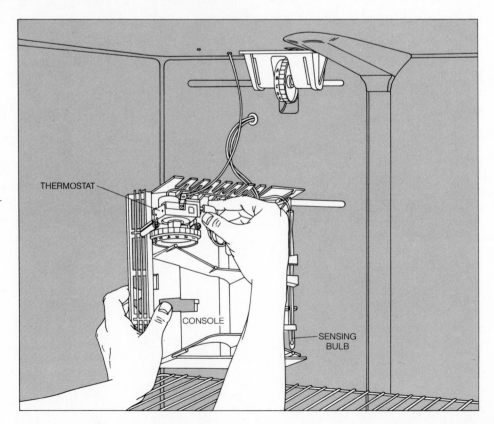

2 **Putting the thermostat through its paces.** Test the thermostat for continuity by turning the control dial to OFF and touching the probes of a multitester to the two terminals; the meter should show no continuity *(page 11)*. Then, with the probes still touching the terminals, turn the dial to ON and gradually rotate it through the entire range of settings. The meter should start showing continuity at some point as the dial is turned, depending on the freezer temperature at the time of the test. If it does not, the thermostat is faulty and should be replaced.

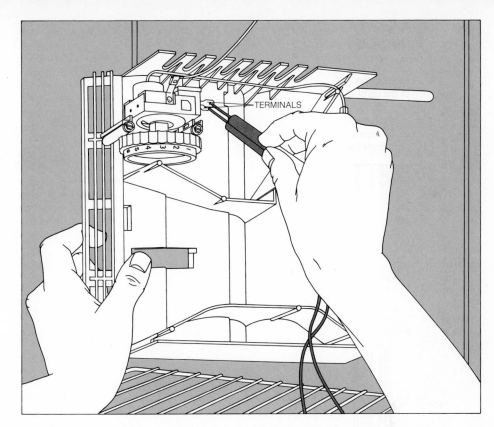

How to Get at the Evaporator Fan

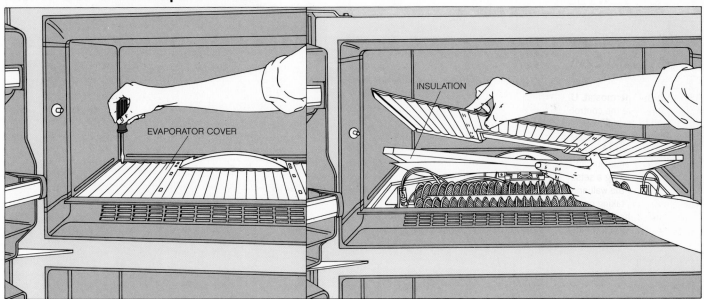

1 **Gaining access to the fan.** Unplug the refrigerator and remove any icemaking devices from the freezer. Remove the louvered cover from the fan assembly, if there is one; unscrew the evaporator cover, which forms the freezer floor *(above, left)*. Lift out this panel and its insulation *(above, right)*. If the sharp edges of the evaporator fins are exposed, cover them with a towel before beginning work on the fan.

2 **Testing the fan motor.** With the power off, remove the retaining screws from each side of the fan's mounting bracket and lift out the evaporator fan. Disconnect the wires and test the motor for resistance *(page 11)*. With the multitester set at RX1, the meter·should read between 50 and 200 ohms. A higher reading or no reading at all indicates that the motor should be replaced. If you save the fan blades and the mounting bracket, you can reuse them with the new motor.

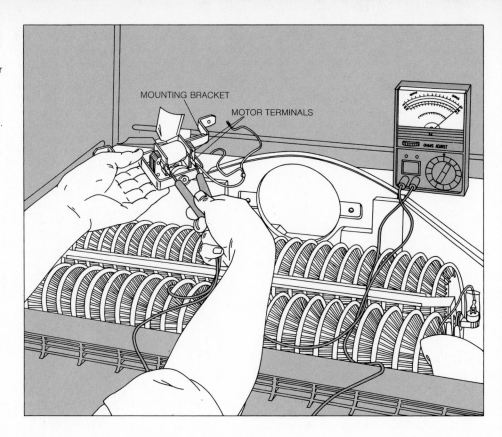

MOUNTING BRACKET

MOTOR TERMINALS

Checking the Condenser Fan

Testing the motor. Unplug the refrigerator and move it away from the wall to remove the rear access panel. Leave the condenser fan in place, but disconnect its wires and test the fan motor for resistance. With the multitester set at RX1, the meter should read between 50 and 200 ohms. A higher reading or no reading at all means that the motor should be replaced.

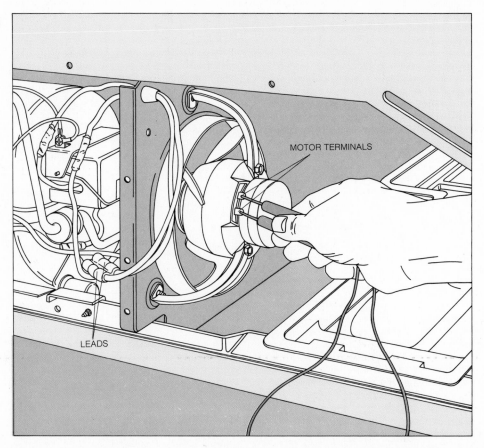

MOTOR TERMINALS

LEADS

Replacing a damaged motor. With the refrigerator unplugged, remove the wires from their terminals and use tabs of masking tape to note their positions. Then unscrew the condenser fan's mounting brackets from the divider panel and lift out the fan assembly. Unscrew the mounting bracket from the motor and unfasten the hub nut that holds the fan blades in place. Reattach both the blades and the bracket to a new motor, and put the fan assembly back into the refrigerator, attaching the wires to their terminals.

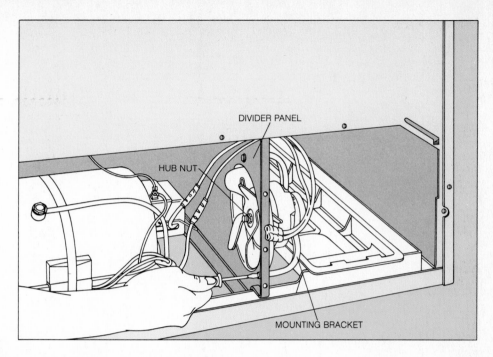

DIVIDER PANEL

HUB NUT

MOUNTING BRACKET

A Mechanical Test for the Defrost Cycle

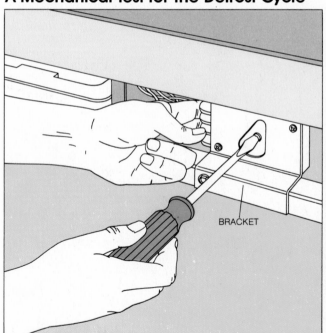

BRACKET

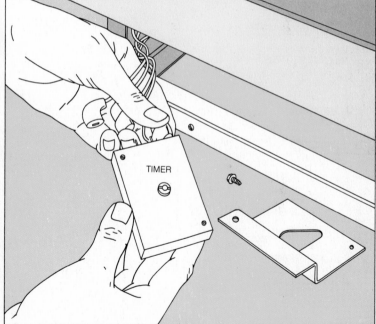

TIMER

Testing the timer. Locate the defrost timer behind the bottom front grille or behind the rear access panel, and advance the timer with a screwdriver while the compressor is not running. Insert the blade of the screwdriver in the timer slot and turn it clockwise until the timer clicks. If the defrost heating element turns on, the defective part is the timer's automatic switch, but the entire timer will have to be replaced.

Replacing a defective defrost timer. Unplug the refrigerator and unscrew the timer's mounting bracket from the refrigerator frame. Remove the timer from the mounting bracket and disconnect the timer's ground wire, if there is one, from the cabinet bottom. Then disconnect the operating wires from the old timer and transfer them to a replacement timer. Screw the new timer to the mounting bracket and connect its grounding wire to the cabinet bottom. Then fasten the bracket and timer back into place on the frame of the refrigerator.

Checking the defrost heater. Unplug the refrigerator, and remove the panel and insulation covering the evaporator. Disconnect the wires of the defrost heating element and, with the meter set at RX1, touch the probes of a multitester to the terminals. The meter should show between 15 and 100 ohms of resistance. If the reading is higher or there is no reading at all, the heater is defective. On this typical model the heater is enclosed in a glass rod running between the evaporator coils; the rod snaps into brackets and is released by a twist of the tabs that hold it in the brackets. If the heater is encased in aluminum tubing and is embedded in the evaporator coils, it should be replaced by a trained technician.

Replacing the defrost-limit switch. Unplug the refrigerator and locate the switch—usually just in front of the evaporator coils. To gain access to it, remove the panel and the insulation covering the evaporator. Remove the screws holding the switch to the freezer floor and lift the switch out of the freezer. Cut the wires to the switch and connect a new switch with wire caps *(page 14)*. Fill the caps with a silicone sealer to protect the wires from the moisture of the refrigerator. Return the switch to its former position on the floor of the freezer.

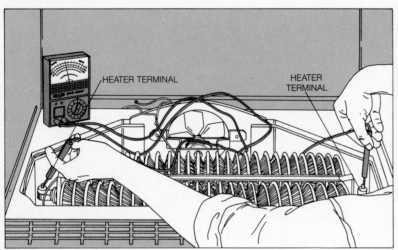

HEATER TERMINAL

HEATER TERMINAL

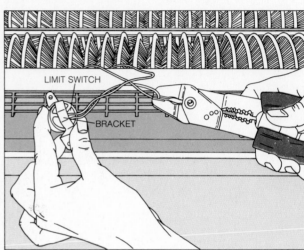

LIMIT SWITCH

BRACKET

A Step-by-Step Approach to Compressor Problems

Testing the components. Unplug the refrigerator and remove the rear access panel. Flip up the retaining wire holding the relay cover in place, and pull the cover straight off. Unplug the relay from the compressor terminals and examine the copper coils of the relay for charring. Test the overload protector for continuity *(page 16).* Then test the compressor itself for continuity *(page 18);* there should be continuity between any two of the three compressor terminals, and no continuity between any one terminal and the compressor housing. If the compressor components fail any of these tests, the compressor is defective. It should be fixed by a trained technician.

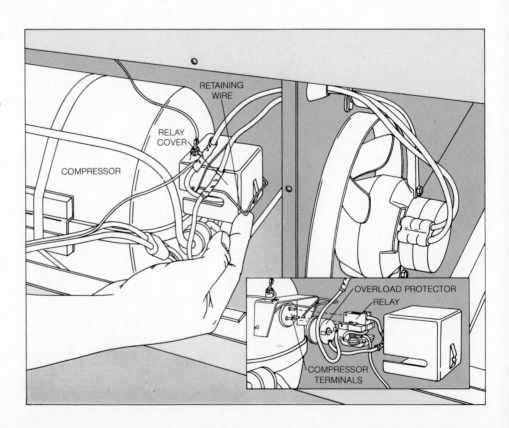

RETAINING WIRE

RELAY COVER

COMPRESSOR

OVERLOAD PROTECTOR

RELAY

COMPRESSOR TERMINALS

The Errant Icemaker

The first step in diagnosing an icemaker's ills is to distinguish what is normal from what is not. In these ingenious machines, the humming of the motor, the sound of water running, and the sometimes disconcerting noise of ice dropping into the device's plastic bin are to be expected. Also, how long it takes the icemaker to produce one batch of ice may vary significantly—from 30 minutes to two hours or more; the amount of time depends on the number of times the freezer door is opened, the temperature of the water entering the mold, the amount of food stored in the freezer and the temperature of the freezer itself.

You will know that the icemaker is malfunctioning when the motor does not start, when there is no ice, or when the icemaker overflows with ice. Testing whether the icemaker is cycling properly will often help you to find the faulty part. You can perform the test by putting the device through its paces manually, using a screwdriver to turn the drive gear (opposite) and studying the sequence of actions that results. Although icemaker models are different in appearance and in installation, most of them operate in the same way.

If the icemaker has stopped, first check to make sure that the shutoff arm (right) is in the correct position at the beginning of the cycle (down in most units). Next, check to make sure that the freezer is cold enough (10° F.) to activate the thermostat that initiates the ice-ejection process. (To test the temperature, put an outdoor thermometer between two food packages in the freezer.) If the thermostat is faulty, it can be replaced, but to attach the new one you will have to use a special manufacturer-approved adhesive that is formulated to make good contact with the cold surface of the icemaker mold.

Any one of the three small on/off switches found in the icemaker (opposite) may also malfunction and cause the device to fail. Although the switches are identical in appearance, they have different jobs to do. The holding switch keeps the power on for the full rotation of the ejector blades, the water-valve switch starts the water flowing during the water-fill period, and the shutoff switch stops

the icemaker when the shutoff arm indicates that the ice bin is full. If a phase of the cycle fails, the switch regulating that particular phase should be tested for continuity (page 11).

Before testing any electrical part, always be sure to disconnect the power to the unit by unplugging the refrigerator. Label each wire you disconnect, so that you will be able to reconnect it in the correct position; this ensures that none of the wires will become entangled in the icemaker's moving parts.

To keep the icemaker working smoothly once it has been repaired and to prevent leaks, keep the ice mold level and coat it lightly with silicone grease, available from appliance dealers.

The mechanics of endless ice. Water entering the icemaker mold at the completion of a cycle is frozen by the cold air of the freezer. When the thermostat in the icemaker senses that the temperature within the mold has dropped to between 10 and 15°, it starts the motor and the mold heater. The heater melts the ice slightly from underneath, while the motor-driven ejector blades slowly but firmly push the ice out of the mold into the bin below (inset). As the ice falls into the bin, the shutoff arm rises.

To make more ice, the ejector blades return to their original position, the thermostat resets, and the mold refills with water. The shutoff arm descends to the level of the new ice in the bin. If the bin is full, the shutoff arm stops the next cycle; if not, the production of ice continues.

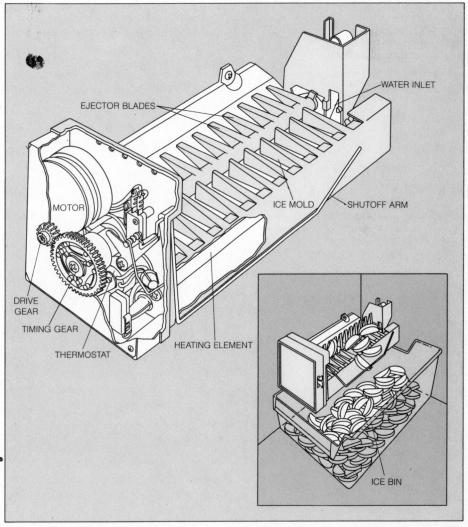

EJECTOR BLADES

WATER INLET

MOTOR

ICE MOLD — SHUTOFF ARM

DRIVE GEAR

TIMING GEAR

THERMOSTAT

HEATING ELEMENT

ICE BIN

Too Much of a Good Thing

Adjusting the water fill. Remove the icemaker cover and unscrew the unit from the freezer but do not unplug it. Place a container marked in cubic centimeters (cc.)—such as a baby bottle—under the water-fill tube. Set a funnel in the bottle. Insert a screwdriver in the slot in the drive gear and gently turn it about one-half turn counterclockwise, until you hear the motor start.

Allow the unit to complete a cycle, then measure the water in the bottle. If it is more than 145 cc., decrease the water flow by turning the water-adjustment screw clockwise; if it is less than 145 cc., turn the screw counterclockwise. One full turn will vary the fill by approximately 18 cc. Do not turn the adjustment screw any more than one and one-half turns in all.

Testing the electrical components. Shut off the power to the icemaker, and test each of its electrical components for continuity. To test the thermostat, first disconnect the leads and touch the continuity probes to the terminals while the icemaker is still inside the freezer; if the freezer temperature is below 10°, there ought to be continuity. Then remove the icemaker from the freezer and allow it to warm to room temperature. Test it once again; this time there ought to be no continuity.

To test the three small on/off switches—the shutoff switch, the water-valve control switch and the holding switch—leave the unit unplugged and label and disconnect the leads, then remove the switches from the icemaker. Test each terminal with the common contact (sometimes marked C) on the side of the switch. When a terminal is marked NC (normally closed), the test should show no continuity when the button is depressed, continuity when the button is extended. A terminal marked NO (normally open) ought to yield the opposite results.

To test the U-shaped heating element for continuity *(page 11)*, first remove the wire nuts from both ends of the element leads. Set the multitester at RX1K, and then touch the probes to the two wires for the heating element.

WATER-FILL TUBE
WATER-ADJUSTMENT SCREW

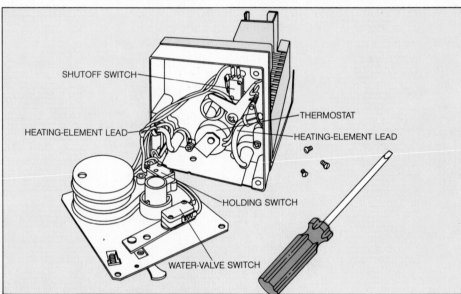

SHUTOFF SWITCH
HEATING-ELEMENT LEAD
THERMOSTAT
HEATING-ELEMENT LEAD
HOLDING SWITCH
WATER-VALVE SWITCH

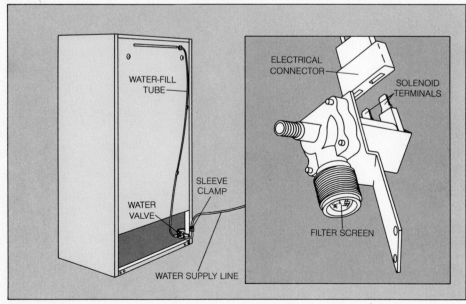

WATER-FILL TUBE
SLEEVE CLAMP
WATER VALVE
WATER SUPPLY LINE
ELECTRICAL CONNECTOR
SOLENOID TERMINALS
FILTER SCREEN

Correcting the water flow. Pull the refrigerator away from the wall and locate the water valve behind the rear access panel. Turn off the water supply at the valve under the sink, disconnect the water line at the sleeve clamp and hold a large container under the line. With the water turned on again, measure the flow; the rate should be several cups a minute. If the flow appears restricted, the valve at the sink may be clogged; clear it by turning off the main cold-water supply, disassembling the valve, and running a wire through it.

If the flow is adequate but insufficient water is reaching the icemaker, unplug the valve on the refrigerator *(inset)* and test the solenoid for continuity with a multitester *(page 11)*. If the solenoid is defective, the valve should be replaced. A dirty filter screen may also be impeding water flow; disassemble the water valve and clean the screen under running water.

When Ice Was Harvested with a Saw

In this mechanized age when the hardest part of chilling a drink is emptying an ice tray (and even this may be done automatically), it is startling to realize that the ice that cooled a Southerner's julep in the 19th Century may have traveled thousands of miles.

Keeping foodstuffs cool in a hot, damp summer—never mind icing a drink—was a problem faced by America's southern colonies from the time of the earliest settlements. Some landowners—George Washington and Thomas Jefferson were among them—solved the problem by building icehouses, large rooms dug into the earth, and stocking them with ice cut from nearby ponds in winter. Insulated with sawdust and straw, about 40 per cent of the stored ice lasted long enough to make an appearance in the summer in a pitcher of water or an iced dessert.

Farther south, warm winters made ice even more of a luxury. In harbor towns such as Charleston, South Carolina, it sometimes arrived as ballast in the holds of cotton-trading ships from New England. Then a shrewd Yankee businessman turned this occasional trade into a regular business. In 1806, Frederic Tudor saw his first ice-filled brigantine set sail from Boston for Martinique, and a new industry was launched.

In the early days, Tudor's ice trade suffered its share of setbacks. His first shipment arrived safely in Martinique, but his profits literally melted away for lack of proper storage. Shortly thereafter, shipping was interrupted by war with Britain. When it resumed, ice supplies were as unreliable as the weather. A warm New England winter in 1818 forced Tudor's brigantine *Retrieve* to head north to Labrador, where the ship's crew attacked an iceberg with picks and crowbars to collect ice for the Caribbean market.

Still, it was not very long before ice-collecting in Northern rivers and ponds was being done with the zeal and efficiency of a Midwestern wheat harvest. Specialized tools and techniques for clearing, marking and cutting the frozen surface created a uniform product relatively easy to move, store and market.

Once cut, the ice blocks were packed with straw and sawdust insulation in huge aboveground icehouses to await transportation by rail to major cities and harbors. Some of the ice traveled halfway around the globe, as Thoreau noted when describing the ice harvest on Walden Pond: "The sweltering inhabitants of Charleston and New Orleans, of Madras and Bombay and Calcutta, drink at my well."

While improved methods of harvesting and transporting ice were making it more affordable, a refrigeration device invented by a Maryland dairyman in the early 19th Century had become common enough that it was dubbed a "household necessity." This invention, a double-walled icebox insulated with cork, ash, charcoal or seaweed, remained standard into the 1930s. Its cooling power came from big chunks of ice delivered door-to-door by the iceman's horse-drawn wagon.

By the 1930s the ice for iceboxes was made artificially. Manufactured ice and mechanical refrigeration first gained acceptance far from American shores, in the breweries of Germany and in the Australian mutton trade. During the American Civil War, two ice-making machines were imported from France by the Confederate States when Northern ice shipments were suspended.

Thereafter, the use of mechanical refrigerators slowly spread—to the meatpackers of Texas and Chicago, to the fruit and vegetable fields of California and the Southwest. But their introduction into the home had to await two technological developments: a compact, self-regulating electric motor and a refrigerant that could be circulated by a small motor-compressor. Once these breakthroughs were made, near the start of the 20th Century, it remained only for mass production to make the new machines affordable.

The first electric refrigerators for home use, marketed in 1917, resembled traditional wooden iceboxes and cost $900, twice as much as an automobile. Twenty-five years later, mass-produced models much like those used today were fixtures in some three million homes. Now, so few American homes are without them that the clink of ice cubes in chilled tumblers is commonplace—even in the hottest of climates.

A 19th Century ice harvest. In this 1883 engraving, newly cut ice is floated to steam-driven conveyors for storage in a huge icehouse. In the foreground, the ice field is cleared of snow and scored with horse-drawn implements —scrapers, ice planes and ice plows— then cut into raft-size slabs with a handsaw.

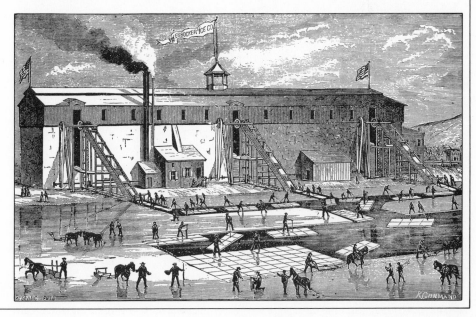

3

Appliances for Cleaning Things

Churning the dirt away. When a clothes washer is operating smoothly, the rippling fins of its plastic agitator swivel back and forth in a 180° arc, squeezing sudsy water through dirty laundry as hands and fingers would. But the agitator is prone to jamming. Small articles such as belts and babies' socks work their way beneath it and wrap around the shaft on which the agitator turns. Freeing the agitator is a simple matter of removing the cap at its top, lifting the agitator from the shaft and removing the caught clothing—a repair usually made so quickly that the machine is only briefly out of service.

Cleaning devices may not be as crucially important to domestic life as those concerned with food preparation, but when they fail, our dependence on them becomes painfully clear. A dishwasher that does not wash takes much of the joy out of a dinner party, and even something as seemingly frivolous as a trash compactor can be hard to do without if you have grown accustomed to its services. Once considered luxuries, some of the machines that help us clean our homes and our belongings are now necessities. They are also likely to represent major investments, and thus are worth fixing.

Although machines that clean appear to have nothing in common, varying widely in design, operation, complexity and size, almost every one of them produces motion. Thus they are full of moving parts. In performing their chores, vacuum cleaners and dishwashers propel air or sudsy water through hoses, while trash compactors and garbage disposers deal directly with refuse by means of mechanical rams and blades. It is the parts producing these motions—pump impellers, agitators, fan blades, drive belts and gears—that are subjected to the greatest stress and are most prone to fail.

In the course of doing their dirty work, cleaning appliances are also vulnerable to their common enemy: dirt. Large volumes of dust, debris and garbage are flushed or wafted through them, leaving behind deposits that can eventually choke major passageways. In appliances that move air or pump water, clogged hoses are a common cause of breakdowns. Similarly, when a garbage-handling appliance fails, the first place to look for the source of the trouble is in the mechanism that is in contact with the garbage. Even water heaters and water softeners are most frequently put out of commission by deposits of ingredients in the water they process.

In considering the repair of a cleaning appliance, you may feel put off by its size: Most of them are large. But bigness is not necessarily synonymous with complexity. Indeed, one of the largest of the appliances in the following chapter is also the simplest—a water heater consists of just two heating elements and several thermostats. All the rest of its bulk is tank. And although some of these large appliances, such as the washing machine, do have complicated timers to control the sequence of actions they are programed to perform, the parts activated by the timer are simple. In fact, there are often striking resemblances between analogous parts in large and small appliances. The valve that lets water into a dishwasher, for example, closely resembles the water-inlet valves of icemakers and clothes washers. Consequently, if you know how to test and repair one valve, chances are you can test and repair any of the three, turning a single skill into a triple play.

Repairs for Water Heaters

Breakdowns of both gas and electric water heaters are caused most often by the malfunction of an easily replaced electrical part. On electric water heaters *(opposite)*, it is the high-powered heating elements or the thermostats that burn out; on gas heaters, the faulty part is usually the electrical safety device *(page 74)* that keeps the gas flowing. Available at home-improvement centers and water-heater dealers, all of these inexpensive parts are simply fitted onto or into the tank wall after the water heater is turned off and, in some cases, drained.

Leaks, however, are far more serious. A water leak in the tank itself calls for replacement of the water heater; leaks in the gas line require the immediate attention of a professional.

The cause for the breakdown of an electric water heater is pinpointed with a multitester *(page 10)*, which isolates a broken electrical connection in a thermostat or a heating element. The elements, particularly the lower element (most electric water heaters have two), are more likely to fail than any other part, and both should be replaced even if only one has failed. The new elements should have the same wattage, voltage and attachment fittings as the old.

The upper thermostat of an electric water heater is harder to test than the lower one, because the arrangement of terminals varies with the model and the thermostat can be hooked up in as many as five different ways. The simplest way to determine whether the upper thermostat has failed is by a process of elimination: Test all the rest of the circuits first. Since upper thermostats differ, a faulty one must be replaced with one of the same type, identified by a number on the dial. All lower thermostats and high-temperature cutoffs *(opposite)*, however, are interchangeable so long as they are made for the same voltage, since they work in the same way.

Unlike electric water heaters, gas models use electricity only in the thermocouple *(page 74)*, a safety device that shuts off the gas when the pilot light goes out. The thermocouple is a short rod that converts heat from the pilot flame into a minute amount of electricity, which in turn holds open the valve that admits gas to the burner. Eventually a thermocouple may become too weak to hold the valve open, so the heater shuts off. Suspect the thermocouple first when this happens, and replace it.

To operate at peak efficiency, both gas and electric water heaters need preventive maintenance. Test the temperature-pressure valve *(opposite)* at the top of the tank every year by pushing down the valve handle and letting out some water. If the valve fails to release water, it is clogged and should be replaced. Unscrew it from the tank top after shutting off the heat and draining the tank *(page 74)*. If the valve leaks after you release the handle, operate it several times to wash out accumulated sediment. Also, once a year open the drain cock and let out about 5 gallons of water to prevent sediment from accumulating on the bottom of the tank.

An Electric Water Heater

How an electric water heater works. The two heating elements of most electric water heaters are controlled by a pair of thermostats wired so that only one element can heat at a time. In normal usage, hot water leaving the tank from the top is replaced by cold water entering the tank through the bottom of the dip tube, and the lower thermostat, sensing the drop in temperature, turns on the lower element. If a great deal of hot water is being used, the upper thermostat turns on the upper element and shuts off power to the lower thermostat and element; thus the water at the top of the tank is heated first.

To protect the tank from corrosion, a magnesium rod—called the sacrificial anode—is slowly consumed by galvanic corrosion, which would otherwise destroy the tank's walls. To keep the tank from overheating, the temperature-pressure valve at the top of the tank vents the water if it reaches a temperature of 210° F., and a high-temperature cutoff preset at 190° turns off the power to the entire heater.

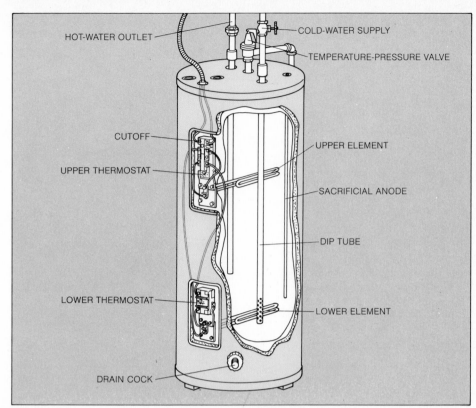

HOT-WATER OUTLET — COLD-WATER SUPPLY

TEMPERATURE-PRESSURE VALVE

CUTOFF — UPPER ELEMENT

UPPER THERMOSTAT — SACRIFICIAL ANODE

DIP TUBE

LOWER THERMOSTAT — LOWER ELEMENT

DRAIN COCK

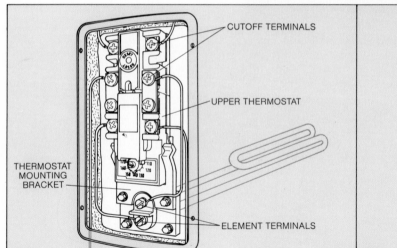

CUTOFF TERMINALS

UPPER THERMOSTAT

THERMOSTAT MOUNTING BRACKET

ELEMENT TERMINALS

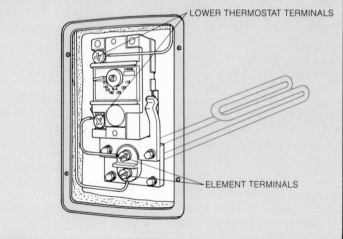

LOWER THERMOSTAT TERMINALS

ELEMENT TERMINALS

Finding an electrical failure. First check the main service panel for a blown fuse or tripped circuit breaker. Then turn off the power to the water heater and remove the cover from the heater controls. Clip the leads of a multitester, set at 250 volts, to the two top terminals of the high-temperature cutoff, and turn on the power at the service panel. If the meter reading is not twice the voltage tested at a standard wall outlet (*page 12*), then the fault is in the house wiring.

If the meter reading is correct, the water heater is at fault; turn off the power to the water heater and let the tank water cool to lukewarm. Then, with the power off, disconnect the heating elements, set the multitester at RX1, and test the

following pairs of terminals for continuity (*page 16*): the two left and two right terminals on the high-temperature cutoff (if there are cutoffs for both thermostats, test both); the upper and lower heating-element terminals; and the lower thermostat terminals. On each test, the meter's needle should indicate continuity. If it does not, the circuitry in the heating elements or the lower thermostat is defective, but the circuitry in the cutoff may be good. Press the cutoff's reset button and test the cutoff again. If the needle still does not indicate continuity, the cutoff circuitry is faulty too.

To test a heating element for a short circuit, touch one meter probe to the tank wall or the

mounting bracket of the element, the other probe to either terminal of the element. If there is continuity, the element is short-circuited.

If your water gets too hot even with the thermostats set low, and the heating elements are good, test the lower thermostat's response to high temperatures by holding it over a lighted candle. Within 30 seconds you should hear a click; test the terminals immediately. If there is continuity, the lower thermostat is broken.

If both of the heating elements—as well as the high-temperature cutoff and the lower thermostat—pass these tests, it is safe to assume that the upper thermostat is broken.

Replacing heating elements. Turn off power to the water heater and remove the panels covering the controls. Connect one end of a garden hose to the tank's drain cock, and run the other end to a floor-level house drain. Turn off the cold-water supply valve (*page 73*) and open the drain cock, as well as all the hot-water faucets in the house. When the tank has been completely drained, disconnect the heating-element wires from their terminals, and unfasten the elements from the tank. Some elements, like the one shown here, bolt directly onto the tank; others (*inset*) screw into it.

Screw or bolt the new heating elements to the tank, using the new gaskets provided. Close the hot-water faucets and the drain cock; then turn on the cold-water supply to refill the tank. To check whether the tank is full, open a hot-water faucet anywhere in the house above the top of the tank and wait for water to gush out; the elements will burn out immediately unless they are covered by water. Reconnect the element wires and replace the cover panels. Then restore power to the water heater.

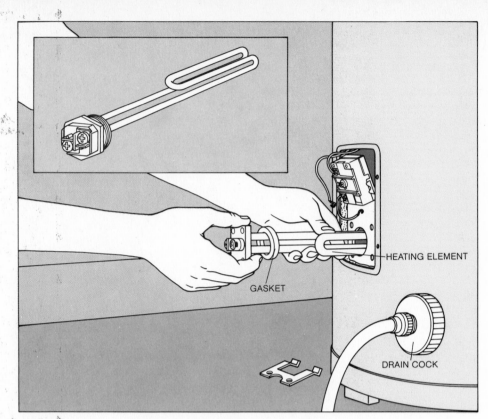

HEATING ELEMENT

GASKET

DRAIN COCK

A Valve to Shut Off the Gas

Replacing a thermocouple. With the gas turned off at the water heater's gas control, unclip the large brazed end of the thermocouple (*inset*) from the pilot bracket underneath the water tank. Then use a wrench to unscrew the small end of the thermocouple from the magnet fitting on the gas control on the side of the tank.

To install the new thermocouple, reverse the procedure. First screw the small end of the thermocouple to the magnet fitting until it is finger-tight; then give it a quarter turn more with a wrench. Bend the copper connecting wire into a gentle curve, then clip the large brazed end into the pilot bracket so that the pilot flame will cover ½ inch of the tip. Turn on the gas and light the pilot according to the manufacturer's instructions printed on the tank.

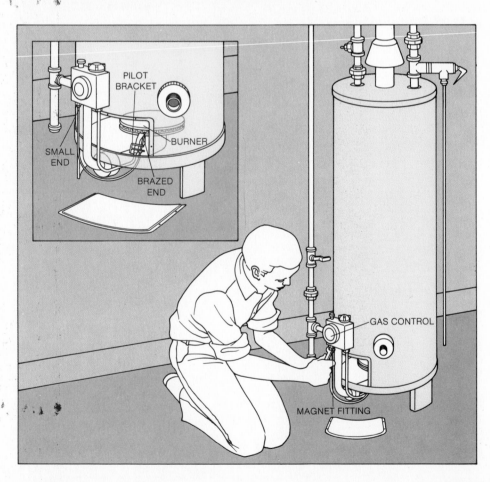

PILOT BRACKET

SMALL END

BURNER

BRAZED END

GAS CONTROL

MAGNET FITTING

Treatments for a Clothes Dryer in Distress

A clothesline filled with wet laundry flapping in the breeze on a sunny day illustrates the three functions a clothes dryer performs: It provides heat, air and motion. Instead of the sun, the breeze and the clothesline, a dryer uses electric or gas heat, a fan, and a revolving drum. All three of them must work together or the laundry will not dry.

The mechanical parts of a dryer are more likely to fail than the electrical parts. So if your dryer stops working, check the mechanical parts first. Gas and electric dryers are similar; they differ only in their source of heat. In either type, suspect a broken belt if the motor is running but the drum does not revolve. Turn the drum manually and listen for a thumping sound, a sure sign that the belt is broken and is hitting the drum as it turns. To replace a broken belt, remove the drum and slip a new belt around it and the pulleys that turn it (page 78).

Any dryer's electrical parts can be tested for continuity with a multitester (page 11), with the dryer unplugged. If the dry-er will not start, check the most likely causes: no power at the outlet (page 12), a faulty door switch, a worn start button or a broken timer. If the dryer runs but does not heat, test the temperature control, the timer, the thermostats and, in an electric dryer, the heating element.

The heating element of an electric dry-er must be replaced when it fails; the burner of a gas dryer can usually be repaired by a professional. But you can safely adjust a gas dryer's air-to-gas ratio for a hotter flame (pages 51-52).

If clothes are drying slowly, check for a clogged lint filter. Then, for an electric dryer, test for voltage at the receptacle (page 12). It should be between 220 and 240 volts. Inadequate voltage to the heating element can cause it to produce insufficient heat. Next test the heating element for continuity (page 76).

A dryer that works only on some settings has either a malfunctioning timer or one or more faulty thermostats. The thermostats, located on the heater duct, the drum bulkhead or the blower-fan hous-ing, control the temperature of the heating element and the air in the drum. Two types of thermostat may be found, usually marked either L or F. The L-type thermostats break the circuit when the heat they are monitoring reaches about 200° F.; thermostats of the F type break the circuit after the temperature drops below a preset point. A safety thermostat breaks the circuit when the other thermostats fail. Most safety thermostats, once triggered, must be replaced; they usually are so marked. But some reset themselves once the dryer has cooled.

If all of the above parts check out but the dryer does not run, check the motor (page 18). A motor fails rarely and is the most expensive part to replace. Purchase of a new dryer may be preferable.

Before making any dryer repairs, turn off power at the main service panel or unplug the dryer. Dryer-cabinet panels disassemble differently, depending on the model. Some are screwed in place; some, like the model shown here, snap together with hidden metal tabs.

A Machine That Tumbles Wet Fabrics through Warm Air

The anatomy of a clothes dryer. Turned by a belt, the steel drum that tumbles the laundry rides on wheel-shaped bearings mounted on the bulkhead. A motor-driven fan blows air heated by the dryer's electric heating element or gas burner (inset) through a perforated opening in the heater duct and the perforated back of the drum. The air then exits into the exhaust duct, laden with moisture absorbed from the laundry. On the way the air passes through the lint screen, which filters out lint and debris.

Several devices determine when and how the dryer runs. For safety, a door switch stops the motor when the door is opened. A timer controls drying cycles, and a thermostat mounted on the heater duct regulates the amount of heat produced by the heater. Operating thermostats, located on the drum bulkhead or the blower-fan housing, control the temperature levels inside the dryer drum. The safety thermostat is designed to shut off the heat if the dryer should overheat.

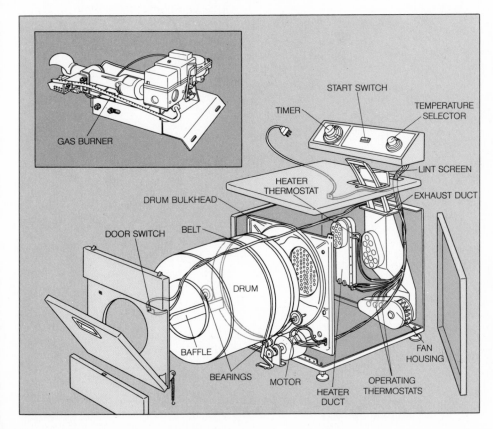

GAS BURNER

TIMER

START SWITCH

TEMPERATURE SELECTOR

LINT SCREEN

HEATER THERMOSTAT

DRUM BULKHEAD

EXHAUST DUCT

DOOR SWITCH

BELT

DRUM

BAFFLE

BEARINGS

MOTOR

HEATER DUCT

OPERATING THERMOSTATS

FAN HOUSING

A Failed Door Switch and How to Fix It

1 **Removing the top panel.** Unscrew the top panel's retaining screws. (They are most commonly located under the lint-screen cover, although on some models they are on the edge of the top panel, near the back.) Unfasten the front edge of the top panel, either by removing screws under the front edge of the panel or, on snap-in models, as shown here, by inserting a 2-inch-wide putty knife under the front corners of the top panel and pressing down on the concealed metal tabs until the panel springs loose. Raise the panel, and rest it on the hinges in the back or lean it against the wall so that it does not fall backward.

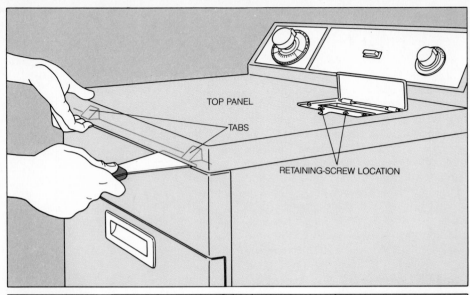

TOP PANEL

TABS

RETAINING-SCREW LOCATION

2 **Testing the circuit.** With the power turned off, remove the two wires from the terminals on the door switch and examine the condition of the terminals. If they are burned, replace the switch; if they are not, test the switch for continuity (*page 16*) with the dryer door closed. If there is no continuity, open the door and depress the switch button manually several times, to make certain that it is not sticking. If the button does not work freely, replace the switch. If you can work it freely, close the door and test the switch again for continuity; if there still is no continuity, replace the switch.

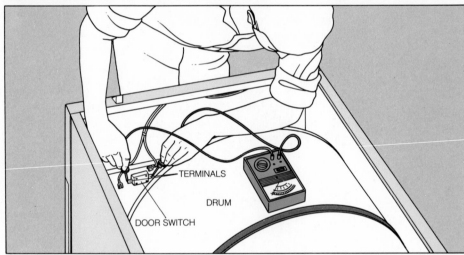

TERMINALS

DRUM

DOOR SWITCH

Replacing a Faulty Electric Heating Element

1 **Testing the heater.** With all power turned off, unscrew and remove the back panel of the dryer cabinet, and disconnect the wires from the terminals of the electric heater. To test for a short circuit, set a multitester at RX1K (*page 15*); place one probe of the tester on a terminal and touch the other probe to the surface of the heater duct. If you find continuity, the heater is short-circuited and must be replaced.

Test the heater for continuity by touching the probes to every combination of terminal pairs; some dryer heaters may have three terminals and thus require three tests. For every pair of terminals the tester should show continuity. Lack of continuity in even one pair indicates that the heater is defective and must be replaced.

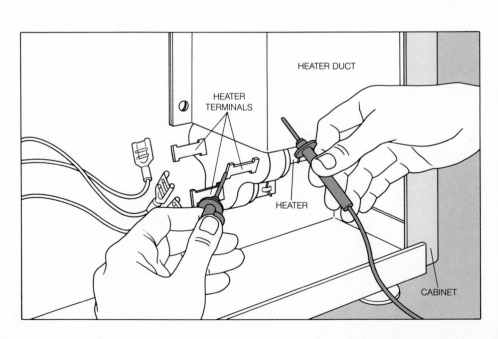

HEATER DUCT

HEATER TERMINALS

HEATER

CABINET

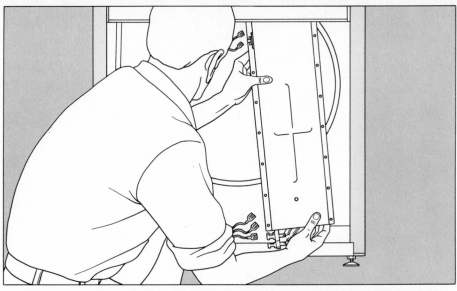

2 **Removing the heater duct.** Remove the retaining screws that hold the duct to the bottom of the cabinet. On some models the duct is also screwed to the top of the bulkhead; to reach these screws, remove the top of the cabinet (*opposite*). Slip the duct out of the cabinet, bottom first.

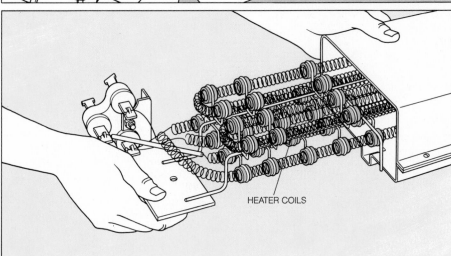

HEATER COILS

3 **Inspecting the heating element.** First remove the screws that fasten the heating element to the heater duct, and slip the element out of the duct. Then examine the heater coils; if you find any burn marks or breaks in the coils, replace the heating element.

To install a new heater element, slip it into the duct and reattach the screws.

A Plan of Attack for a Broken Drum Belt

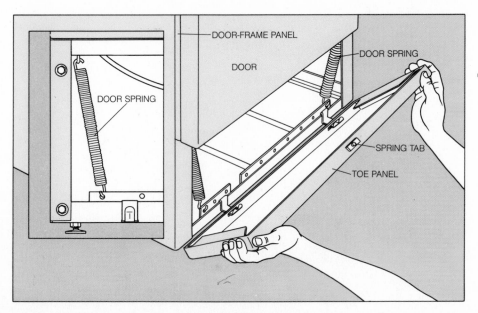

DOOR-FRAME PANEL

DOOR

DOOR SPRING

DOOR SPRING

SPRING TAB

TOE PANEL

1 **Getting at the belt.** Remove the top of the cabinet (*page 76*), then remove the front panels. The typical dryer shown here has two front panels—a door-frame panel, to which the door is permanently hinged, and a toe panel. Remove the toe panel first. Unhook the top of the panel by depressing the spring tabs at the center or ends of the panel with a putty knife. Pull the top of the panel toward you, and lift it off the brackets at the bottom.

To remove the door-frame panel, unhook the door springs, located behind the toe panel (*inset*), and unfasten the screws that hold the top of the door-frame panel to the top of the side panels. Remove the door-frame panel.

2 Removing the drum. In some dryers, to remove the drum you must first unscrew it from drum-support brackets or slides on each side of the cabinet *(inset)*; in others, you must unscrew a metal strap on the inside back of the drum, which secures the drum to a bearing on the back of the cabinet. Then, with the drum detached from the cabinet, pull out the broken belt and lift the drum off its bearings; hoist it up and out, bracing it against one knee to distribute the weight. If the front and back openings of the drum look the same, mark the front before setting the drum aside.

Remove pieces of broken belt and any lint or debris. Check the drum bearings for broken or worn spots and replace the bearings if necessary. Spin the motor pulley with your hand to make sure it is rotating freely while the pulley shaft remains stationary. If the pulley binds or wobbles, or if the shaft rotates, replace the pulley. To remove the faulty pulley, unscrew its mounting bracket from the cabinet bottom and pry the pulley out of the bracket; then place a new pulley on the mounting bracket and reattach the bracket. Lift the drum back into position inside the cabinet.

3 Replacing the belt. Loop the belt around the drum, centering it on the dark line left on the drum by the previous belt. In most dryers the belt is placed with the grooved side against the drum, but follow the instructions that come with the belt. Loop the belt around the idler, and then snake it around the motor pulley *(inset)*.

Reattach any drum brackets, slides or tabs, the door springs and all of the panels.

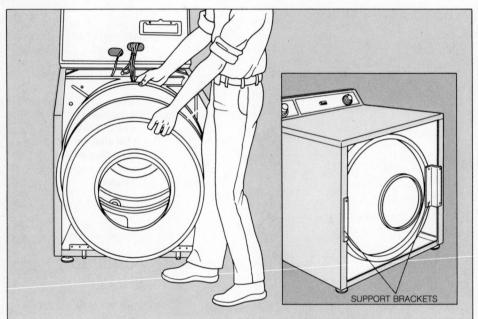

SUPPORT BRACKETS

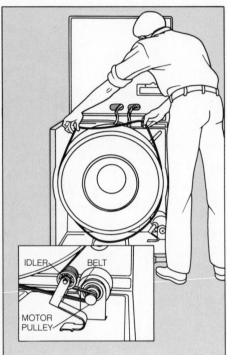

IDLER BELT

MOTOR PULLEY

Servicing the Dryer Controls

The start switch and temperature control. With all power turned off, unscrew the control panel and remove the backplate; the screws usually are along the panel's bottom edge. To check the start switch, disconnect the wires at the start-switch terminals. If the terminals are not burned, depress the switch in the on position and check for continuity *(page 16)*; there should be continuity. Then test the switch in the off position; there should be no continuity. If your results differ, replace the switch.

To check the temperature control, mark and remove the wires leading to it. If any terminal is burned, replace the temperature control; if not, lift the control panel and set the temperature-control knob on any heat setting. Test for continuity; you should find continuity between at least one pair of terminals. Mark the pair. Repeat the test; at each temperature setting you should find continuity between a different pair. If you do not, replace the temperature control.

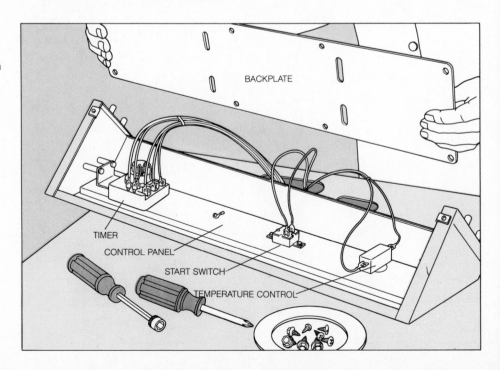

BACKPLATE

TIMER

CONTROL PANEL

START SWITCH

TEMPERATURE CONTROL

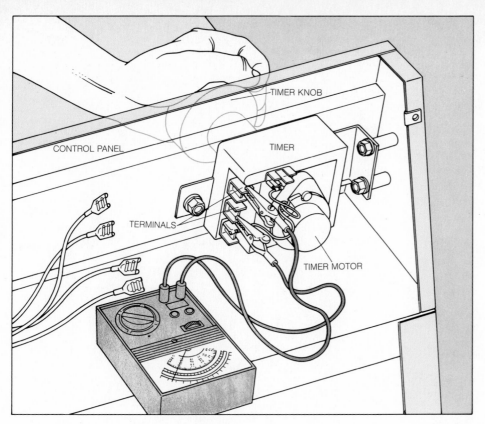

The timer and the timer motor. With all power turned off, remove the control panel and backplate *(opposite)*, and disconnect the wires from the timer terminals, marking their location on a diagram. If the timer terminals are burned, replace the timer. If they are not, test the terminals for continuity *(page 16)*. First turn the timer knob to a setting, then check all the terminals for continuity at this setting; you should find continuity between at least one pair. Mark this pair, then repeat the test at each of the other settings. There should be continuity between at least one pair of terminals at each setting except off—at this setting, no pair should show continuity.

To test the timer motor, unscrew it from the timer, set the timer on any setting, restore power to the dryer and observe the small timer-motor gear. If it does not rotate, replace the timer motor.

To replace the entire timer and its motor, pull off or unscrew the timer knob, then unscrew the timer from the control panel. Following the diagram you made when the wires were disconnected, attach the wires to the new timer. To replace only the timer motor, connect it as the original motor was connected.

Three Thermostats to Check

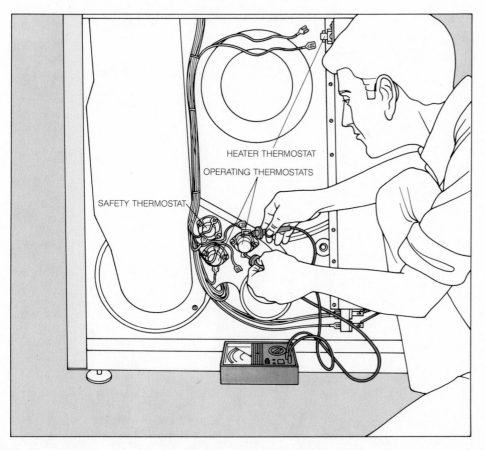

Testing for lack of heat or overheating. With the power turned off, remove the back panel of the cabinet and locate the thermostats. If the problem is inadequate heat, test the thermostats at room temperature. First disconnect the heater thermostat and test its terminals for continuity *(page 16)*. The heater thermostat is always of the L type and should register continuity between one pair of terminals; if it does not, replace it. Test L-type operating and safety thermostats in the same way. However, if the operating and safety thermostats are of the F type, the test should yield reverse results: When operative, F-type thermostats should show no continuity between any pair of terminals.

If the problem is overheating, test the operating thermostats in the presence of heat. Remove them one at a time and hold them with pliers ½ inch above a candle flame for no more than a minute, until you hear a click. Then test immediately for continuity. If they are L-type thermostats, there should be no continuity between any pair of terminals; if they are F-type thermostats, the results should be the reverse. Test a safety thermostat in the same way unless it bears a warning label. Some L-type safety thermostats are designed for one-time use, and when overheated will click open and stay open.

Step by Step through Clothes-Washer Repairs

A modern clothes washer does more than agitate dirty clothes through a detergent solution. It regulates water temperature, adds bleaches and rinsing agents, fills and empties itself, rinses the clothing and finally spins it damp-dry. To perform these varied functions, the clothes washer has become a complicated assemblage of mechanical and electrical parts. Some of these parts are more susceptible to trouble than others.

The water system—with its clog-prone pump, hoses and valves—is the most troublesome, followed by the timer. And although the transmission system, which agitates and spins the clothing, seldom breaks down, other parts associated with it do: The transmission's drive belt can slip, or the plastic agitator can crack or break. With the exception of the transmission, which only a professional should dismantle, most parts can be serviced by a homeowner.

When the washer does not start, first check out the obvious causes. Make sure the load is evenly distributed, the lid is closed and the machine is plugged into a live receptacle. Also check the lid button or switch. If water does not enter, check that the hot- and cold-water faucets are on, then look for kinks in the water-inlet hoses. Next examine the screens inside the hoses and the water-mixing valve for clogging (opposite, bottom) and, with the washer unplugged, test the valve terminals for continuity (page 83).

If the machine fills incompletely or overfills, the water-level switch (page 84) is probably malfunctioning. If the washer leaks, check for breaks or loose connections in the hoses to the water-mixing valve and the pump. Also inspect the pump, and replace it if it is leaking (page 86). If the washer does not drain, the pump may be clogged or stuck, or the drain hose that leads from the tub to the pump may be clogged. Then test the tightness of the drive belt (page 87). Finally, test the machine's timer and the motor (page 85).

If the washer does not agitate, the agitator may be slipping on its shaft (opposite, bottom) because the gear teeth are worn. Or the drive belt may be loose or broken. Since agitation does not begin until the water reaches a preset level, the water-level switch may be the cause. Finally, check the timer. If none of these parts are faulty, the problem probably is in the transmission.

If the washer does not begin the spin cycle, lift the lid and redistribute the clothing. Close the lid, rotate the timer dial into the spin cycle and start the machine. If the basket does not spin but the motor is running, look for a blockage, such as a handkerchief caught between the tub and the basket (page 83). If you find no obstruction, the drive belt may be loose or broken, the basket lock nut may be loose or the transmission may not be working. Also check the timer.

If the washer vibrates a lot, the cabinet may need leveling (opposite, top), or the snubber—a pad that absorbs the vibration of the tub—may need replacing.

Before taking a washing machine apart, unplug it from the wall outlet. In addition, before disconnecting any water hoses, turn off the hot- and cold-water faucets to the washer, spread a plastic dropcloth over the floor and have containers ready to catch water draining from the pump and from the hoses.

Anatomy of a clothes washer. When the timer is turned on, the water-mixing valve lets the selected mixture of hot and cold water into the tub until the water-level switch stops the flow. Then the agitator, turned by the motor-driven transmission, churns the laundry back and forth in the basket. At the end of the wash cycle and again at the end of the rinse cycle, the timer signals the pump to drain the tub and the transmission begins to spin the basket at high speed, squeezing the water out through its perforated sides by centrifugal force. The water drains down through a hole in the tub and is lifted by the drain pump into a standpipe behind the machine.

For safety, a lid switch stops the motor when the lid is raised—in some models during all cycles and in all models during the spin cycle. To keep the machine from vibrating excessively, an overload switch stops the motor when the load is unbalanced. In some machines, a snubber—a small rubber pad held by an armlike spring—rubs along the tub's top cover to keep the tub from shimmying and hitting the sides of the cabinet. In other models a shock-absorbing suspension under the tub performs this function.

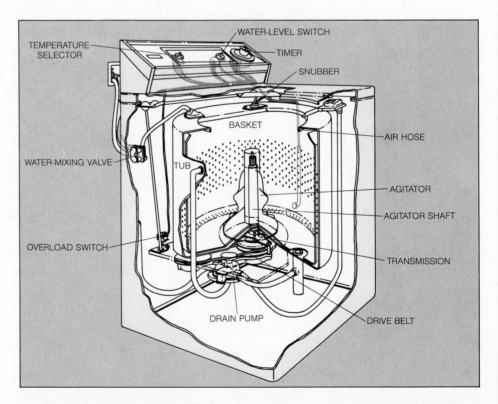

A Lopsided Cabinet Leveled

Adjusting the legs. Rock the cabinet from side to side to determine which side is lower. Then set a carpenter's level along the front edge of the cabinet top, and raise the lower side by reaching beneath the cabinet to extend the legs on that side—either by twisting them or by loosening lock nuts on the legs and sliding them farther out of their sockets. Next level the cabinet from front to back by placing the level first along one side of the cabinet, then the other, while adjusting both front legs and both rear legs.

If the machine is badly unbalanced, slip a piece of wood under the low corner to hold the machine up while you adjust the leg.

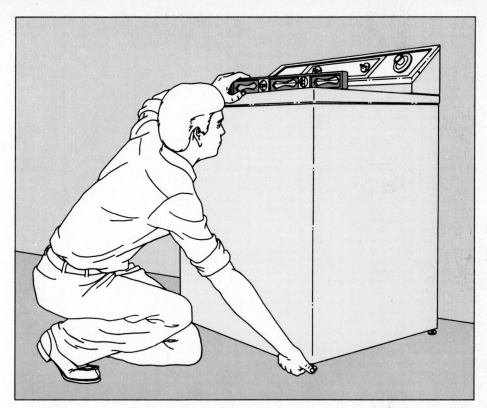

Obstructions That Stop the Flow of Water

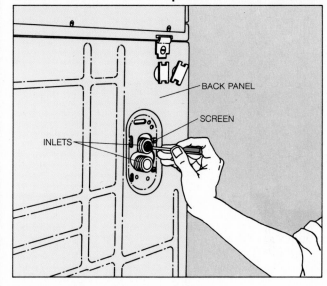

BACK PANEL

SCREEN

INLETS

Cleaning screens. Using pliers, unscrew the two water hoses from the water-mixing valve on the back of the machine and, with a small screwdriver, carefully pry out the screen inside each inlet; be careful not to damage the screens. Also pry out any screens inside the hoses. Clean the screens under running water and reinsert them. Reattach the hoses. Before tightening the hose coupling, run your hand along each hose from the house plumbing valve to the water-mixing valve, to check them for any bends or kinks that could obstruct the water flow.

What to Check When the Agitator Fails

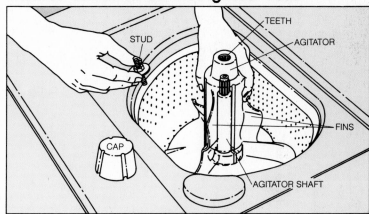

TEETH

STUD

AGITATOR

CAP

FINS

AGITATOR SHAFT

Replacing the agitator. Remove the agitator from the agitator shaft either by pulling it upward to slide it off the shaft or by unscrewing a plastic cap that holds the agitator down. In the example shown here, the cap covers a threaded metal stud-and-nut assembly. To take off this stud, turn the nut with a wrench until the stud can be freed from the shaft. Then pull the agitator straight up. If the agitator does not budge, rock it at its base or enlist a helper.

Examine the agitator fins for cracks or breaks; if any fins are damaged, replace the agitator. Do the same if the agitator fits too loosely on its shaft. Inspect the teeth inside the top of the agitator column for signs of wear; if the teeth are worn smooth, replace the agitator.

The Critical Lock Nut That Secures the Spinning Basket

Removing the nut. To loosen the lock nut that secures the basket to the agitator shaft, remove the agitator *(page 81)* and wedge a blunt tool, such as a steel rod or a cold chisel, in one of the notches at the edge of the nut. Hit the tool with a hammer to move the lock nut counterclockwise. If the lock nut is corroded, spray it with penetrating oil and wait a few minutes before attempting to dislodge it.

To install a new nut, place it on the agitator shaft and tighten it clockwise, again using a hammer and rod or chisel to seat it firmly.

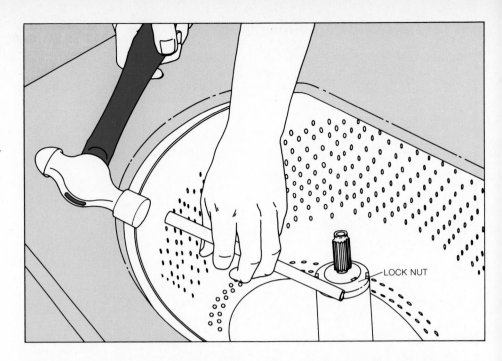

LOCK NUT

Getting Inside a Washer

Releasing the hinged top panel. If the top panel is held down by tabs *(page 84)*, use a putty knife to free it; if it is held by visible screws, remove them; if the screws are hidden, remove the front panel to gain access to them. To do this, remove the screws located under the lip of the kickplate at the bottom of the front panel. Next swing the bottom of the front panel up toward you, and lift the panel off its hinges at the top. Then free the top panel from the side panels by removing the screws inside the cabinet that hold the panels together. Swing the top panel back on its hinge, and lean it against the wall or prop it up from underneath.

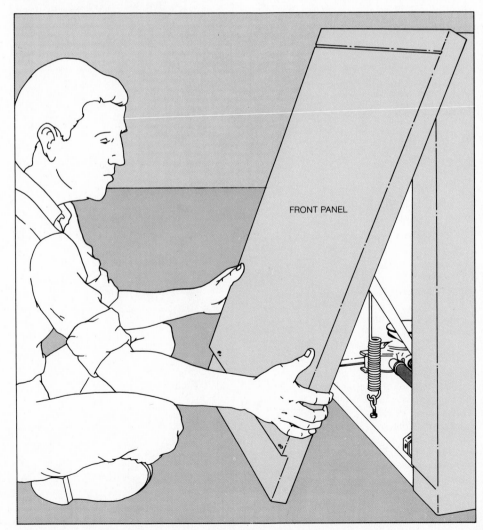

FRONT PANEL

A Cure for Vibration: The Snubber

Replacing the snubber. After raising the top panel, disassemble the snubber assembly by lifting the snubber's wishbone-shaped spring off the top of the snubber. If the snubber sits on a friction pad, run your fingers over the pad; if the pad feels sticky or is caked with detergent, clean it with an emery cloth or sandpaper. If the snubber is worn, replace it.

To replace the wishbone spring, you must begin by unfastening both of its legs from the clothes washer. First free one leg by unscrewing the nut and bolt that secure the leg to the snubber bracket *(inset)*. Then slide the spring's other leg out of the slot in the bracket. Finally, insert the new wishbone spring, and reattach its legs to the snubber bracket.

Testing a Water-mixing Valve

Replacing a faulty valve. With the washer unplugged, test the water-mixing valve for continuity with a multitester set at RX1 *(page 17)*. To gain access to the valve, remove the top panel and unhook the wires from the valve terminals. Test both pairs of terminals; if either pair shows no continuity, disconnect the valve and replace it. To do this, first remove the two hoses from the valve inlets on the back of the machine *(page 81)*, then remove the single hose from the valve outlet inside the machine. Unscrew the valve from its mounting on the back of the machine. In order to install a new valve, reverse the steps of this procedure.

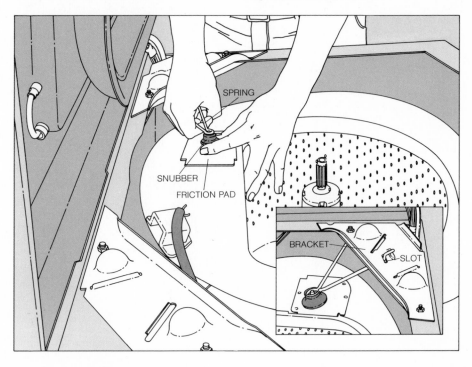

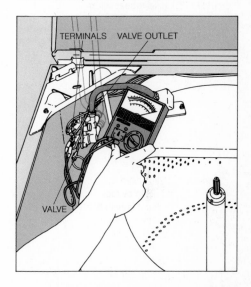

A Routine Inspection for Obstructions in the Tub

Lifting out the basket. To examine the tub, you must first free the basket from the agitator shaft. Raise the top panel, then remove the agitator, the snubber and its wishbone spring, the tub cover, and the lock nut on the agitator shaft *(pages 81-83)*. Next loosen the basket from the agitator shaft by having a helper rock the basket back and forth, or dislodge the basket by striking the basket's flared top in the center sharply with a hammer and a scrap of wood. If the agitator shaft is rusted or corroded, lubricate it with penetrating oil to loosen it. Then, once the basket has been loosened, you will be able to pull it straight up, off the shaft, to lift it out of the machine.

Examine the drain hole in the bottom of the tub for blockage *(inset)*. Scrub the tub bottom with a stiff-bristled brush to clear it of any mineral deposits that may obstruct the rotation of the basket. Then reassemble the parts, reversing the order in which you removed them.

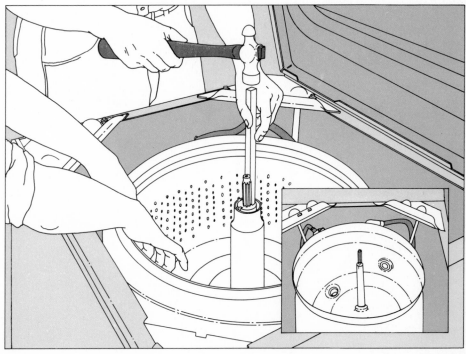

For Water Trouble, Check the Water-Level Switch

1 **Testing the switch in the empty position.** If the tub overflows or does not fill at all, unplug the machine and siphon or bail out any water standing in the tub; then remove the backplate from the control panel. Disconnect the wires from the terminals of the water-level switch, and test the terminals for continuity *(page 16)*. The tester should show continuity between only one pair of terminals; mark that pair with tape. If there is no continuity at any pair of terminals, the switch is defective and must be replaced.

Check the switch's air-pressure hose for pinholes and obstructions by following it from the switch to its juncture with the reducer coupling *(inset)*, where the small air-pressure hose and the larger water-pressure hose meet. If you discover any pinholes in the air hose, pull it off the switch and coupling and replace it.

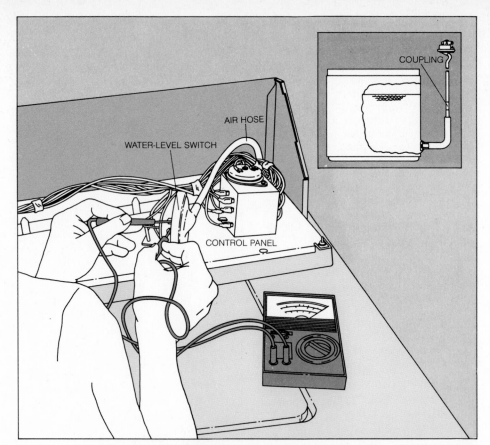

COUPLING

AIR HOSE

WATER-LEVEL SWITCH

CONTROL PANEL

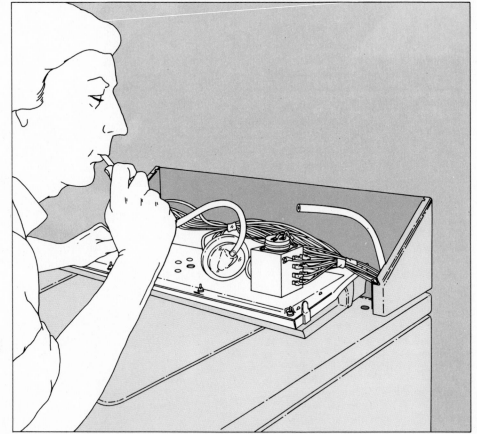

2 **Testing the switch in the full position.** Pull the air-pressure hose off the neck of the water-pressure switch, and attach a shorter length of hose of the same diameter. Blow gently through the hose and listen for a clicking sound. Then blow into the hose again, simultaneously testing the switch terminals for continuity *(page 16)*. You should find continuity between a pair of terminals other than the pair that showed continuity in Step 1, above. If your results differ, the switch is defective and must be replaced.

A Dry Run for the Timer and the Timer Motor

1 **Testing the timer's electrical circuit.** Unplug the washer and unscrew the control panel and the backplate *(page 78)*. Disconnect the two wires of the timer motor from their terminals on the timer, and clip the probes of a multitester—set at 250 volts—to the terminals. Close the washer lid, rotate the timer knob to the spin cycle, turn the machine on and plug the washer into the wall outlet. If the multitester does not show the same voltage tested at a standard wall outlet *(page 12)*, the timer has an electrical defect. If the voltage reading is correct, proceed to test the timer motor *(Step 2)*.

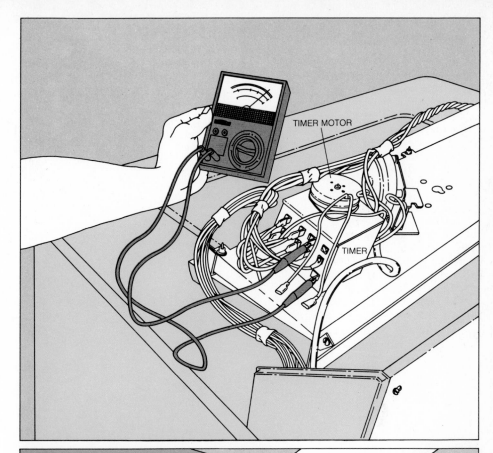

2 **Testing the timer motor.** Unplug the clothes washer and reconnect the timer-motor wires, disconnected in Step 1, above, to their terminals on the timer. Unscrew the timer motor from the timer, revealing the small gear on the underside of the timer motor. With the washer lid closed, set the timer on the spin cycle, turn the washer on and plug it in. Observe the small gear; if it does not turn, replace the timer motor.

If the small gear does turn, test the timer's mechanical parts. Unplug the washer and reattach the timer motor to the timer. With the washer lid closed, set the timer to SPIN and plug in the machine. If the timer does not advance through the spin cycle, replace the timer.

To replace either the timer or the timer motor, remove them as a unit by removing the timer knob *(page 28)*, then unscrewing the timer from its mounting on the control panel.

Cleaning Out the Drain Pump

1 Removing the drain pump. With a helper, lay the washer face down on a padding of soft rags, exposing the underside of the machine. Disconnect the hose clamps with pliers *(page 29)*, and slip the drive belt from the pump pulley. Remove the pump by unscrewing its mounting bolts with a socket wrench. Lift the pump out of the machine, and place it on a sheet of plastic to catch any dripping water.

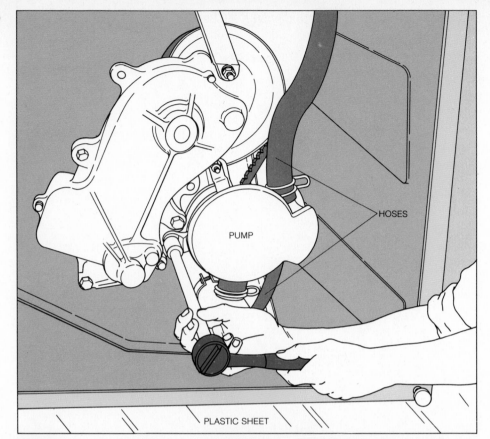

HOSES

PUMP

PLASTIC SHEET

2 Cleaning the pump. Working above the plastic sheet, clear the hoses of any obstructions. Also clear the pump-protector tube, if your machine has one; the protector tube traps small objects such as handkerchiefs and babies' socks. If the pump itself appears to be clogged but cannot be disassembled because it is permanently sealed, replace it. If the pump can be disassembled, remove the screws or clips holding it together *(inset)*, and remove any obstructions. Then reassemble the pump.

Next turn the pulley on top of the pump with your fingers. It should turn easily in both directions. If it does not turn, the pump bearings are jammed, and the pump must be replaced.

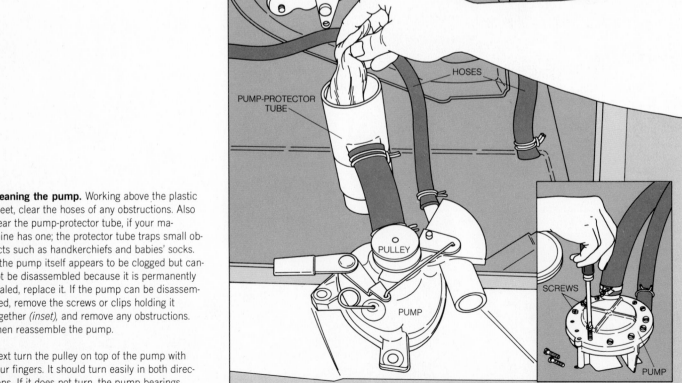

PUMP-PROTECTOR TUBE

HOSES

PULLEY

PUMP

SCREWS

PUMP

Adjustments for the Tension of the Drive Belt

Tightening or loosening the drive belt. Unplug the washer and disconnect its hoses, remove the back panel, then lay the machine face down on a padding of soft rags, exposing the motor and the drive belt, which are at the bottom of the washer. Press the drive belt; it should have about ½ inch of play. If it is slacker than this, tighten it by repositioning the motor. To do this, loosen the motor mounting bolts with a socket wrench *(below, left)*, and slide the motor away from the drain pump; then retighten the bolts. Make certain that the drive belt is positioned securely in the pulleys.

To install a new belt, loosen the mounting bolts *(below, right)*, and pull the motor toward the drainpipe to make installation of a new belt easier. If the motor will not budge, use pliers to pull it. Slip the new belt around the motor, transmission and drain-pump pulleys, following the installation instructions that are provided with the belt made for your clothes washer. Adjust the position of the motor to tighten the new belt, then retighten the mounting bolts.

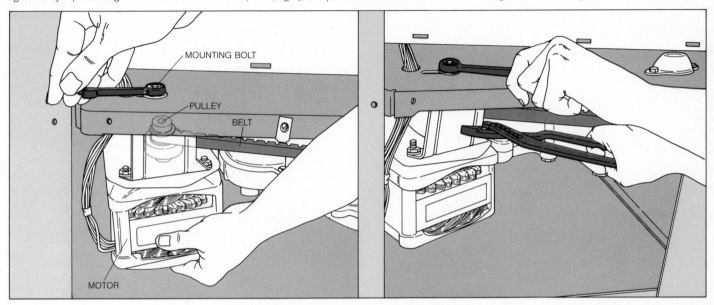

MOUNTING BOLT

PULLEY

BELT

MOTOR

Examining a Motor for Flaws

Testing the motor switch. Unplug the washer. To reach the terminals on the motor, you must remove the back panel and, in some cases, place the washer face down on a padding of soft rags. Next clip the probes of a multitester— set at 250 volts—to one pair of terminals. Slip the drive belt from the motor pulley, close the washer lid, rotate the timer knob to the spin cycle, turn the machine on and plug the washer in. Check each combination of terminals, unplugging the washer when you move the probes from one pair of terminals to another; do not touch the machine when it is plugged in. If you find current in at least one pair of terminals but the motor is not running, the motor is faulty. If you find no current at the motor switch, the problem lies elsewhere in the washer.

To examine the motor pulley, with the machine unplugged remove the drive belt and rotate the pulley in both directions by hand. If the pulley binds, have the motor repaired. If the pulley is loose, tighten the setscrew on the pulley hub; if the setscrew quickly works loose again, loosen the setscrew, slide the old pulley off the motor shaft and put a new pulley in its place.

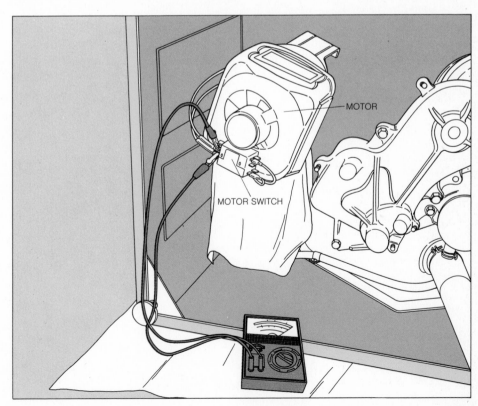

MOTOR

MOTOR SWITCH

The Dishwasher: A Kitchen Aid with Four Tasks

Unlike some other under-counter kitchen cleaning appliances, such as the garbage disposer *(page 96)* and trash compactor *(page 98)*, which work on the principle of the chain reaction, the dishwasher is controlled by a central timer that puts it through its paces. This timer commands the dishwasher to perform its four basic tasks: filling with water, spraying dishes to wash or rinse them, draining water out and drying the dishes with heat and circulating air.

When a dishwasher malfunctions, the trouble is often signaled by a failure to perform one of these tasks. Water does not enter the machine, dishes emerge from the appliance dirty, water remains in the bottom of the tub after the drain cycle is over, or the dishes do not dry. But pinpointing the actual source of the trouble can be difficult.

Most commonly the problem is clogging. If there is no clog, look for a mechanical or an electrical failure. Only then should you check the timer; although the timer makes everything happen, it rarely is responsible for breakdowns. Suspect the timer only when the dishwasher does not advance.

A dishwasher that drains poorly is in many cases suffering from a clogged air gap *(page 90)*, which is easily cleared. The air gap is a plumbing part—required in many, though not all, local codes—that prevents water in the sink drain from backing up into the dishwasher.

If the air gap is not responsible for the poor drainage, look next at the dishwasher's pumping mechanism. Occasionally the pump impellers become clogged or broken, so water is not pumped through the spray arms during the wash or rinse cycle, or out during the drain cycle. The pump can be disassembled so that impellers can be replaced *(page 91)*.

If the pump motor itself wears out, it too can be replaced. It is usually removed as a unit: Release the clips that lock the motor in place under the tub, and lift it up through the tub. On a few dishwasher models, water is drained not by a reversing pump motor but by a drain valve *(page 92)*; this valve may clog or stop working because of an electrical problem. To clear an obstruction, flush the valve with water; for an electrical problem, replace the solenoid that operates the valve. If necessary, the entire valve can be replaced.

When a dishwasher does not clean dishes well, it usually is because the water entering the dishwasher is not hot enough. Check the temperature of the hot water at the sink by running water over a meat or candy thermometer for two minutes; if the thermometer reads less than 140° F., turn the water heater's controls to a higher temperature setting. If this measure fails (which can happen if the hot-water pipes run through unheated parts of the house, such as a crawl space or a basement) wrap the pipes with pipe insulation, available at home-improvement centers.

If water temperature is not the problem, it may be that your detergent is too old. If it dissolves too slowly and leaves a gritty residue when placed in a glass of hot water, replace it. Sometimes, too, using a different brand of detergent will improve the dishwasher's performance, especially in hard-water areas.

If the movement of the spray arms is blocked by debris or improperly arranged dishes, cleaning performance will be poor. Test the action of the arms by closing the dishwasher and running it briefly on the wash cycle, then open the door; if it looks as though the arms have not moved, clean them *(page 90)*. If this remedy does not produce clean dishes, disassemble the pump and inspect the upper impeller for teeth that are broken or clogged. Then examine the water-inlet valve *(page 91)*, which may be failing to allow enough water to enter the tub; or a float may be sticking, shutting off the water-inlet valve.

Finally, poor cleaning may be the result of low water pressure in the house water lines. Since the timer lets hot water into the dishwasher for a preset period of time, less water enters the machine when the pressure is low. To test the water pressure, turn on the dishwasher and let it fill. Then siphon out the water into containers; there should be 2½ U.S. gallons (2 imperial gallons). If water pressure is the problem, run the dishwasher only when no water is being used elsewhere in the house.

When a dishwasher does not run at all, the trouble may be simply a defective door latch or switch *(page 93)*. If the dishes do not dry well, check the heating element *(page 93)* or, in a model that has one, the blower *(page 93)*.

Dishwashers can leak either through a slipped or worn gasket or through poor hose connections and pump seals. Reseat a slipped door gasket with a screwdriver or a pair of pliers. Replace a worn gasket by following the manufacturer's instructions for inserting a new one. To trace hose leaks, observe the character of the water. Clear water indicates a leak during the fill cycle, which means a faulty hose connection at the water-inlet valve. Sudsy water is a sign of leaks during the wash, rinse or drain cycles, from hose connections at a pump or, in a model that has one, the drain valve. If a hose is simply loose, tighten or replace its clamp; if it is cracked or brittle, replace the entire hose assembly *(page 30)*.

Before attempting any repair on a dishwasher, turn off the power to the machine at the house service panel. To work on parts located on the underside of the tub—the water-inlet valve, drain valve, pump motor, float switch or pressure switch, heating element or blower—unscrew the lower access panel. Before removing a water-inlet valve, shut off the hot-water valve under the sink or the hot-water supply valve at the water heater. To replace a faulty detergent dispenser, unscrew and remove the panel on the front of the door; to service the timer, remove the control panel over the door.

Anatomy of a dishwasher. Almost every part of a dishwasher is operated by the timer, which opens the water-inlet valve to fill the tub, turns on the pump and opens the detergent dispenser to wash the dishes, reverses the pump to drain the tub, and turns on the heating element to dry the dishes. Only the float switch, an emergency device that turns off the water-inlet valve to prevent the tub from overfilling, works independently of the timer.

Although all dishwashers have wash, rinse and dry cycles, some models have special features—such as a selector switch, which alters the oper-

ation of the timer to provide a choice of short or long wash cycles. Also, the mechanical parts may differ. On the model below, a spray tower guides water, pumped at very high pressure, up into the upper spray arm; on other models there is a pipe that performs this function. On some machines, a drain valve *(page 92)* and a one-way pump replace the two-way pump shown here. To dry dishes faster, some dishwashers have a blower unit in addition to the heating element. And the job that is usually handled by a float switch is, in a few models, performed instead by a pressure switch *(page 92)*, which is mounted either inside or under the tub.

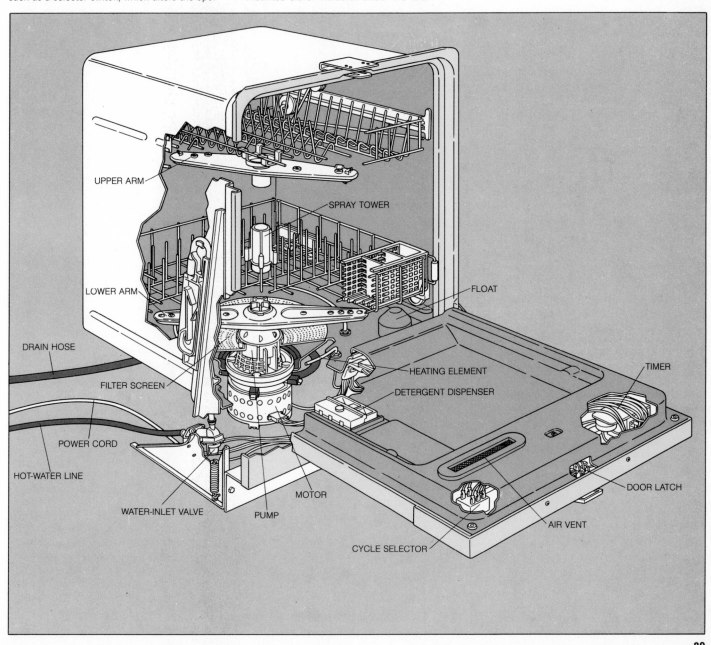

Five Places to Look for a Dishwasher Obstruction

Opening a clogged air gap. Pull the chrome cover off the air gap, located next to the faucet at the sink, and unscrew the plastic cap under the cover. With tweezers, remove any debris such as glass, bones or toothpicks from the small tube in the center of the air gap. Run the cover and cap under water to clean them. Screw the cap back and put the cover on again.

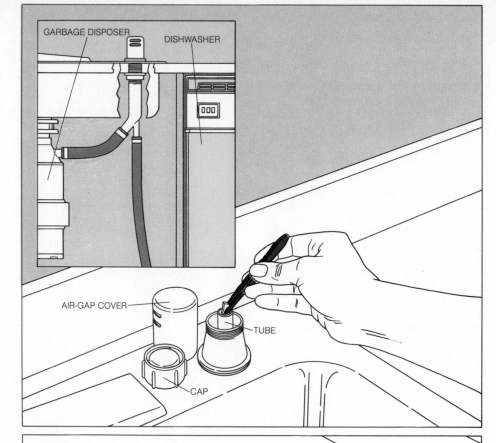

Cleaning the spray arms and filter screen. Slide out the lower dish rack, unscrew the plastic hubcap that holds the lower spray arm in place and lift off the spray arm. Unsnap the coarse strainer and lift out the filter screen. Clean the slotted holes on both sides of the spray arm with a stiff wire, bent at a right angle at the tip. Then rinse the spray arm, the strainer and the screen under running water, scrubbing the screen and strainer with a stiff brush, if necessary, to clear their perforations.

Unclog the holes in the upper spray arm without removing the arm from its holder. If there is a spray arm at the top of the dishwasher tub, clean it while it is in place also.

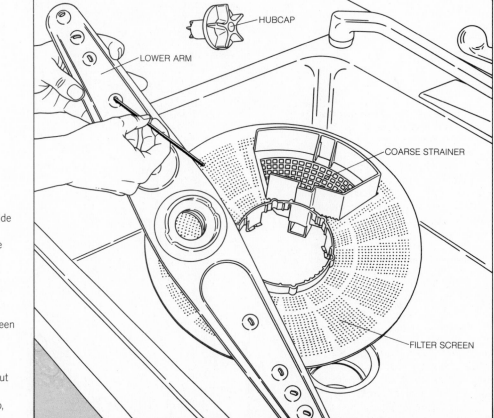

Servicing the pump. On this typical pump, take off the lower spray arm *(opposite, bottom)*, and remove the pump cover by turning and lifting it, exposing the upper impeller. To remove the upper impeller, bend the bolt-locking tab up to clear the bolt; unscrew the bolt, freeing the impeller. Check the impeller for debris and for worn or broken blades; clean or replace the impeller as necessary. Next, lift out the spacer plate and the food-disposer blade under the impeller; clean the blade.

To clean the lower impeller, unfasten the screws holding the pump guard and remove the guard. Then pull off the pump plate, but do not remove the lower impeller unless it has broken blades and needs to be replaced. To replace the lower impeller, pry if off with a screwdriver or pull it straight off the shaft with a pair of locking pliers. When you install a new impeller, replace the existing seals as well.

Reassemble the pump by reversing this procedure, reattaching the screws first by hand and then driving them in with a screwdriver until the parts fit snugly together.

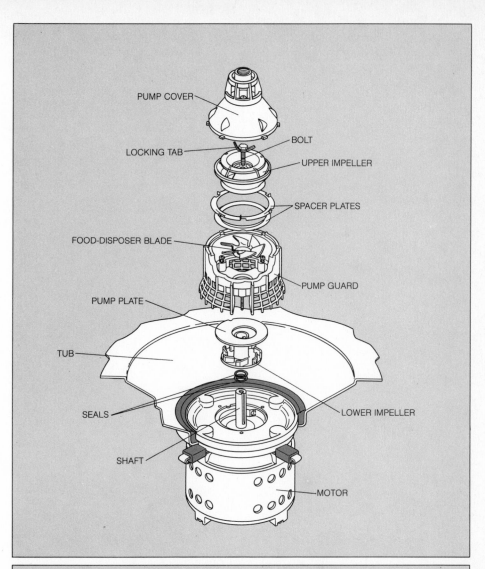

Repairing the water-inlet valve. With the power to the dishwasher off, test the solenoid terminals of the water-inlet valve for continuity, using a multitester *(page 17)*. If there is no continuity, replace the solenoid; if there is continuity, clean the valve filter or replace the diaphragm. To disassemble the valve, first turn off the hot-water supply and drain the two hoses into a pan. Then unscrew the valve from its mounting bracket and detach it from the water connections. To clean the filter screen, unscrew the mounting bracket from the valve body, remove the filter screen and run water through it. Check the flow washer for wear and replace it if necessary. Then unscrew the solenoid from its mounting and run water through the valve body.

If the filter is clean, check the condition of the diaphragm in the solenoid assembly that controls the operation of the valve. Unscrew the solenoid mounting, disassemble the spring-activated plunger and its guide, and replace the diaphragm. Then reassemble the valve and reattach it to the dishwasher water connections.

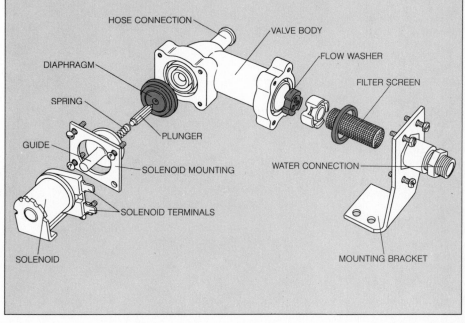

Repairing a drain valve. Test the drain-valve solenoid for continuity in the same way as in a water-inlet valve *(page 91)*; then remove the valve to examine its mechanical parts. First bail out any water standing in the dishwasher tub, then unscrew the valve from its mounting bracket. If the valve resembles the one shown here *(inset)*, pull back the plunger to see whether the rubber seal opens freely. If the seal sticks or is clogged, unscrew the valve body from its solenoid assembly and flush the valve body with water. If the seal is deteriorated, replace the valve.

If the drain valve resembles a water-inlet valve, repair it as you would the water-inlet valve.

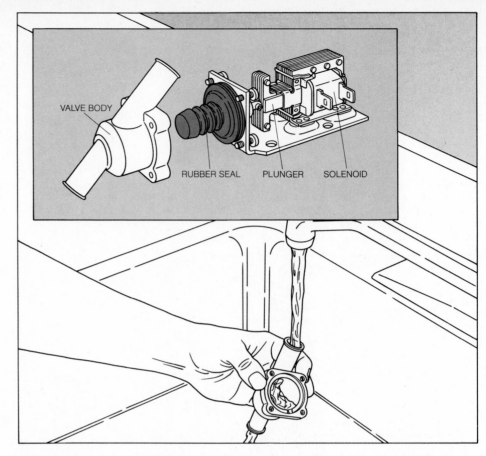

VALVE BODY

RUBBER SEAL   PLUNGER   SOLENOID

Checking Overflow Controls

Repairing a float or pressure switch. Jiggle the float up and down in its sleeve, and pull it out of the sleeve to clear the shaft of any impediment to its movement. If the float moves freely but water does not enter the machine, or if it overflows, turn off the power to the dishwasher at the main service panel, bail out any water in the tub and remove the bottom access panel. Test the float-switch terminals *(top inset)*, located under the tub, for continuity *(page 16)*. If there is no continuity, replace the switch by unscrewing the retaining nut and lifting the switch off its mounting; screw on a new one.

If the overflow is controlled instead by a water-pressure switch mounted inside the tub *(bottom inset)*, test the terminals for continuity as above. If there is no continuity, replace the switch. To replace a water-pressure switch, unfasten the switch wires, unscrew the nuts under the tub that hold the switch, and lift it out of the tub. Install a new switch by reversing these steps.

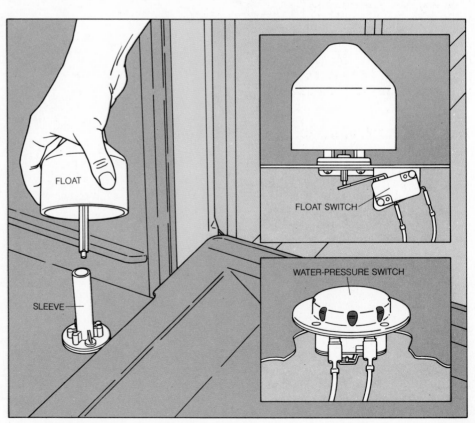

FLOAT

SLEEVE

FLOAT SWITCH

WATER-PRESSURE SWITCH

What to Do When Dishes Do Not Dry

Replacing the heating element. With the power turned off, remove the lower access panel, disconnect the leads to the heating-element terminals and test the element for continuity, using a multitester *(page 15)*; if there is no continuity, the element is defective. If the test does show continuity, check the element for a short circuit by touching one probe of the multitester to a terminal and the other to the element's sheath; in this test, continuity indicates that the element is short-circuited. To replace a damaged element, remove the bottom access panel and detach the leads from the nuts under the tub *(inset)* that hold the element in place. Unscrew the nuts and remove any sealing gas-

kets. Then unhook the element from the fasteners that hold it in place inside the tub, and remove the heating element along with the gaskets that seal its mounting holes.

In order to install a new heating element, position a pair of new gaskets over the holes in the tub and insert the two ends of the element through the holes. Then fit two new gaskets over the protruding element ends on the underside of the tub, and screw the nuts back into place. Reattach the leads. Turn on the power to the dishwasher, run the machine and look for leaks around the mounting. If you see that water is leaking out, tighten the nuts.

Repairing a blower heater. With the power off, remove the bottom access panel and detach the wires to the terminals of the motor, the thermostat and the heating element. Test each pair of terminals for continuity with a multitester *(page 15)*; any part that does not show continuity is defective. Test for a short circuit in the heating element by touching one probe of the multitester to a terminal of the element and the other to the mounting bracket; if there is continuity, the element is short-circuited.

To check the heater's mechanical parts, unscrew the blower unit and pull it down and out of the dishwasher. Check the fan for obstructions by rotating the blades with your hand. If the motor has been noisy and there are oil holes, oil it with a light oil such as sewing-machine oil.

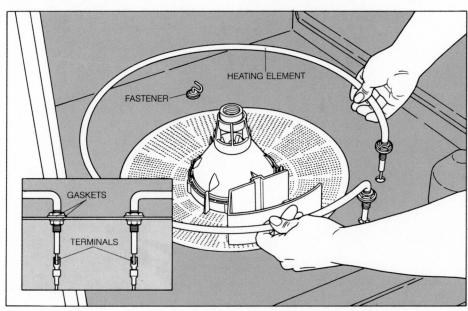

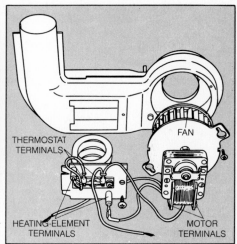

Isolating Control Troubles

Testing the door-latching mechanism. If the machine does not start, turn off the power at the main service panel and remove the control panel to expose the latch and its switch. With the door closed and locked, disconnect the wires on the latch leading to the switch terminals—in this case located behind the latch—and test the terminals for continuity *(page 16)*. If there is no continuity, replace the switch. If there is continuity, the switch is operating, but the latch may not be hitting the strike. Unscrew the retaining screws and adjust the position of the strike, pulling it out until it hits the interlock lever when the door is latched; then tighten the retaining screws, securing the strike in position.

With the door open, test the switch terminals a second time for continuity. If there is continuity this time, the switch must be replaced.

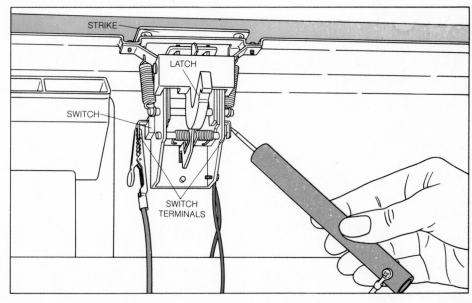

Testing the cycle selector and timer. With the power turned off, remove the control panel, exposing the mounting plate to which the selector and timer are attached. Examine the wires connected to the terminals of the timer and the cycle-selector switch. If any terminal is burned or the wire insulation is discolored, replace the entire timer or selector switch, making a diagram to record wire locations as you disconnect the wires. Unscrew the bracket that holds the selector switch against the mounting plate, and slip the switch out of its opening. Remove the screws that hold the timer against the plate. Install a new switch or timer, reconnecting the wires and repairing any that may be damaged.

If the wires and terminals are sound, check the switch terminals for continuity (*page 79*). If the switch is defective at any setting, replace it.

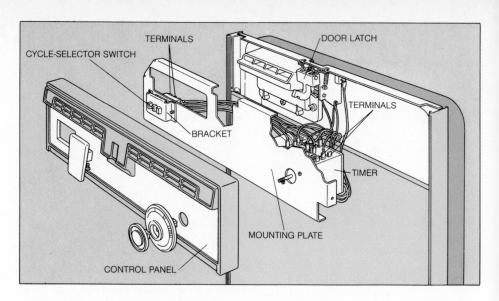

The Special Problems of Portable Washers

Portable dishwashers, once more common than the built-in variety, work in the same way as their under-counter cousins. But they have extra parts that may present special problems: casters that can stick, for example, a retractable electric cord that may not rewind, or a faucet coupler that can leak.

When a portable does not roll easily, spin the casters to see whether they turn. Clean a dirty bearing with a damp cloth and lubricate it with light oil; replace the entire caster if the tire is split. If the caster does not swivel, the shank may just need tightening; if the shank is bent, replace the entire caster.

When the electric cord does not retract, unscrew the back service panel or lay the dishwasher on its side, and check the rewind reel. If the spring or cable holding the reel is disconnected or broken, reconnect or replace it. If the cord winds so loosely that it comes off the reel, adjust the cord-guide bracket, located where the cord enters the reel, until the cord rewinds properly.

The parts of a leaky faucet-coupler assembly that can be replaced separately are the washers and adapters that connect the head to the coupler. If the coupler leaks anywhere along its two hose lines, the water-inlet hose or the coupler must be replaced. To replace the coupler, remove the top from the machine and tip it over on its side.

Disconnect the drain hose from the pump and the fill hose from the water-inlet valve. Set the machine upright and remove the hoses. Then feed the hoses of a new coupler into the machine, threading them through the hose guides. Once again turn the dishwasher on its side, and reconnect the hoses.

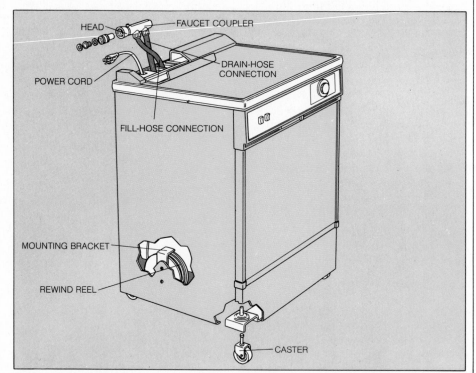

A portable dishwasher. Only two operating parts—the faucet coupler and the reel-mounted electric cord—distinguish a portable dishwasher from a built-in. The coupler has a head, a fill hose and a drain hose that connect the dishwasher to the sink's hot-water supply and drain. Retracting on a spring-operated rewind reel, the electric cord can plug into any outlet. Casters allow the dishwasher to be rolled to and from the sink.

Servicing a Water Softener

Water softeners condition water by circulating it through a tank, where the water's hard minerals such as calcium and magnesium are replaced with a soft mineral—sodium. Periodically, to regenerate the mineral tank's softening ability, salty water flows from a second tank—called the brine tank—through the mineral tank. The salt pellets (sodium chloride) in this brine tank sometimes cake up, the inlet valve can clog, and in rare instances the timer that operates both tanks can fail to start the regeneration cycle. But before assuming that a water softener is malfunctioning, make sure that the timer dial is set for the time of day when you want regeneration to take place, usually at night when water is not being used.

Clogs occur most often where the house water supply enters the water softener, at the inlet valve, causing incomplete regeneration. The internal screen cartridge at the inlet can be taken out for cleaning or replacement (bottom).

Problems with the regeneration cycle also occur when salt in the brine tank congeals into a solid mass, a condition called salt bridging. You can spot this problem by poking at the salt bed with a broom handle—the salt pellets should be loose. If they are not, try to break them up with the broom handle. If this fails, disconnect and empty the tank, then poke at the salt lump with the broom handle, to crack the lump into pieces small enough to remove. Refill the tank with fresh salt pellets.

The water softener's timer seldom fails, but the spring-arm assembly that trips the timer may wear out. For some models, a replacement can be purchased separately; for others the whole timer assembly must be replaced.

Anatomy of a water softener. Water flows from the house water-supply pipe into the softener's mineral tank through an inlet valve. As the water filters down through the bed of plastic beads inside the tank, its hard mineral ions of calcium and magnesium are replaced by soft ions of sodium. The softened water flows up the riser pipe from the tank bottom, through the outlet valve and into the house plumbing.

Usually once a week, accumulated hard minerals are flushed out of the mineral tank, and the sodium ions are replenished from a brine tank. To begin this regeneration cycle, the timer disconnects the mineral tank from the house plumbing. Then a cleansing solution of brine (salt water) is drawn from the brine tank into the mineral tank, to remove hard ions from the plastic beads and add sodium ions. After doing its work, the brine is flushed out through the mineral tank's drainpipe. Finally, fresh water rinses any remaining brine out of the mineral tank and sends it back to the brine tank, where it dissolves more salt for the next regeneration cycle.

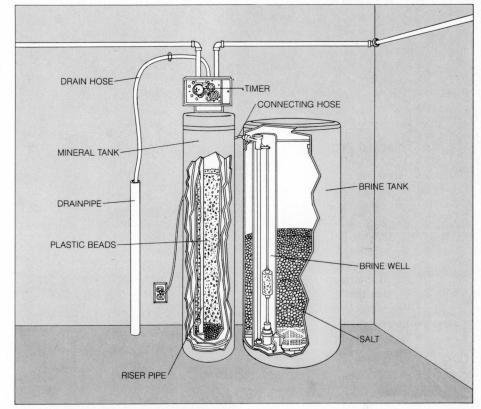

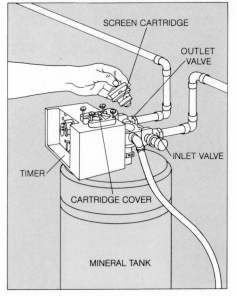

Replacing the screen cartridge. Shut off the house water line and open a faucet at a sink or lavatory to release pressure on the line and lower the water level in the softener below the inlet valve. Remove the four screws holding the cover over the screen cartridge. Clean off the cartridge if it is not badly clogged; otherwise replace it. Reattach the cartridge cover, turn off the faucet and reopen the water-supply line.

Getting a Garbage Disposer to Dispose Properly

A garbage disposer is a small device designed to do a big job. Grinding away under the sink, it chews up all sorts of kitchen waste, from tough vegetable skins to eggshells and chicken bones. With reasonable use, it should last for years. A disposer requires a steady stream of cold water to flush waste through the unit and to prevent congealed grease from clogging the drainage holes in the grinding mechanism. Finally, disposers should never be subjected to chemical drain cleaners, which can damage plastic and rubber parts.

When a disposer stops working, it is usually because the grinding mechanism has jammed, which in turn overheats the motor and causes it to cut off. The motor may also stop if you pack the hopper too solidly with garbage. Most disposer jams are caused by food particles caught between the spinning flywheel and the stationary grind ring, though bits of glass, metal or rubber trapped between the wheel and the ring can also immobilize the mechanism.

Freeing a jammed flywheel is a relatively simple procedure. It involves backing up the flywheel, either with a special wrench provided by the manufacturer or with the handle of a broom. On some models there is even a motor-reverse button to back up the wheel automatically. Such a motor reverse also prolongs the life of the grind ring by allowing the unit to use both sides of its blades.

Before you begin any repair, however, it is important that you understand how your disposer works. Although all disposers operate on the same principle, they are activated in two distinct ways. In one type, called a continuous-feed disposer, the motor is controlled with a wall switch. In the other, called a batch-feed disposer, the motor is activated when you turn a stopper in the sink opening. A continuous-feed disposer is somewhat more expensive to install, but its switch, located outside the unit, is easier to service. To gain access to the switch of a batch-feed disposer, you must disassemble the machine.

Never attempt any repair—or even a simple unjamming—without cutting off the power at the main service panel of your house. Take the added precaution of attaching a note to the service panel to alert other members of your household. Never put your hand inside the unit while the power is on.

Before you restart a motor that has been overloaded, give it at least 15 minutes to cool off. Then turn on the power and press the reset button on the bottom of the unit. (Professionals note that they answer many unnecessary service calls, in cases when the reset button simply was not pushed hard enough.) If the disposer does not start, check the service panel to see if a fuse has blown or a circuit breaker has been tripped. As a last resort, check the control switch—either wall-mounted or inside the machine—with a multitester *(page 16)*.

Apart from jamming and overloading, older disposers suffer from two other common ailments: leaks and worn parts. To remedy either, you will have to disassemble the unit.

A leak around the sink drain probably is the result of a worn gasket or loose nuts in the brackets that support the disposer. If water is leaking from the bottom of the unit or from a weep hole in the side, inspect the seal around the motor shaft at the bottom of the drain chamber. A leak of this type is more serious than one at the top, since the water can trickle down into the motor and damage it; replace the worn seal immediately.

If an old disposer still functions but grinds slowly, the grind ring probably needs to be replaced. If the disposer is especially noisy, one of the impeller blades on the flywheel may have worked itself loose; the flywheel should be replaced. Another possible cause of excessive noise is a damaged bearing in the motor. If disposer problems can indeed be traced to the motor, take the unit to the manufacturer's service center. Repairing the sophisticated capacitor-start, split-phase motor *(page 19)* is a job for a professional.

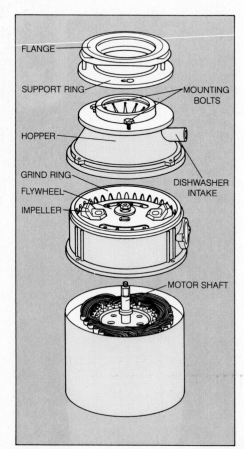

FLANGE

SUPPORT RING

MOUNTING BOLTS

HOPPER

GRIND RING

FLYWHEEL

IMPELLER

DISHWASHER INTAKE

MOTOR SHAFT

Anatomy of a garbage disposer. A garbage disposer consists of three main assemblies suspended beneath the sink by a flanged mount and a support ring. Garbage enters the upper assembly—called the hopper—through the sink opening and perhaps also an intake pipe connecting the unit to a dishwasher. The next assembly contains a grind ring, fluted with sharp cutting edges, and a perforated flywheel, the latter turned by the shaft of the motor. The centrifugal force of the flywheel hurls the garbage against the grinding ring, where it is shredded by the blades of the flywheel. The waste particles wash through perforations in the flywheel and the grind ring into a drain chamber, which has an outlet that disposes of the waste. The bottom assembly contains the motor, and the whole unit is enclosed in an insulated cover.

Unjamming a Stuck Disposer

Freeing the flywheel. With power to the disposer shut off at the main service panel, wedge the end of a broom handle against one of the impeller blades on the flywheel; apply force until the wheel begins to turn backward. Then work the wheel back and forth until it moves freely. If the jam was caused by a piece of glass, rubber or metal, take the object out of the disposer. Then restart the unit.

If your disposer came with a Z-shaped hex wrench *(inset),* insert one end of the wrench into the hexagonal hole at the bottom of the motor housing. Turn the wrench back and forth to rotate the motor shaft, until the flywheel is free.

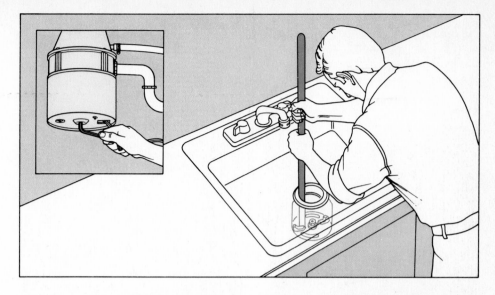

Fixing Leaks, Worn Parts

1 Disconnecting the disposer. With power to the disposer cut off and the electrical and plumbing connections uncoupled, loosen the bolts at the top of the disposer and twist the unit free of its top support ring. If your disposer is fastened with a twist-lock action, there will be no mounting bolts; simply turn the unit counterclockwise until it slips free.

With the tip of a screwdriver, pry open the cover of the disposer along its middle seam. Remove the bolts that join the three assemblies of the disposer — hopper, grinder and motor.

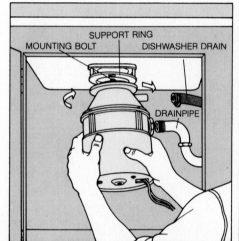

SUPPORT RING
MOUNTING BOLT
DISHWASHER DRAIN
DRAINPIPE

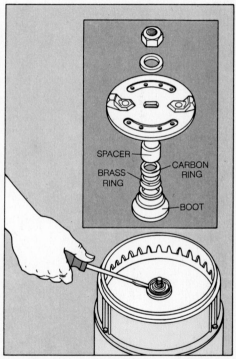

SPACER
BRASS RING
CARBON RING
BOOT

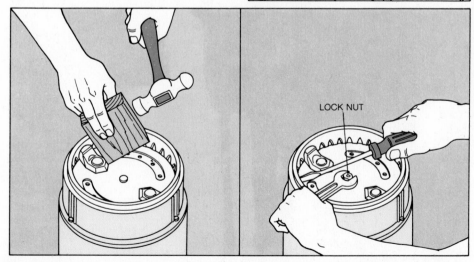

LOCK NUT

2 Removing a worn flywheel. If the flywheel is threaded directly onto the motor shaft, hold a block of scrap wood against an impeller blade and strike the block sharply with a hammer *(above, left),* driving the wheel counterclock-

wise; continue until the flywheel unwinds from the shaft. If the flywheel is held by a nut *(above, right),* keep the wheel stationary by wedging a screwdriver between an impeller blade and the grind ring; then loosen the nut with the wrench.

3 Replacing a leaking seal. If the motor shaft is sealed with a neoprene ring on the bottom of the drain chamber, wedge the tip of a screwdriver under the ring and pry it up. Scrape out the seal cavity, and spread a few drops of machine oil on the replacement neoprene ring before pressing it down into the cavity.

If the seal is a series of brass and carbon rings and spacers that fit around the shaft, lift these parts off the shaft *(inset),* taking care not to scratch the rings. Clean the parts and examine them for signs of wear; if any ring is nicked or worn, replace all of the rings and spacers. In reassembling a brass-and-carbon seal, do not scratch any of its metal surfaces.

Repairs for a Trash Compactor

Devotees of the space- and time-saving trash compactor, accustomed to fewer trips outside to the garbage can, may feel a real pinch if the masher runs amok. Luckily, repairs usually are simple.

A malfunctioning compactor either will refuse to run at all, will stop in mid-cycle or will run continuously. In each case, the problem probably is electrical. The six switches (opposite, bottom left) that control the up-and-down motion of the metal ram are quite vulnerable to the movement of this ram, which exerts up to 3,000 pounds of pressure to crush into a hatbox-sized space the trash that would normally fill two 20-gallon cans.

If the compactor fails to start, make sure the problem is not caused by a simple oversight—an unplugged cord, a tripped circuit or blown fuse, or your own failure to unlock the safety switch or to close the drawer completely before pressing the start button. If everything is in order and the compactor still will not run, the problem is within the machine and you must expose its innards.

Most compactors are serviced from the bottom or the back; after unplugging the unit, simply unscrew and remove the appropriate panel. If necessary, you can also remove the side and top panels the same way. To remove the drawer, pull it all the way out and lift it off its tracks.

Once the circuitry is exposed, perform a continuity test at each switch (page 16). You may find that a nonfunctioning switch arm is not making proper contact and needs only to be bent back into position. If a switch is otherwise faulty, replace it with one of the same type, using the guidelines on page 15.

If the continuity tests reveal no malfunctions in the electrical system, the problem is a mechanical one. There are several parts that may break down with normal day-to-day use, and they usually have telltale symptoms. If there is excessive machine noise, or if the motor runs but the ram does not move, there are damaged gears in the motor or a loose or broken drive chain. You can tighten the chain by repositioning the motor as shown at top, opposite; if the chain is broken, it can be replaced. Damaged gears are trickier to remove and replace, and may warrant a call to a professional.

Occasionally, the ram will complete only half of its cycle, refusing to budge from the bottom of the compactor because the power nuts are worn or stripped. The power nuts, which are part of the screw-and-nut system that pushes the ram down and pulls it back up (below), are mounted on top of the ram and can be replaced by the method shown at lower right, opposite.

How a compactor mashes trash. During the 30- to 60-second work cycle of the trash compactor, the metal ram located in the center of the machine travels down into the trash container and then moves back up to its starting position above the top of the container. This action is initiated by a ⅓-horsepower motor. The motor drives a chain around three sprockets, causing two power screws—one situated at either side of the ram—to spin slowly, threading their way through the two power nuts that are mounted on top of the ram.

When the machine starts, the power screws turn in one direction to draw the ram down into the trash compartment. The ram descends until it exerts a set amount of pressure—generally 2,000 to 3,000 pounds—either on the trash in the container or, if there is not enough trash, on four rubber bumpers at the sides of the compactor. At this point the motor pauses and then, directed by the reversing switch at the top of the unit, begins to turn in the opposite direction. The power screws turn in the opposite direction too, and the ram returns to starting position.

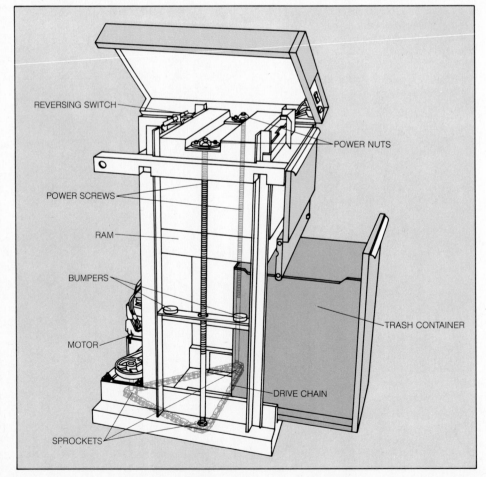

REVERSING SWITCH

POWER NUTS

POWER SCREWS

RAM

BUMPERS

MOTOR

TRASH CONTAINER

DRIVE CHAIN

SPROCKETS

The electrical system of the machine. A standard trash compactor has six electrical switches that direct the ram through its cycle. The on/off switch, manually controlled, begins the cycle and can also be used to stop the ram's cycle at any point. The key-operated safety switch beside the on/off switch locks the system so that neither a child nor an inadvertent flick of the wrist can turn the power on.

The limit switch has a levered arm that flips to the on position as the ram begins its downward path, supplying the current to run the motor. When the ram returns to the top, at the end of the cycle, the arm flips to the off position and the current is shut off. The reversing switch, beside the limit switch, works in the same way, flipping on as the ram passes. This switch changes the polarity of the current reaching the motor so that when the ram ends its downward movement and the motor pauses, the motor reverses the drive chain and power screws to pull the ram upward.

The two drawer switches are safety switches. The rear switch interrupts the flow of current when the drawer is open; the front switch lets the current flow when the drawer is shut tightly.

The switches are tested for continuity as on page 16; all should show continuity with contacts closed. If you must replace the limit switch, position the new one so that its levered arm is up when the ram is at its highest point. Similarly, position a new rear drawer switch so that the drawer will slide underneath the levered arm to lift the switch into the on position.

Adjusting the drive chain. Unplug the compactor, lay it on its side and remove the bottom panel to expose the drive chain, the motor sprocket and the two drive sprockets. Loosen the nuts in the elongated adjustment holes on the motor mount plate and, gripping the motor-pulley wheel, push or pull the entire motor assembly to adjust the tension in the chain; there should be about ¼ inch of give when the chain is pressed from the side. Tighten the adjustment nuts on the motor mount plate and lubricate the drive chain lightly with No. 30 motor oil.

If the drive chain is broken, replace it with a new chain, available from the manufacturer. Assemble the new chain with its master link *(inset)* and, after loosening the motor assembly and pushing it as far toward the front of the machine as it will go, install the chain on its sprockets. Adjust the tension in the new chain as before.

On some compactors you may find a tension-regulator spring attached to the old chain. Remove the spring before you remove the chain, then replace it when the new chain is installed.

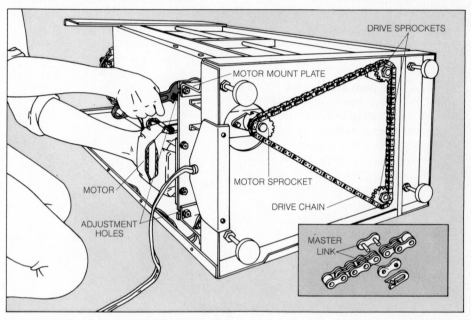

DRIVE SPROCKETS

MOTOR MOUNT PLATE

MOTOR

ADJUSTMENT HOLES

MOTOR SPROCKET

DRIVE CHAIN

MASTER LINK

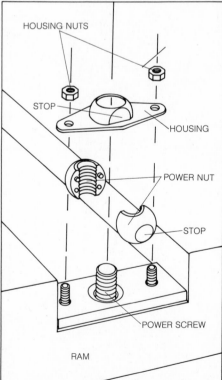

HOUSING NUTS

STOP

HOUSING

POWER NUT

STOP

POWER SCREW

RAM

REVERSING SWITCH

ON/OFF SWITCH

SAFETY SWITCH

LIMIT SWITCH

FRONT-DRAWER SWITCH

REAR-DRAWER SWITCH

Replacing a worn power nut. The exploded view at left shows how the two halves of the power nut fit around the power screw and how the power-nut housing, which is secured to the top of the ram with two nuts, encases the power nut to hold it securely in place.

To replace a stripped power nut, unplug the compactor and remove the top panel to expose the top of the ram. Tape the limit switch and reversing switch *(far left)* out of the way of the ram. Then tilt the machine to one side and reach beneath it to turn the chain sprockets by hand, moving the ram up until it can be lifted off the tops of the power screws. Remove the power nut and its housing from the top of the ram; set the new nut and housing in place, aligning the stops on both sides of the nut with the stops in the housing. Hand-tighten the housing nuts.

Replace the ram on the power screws, and turn the chain sprockets to lower the ram 1 inch. Tighten the housing nuts with a wrench, making sure the housing's outer edge does not protrude beyond the edge of the ram. Lubricate the power-nut assembly with molybdenum-and-lithium grease, available at hardware stores. Then remove the tape, releasing the switches.

The Vacuum Cleaner: A Much-Abused Machine

Perhaps the most abused of all home appliances, the vacuum cleaner is prone to three common problems: poor suction, electrical failure, and excessive noise. But the simplicity of the machine, which is essentially a motor-driven fan that draws debris into a bag, makes the cause of a breakdown easy to find.

Of the two basic types of cleaners, uprights have a greater number of serviceable parts than canister models. In both types, poor suction is most often caused by an overfull dust bag, which restricts the flow of the air; it can also cause the fan motor to overheat and even burn out. Always discard or empty a bag when it is 75 per cent full.

In canister cleaners, the hose is the next place to look for obstructions. To determine whether the hose is clogged, disconnect it, turn on the power and place your hand over the cleaner's intake port; if you feel strong suction, the blockage is in the hose. To clear the hose, take the cleaner outdoors, attach the hose to the exhaust port, and turn on the power to blow out the obstruction. If this fails, ease a broom handle through the hose.

Other causes of reduced suction in a canister cleaner are a clogged filter, which should be either washed clean (opposite) or replaced, and leaks in the hose, the intake port or the lid gasket. Test these parts by holding your hand over them with the cleaner running. Wherever you feel suction, the machine is leaking. A leaky hose can be salvaged or replaced (opposite). The intake port and the lid gasket are detachable and also can be replaced.

In an upright cleaner, poor suction can be caused by obstructions in the intake port or in the fan; blades of the latter can be jammed by the debris they suck in. The efficiency of an upright may in addition be affected by wear in the drive belt and beater bristles. You can get at any of these parts by removing the bottom cover plate; the belt and bristles can be replaced as shown on page 102.

When a vacuum cleaner of either type does not run at all, check first for a blown fuse or a tripped circuit breaker at the house service panel. Then test the power cord and the on/off switch for continuity. Most upright cleaners have a special socket connection inside the bottom of the handle, which you can test for continuity (page 102). The power-head attachment that comes with some canister cleaners is connected to a cord that runs down through the hose. If the power head does not run, this cord may be defective; test it for continuity between the on/off switch and the power head.

Any cleaner motor will eventually fail, but only an upright's motor is accessible for testing (page 103) and repair. The motors of most canister cleaners are sealed permanently and can be repaired only by a professional, if at all. And if the motor in a power-head attachment fails, the attachment must be replaced.

Although most vacuum cleaners are naturally noisy, listen for unusual sounds as indications of trouble. An upright makes a distinctive rattling sound when the bearings in the cylindrical beater brush are worn or when the fan blades break or become unbalanced. You can replace the bearings in the beater brush simply by taking off the ends of the cylinder (page 102), but to install a new fan you must first remove the motor.

Two Approaches to Ridding a Home of Dust and Debris

Upright and canister cleaners. In an upright cleaner (left), the motor-driven belt turns the cylindrical beater brush that loosens carpet dirt, which the fan then sucks in and deposits in the dust bag on the handle. The exhaust air is pushed out through the pores in the bag. Since the fan blades are directly in the path of the dirt, an object inadvertently sucked into the machine can lodge in the blades and jam the fan.

In the canister cleaner (below), the fan draws dirt through the hose directly into the dust bag, pulls the air through the bag and pushes it out the exhaust port. Only very fine particles can ever get as far as the fan blades.

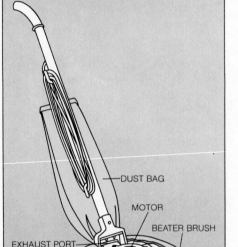

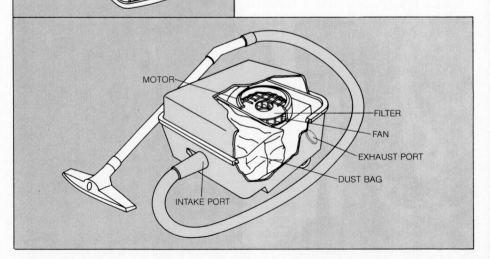

Maintenance of a Canister-Type Cleaner

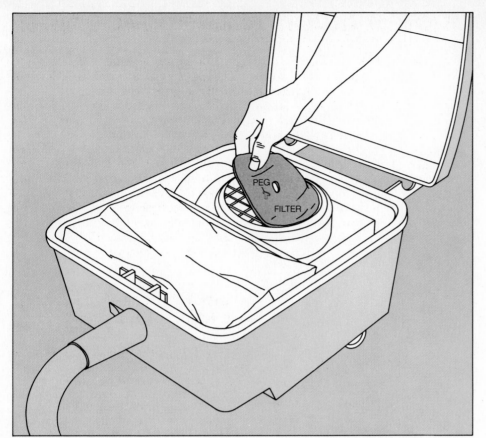

Cleaning a felt or foam-rubber filter. Remove and examine the dust filter that lies on top of the fan housing of a canister cleaner. On some cleaners, such as the model shown here, the filter is held in place by a small peg at the top of the housing; on other models, it is held by a metal rim that unscrews or unclamps. Hand-wash the filter in warm soapy water, and allow it to dry thoroughly before reattaching it.

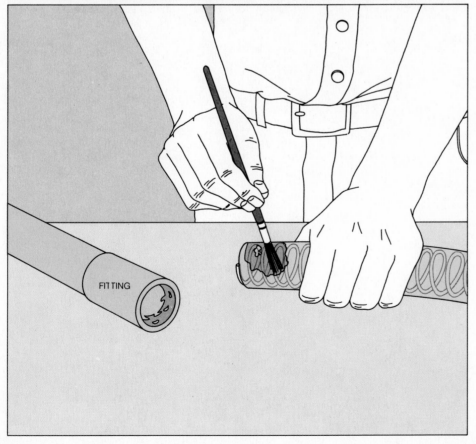

Replacing the hose. If the old canister hose has rubber fittings, twist the fittings off the hose; if the fittings are metal or plastic, cut the old hose 2 inches from the fittings, using wire cutters to cut the coiled wire. Pull the wire out of the fittings and, with a utility knife, scrape any remaining hose fabric from inside the fittings. Coat the ends of the new hose and the inside of the fittings with rubber-based glue, and push the new hose into the fittings.

The Belt and Brushes
of an Upright Cleaner

Replacing the drive belt. With the cleaner resting in an upside-down position, take off the bottom cover by releasing its clamps. Once the cover has been removed, you can examine the drive belt. If the belt is stretched or worn, lift it off the motor-shaft pulley, snap one end of the beater brush out of its spring slot, and slide the belt off the beater brush. Then fit a new drive belt into the groove on the beater-brush cylinder, and snap the end of the beater brush back into place. Align the lower loop of the belt with the arrow that is embossed on the sloping trough, and slip the belt over the motor-shaft pulley. Finally, put the bottom cover back into position.

Replacing worn beater-brush bristles. Snap the beater brush out of its spring slots, and twist its metal end caps in opposite directions until one unscrews from the shaft that runs through the beater-brush cylinder. With a screwdriver, pry the metal flange *(inset)* out of the end of the cylinder. Then remove the shaft and the other end cap, and pry out the metal flange at that end of the cylinder. Pull out the strips of bristles with pliers, and replace them with new bristles.

Before reassembling the beater brush, place a few drops of oil in each bearing assembly. When you are replacing the shaft, make sure that the shaft key at the edge of the flange is properly aligned with the notch in the cylinder.

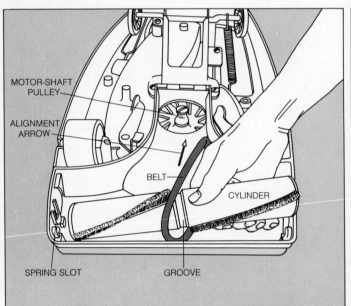

MOTOR-SHAFT PULLEY

ALIGNMENT ARROW

BELT

CYLINDER

SPRING SLOT

GROOVE

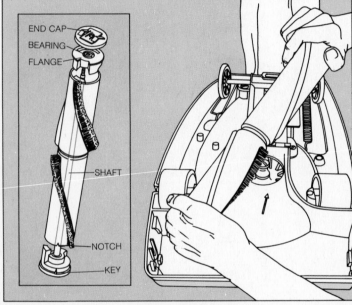

END CAP

BEARING

FLANGE

SHAFT

NOTCH

KEY

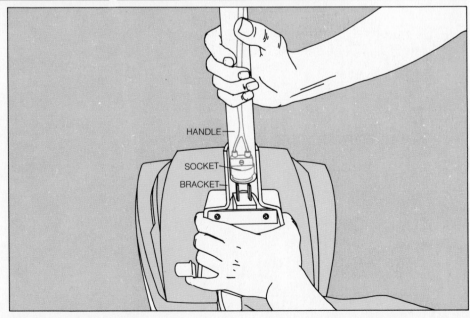

HANDLE

SOCKET

BRACKET

Checking the power supply. With the cleaner unplugged, release the spring lever to free the lower end of the dust bag from the machine, and then unfasten the handle from its bracket on the cleaner frame. With the handle switch turned to ON test the electric cord for continuity by touching one tester probe alternately to both slots in the socket at the bottom of the handle and the other probe alternately to both prongs of the plug for the wall outlet. The meter should show continuity on two of the four combinations. If it does not, test the handle switch for continuity. If the switch shows continuity, the electric cord is defective and should be replaced. If the switch does not show continuity in the ON position, it should be replaced.

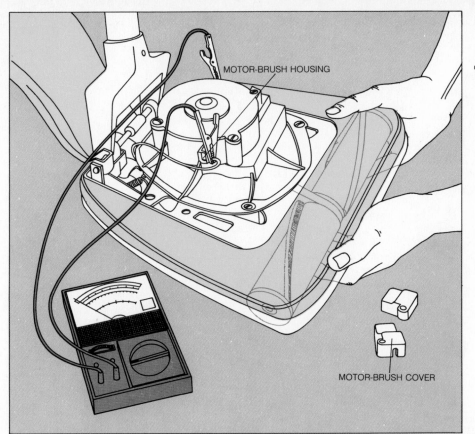

MOTOR-BRUSH HOUSING

MOTOR-BRUSH COVER

Testing and Replacing the Motor's Brushes

1 **Testing the motor brushes.** With the machine unplugged, unscrew and remove the motor cover from the top of the cleaner; then unscrew the small plastic covers over the two motor-brush housings. Test the motor brushes for continuity *(page 18)* by setting the multitester at RX1K and clipping the two probes to the terminals at the side of the housings. Reach under the cleaner and rotate the beater brush slowly by hand, watching the meter for intervals of no continuity. If at any point the meter shows no continuity, the motor brushes are worn and should be replaced.

2 **Replacing motor brushes.** Press a screwdriver against the end of a terminal on one motor brush, forcing the terminal into its slot in the housing until the catch on the terminal is released; pull the terminal out of the slot *(inset)*. The spring and the motor brush will pop out. To install a new motor brush, insert the brush into the brush housing and, with a screwdriver, press the spring in behind it until the spring is clear of the terminal slot. Then slide the terminal into the slot until the metal catch engages, locking the terminal in place.

Repeat this procedure to replace the other motor brush, and reattach the plastic covers on both of the motor-brush housings.

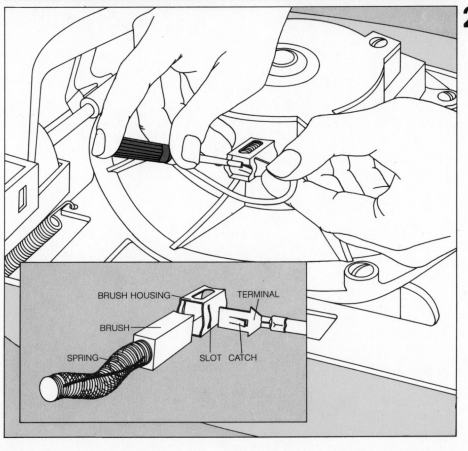

BRUSH HOUSING

TERMINAL

BRUSH

SPRING

SLOT CATCH

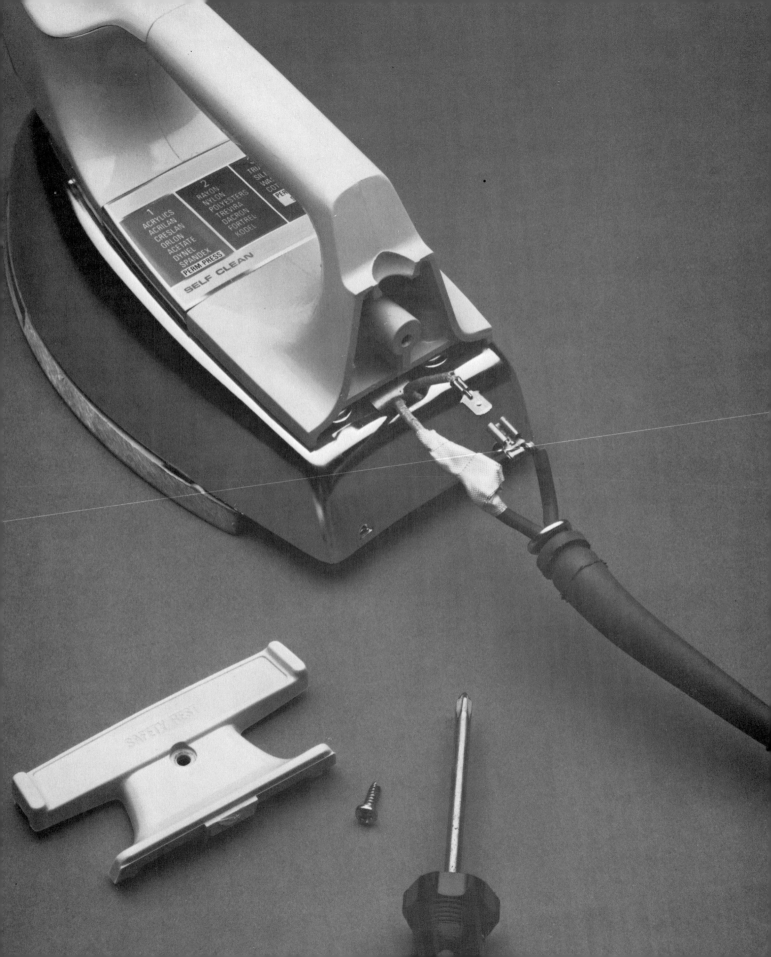

4 Little Things That Mean a Lot

Back in the days when electricity was used only for light and was generated only at night, various manufacturers tried to convince power companies that there could be a huge market for daytime electricity to run small appliances such as irons and space heaters. But most companies remained unpersuaded until one meter reader for a California utility suggested that the company run its generators all day long one day a week. He proposed Tuesdays, which happened to be the traditional day for doing the family ironing—and quickly made a fortune selling housewives an electric iron he had designed. Power companies got the message and soon it became customary, in applying for electric service, to pick up a few small electric appliances, which the power company also sold. Thus did small appliances promote the use of electricity and provide the springboard for the development of larger, more complex appliances with bigger jobs to do.

Today many of these appliances devoted to comfort and personal care would be difficult to live without. Air conditioners, once a frill that enticed customers into bars and movie houses, are considered life-supporting systems in some parts of the country. And the electric hair dryer can create a small crisis if it fails to function after the morning shower. In fact, the urge to immediately fix the broken hair dryer, electric shaver or window fan is often the spur that introduces novices to the mysteries of appliance repair. In many cases, it is a very good place to start. Most of the smaller appliances are simple in design, with only a few parts and relatively uncomplicated circuitry. Opening them up is not as daunting as, for instance, unveiling the circuitry of a dishwasher. Also, their initial cost usually is much lower, so not as much money is at stake if the attempt at repair should happen to go wrong.

Technological improvements have, on the other hand, limited the repair possibilities on some of these smaller appliances. In cutting production costs, manufacturers have incorporated many elements in sealed modules that, once they are disassembled, cannot be put back together again.

On the plus side, however, many of the repairs on these smaller appliances—especially those intended for personal care—have less to do with replacing mechanical parts than with keeping them clean. Hair dryers and electric razors often break down because their working parts get clogged with debris connected with their function—loose hair or whiskers. Similarly, repairing a humidifier or a window air conditioner may be a simple matter of hosing down the filters and vacuuming the refrigeration coils. Even a novice can deal easily with this kind of problem.

Small Aids to Personal Comfort

An array of personal-care appliances— shavers, hair dryers, shower-massagers— help busy people face each day looking and feeling their best. Among the simplest and least expensive of appliances, they are so important to personal comfort that many are available in cordless versions, either for traveling or just for added convenience.

All cordless appliances contain batteries that can be recharged with current from a wall outlet through a charging unit—a useful appliance in itself. Inside the charger is a transformer, a wire coil that reduces household voltage to a low enough level—usually five to seven volts—to charge the batteries safely.

In addition to reducing the voltage level, the charger must also change the alternating current of the house wiring into direct current—the form of electricity accepted and discharged by batteries. A small electronic part called a rectifier handles this conversion task. Though often built into the circuitry of the charger, between the transformer and the batteries, the rectifier is sometimes made a part of the appliance itself. If the label on the charger lists an output of 5-7 VAC, the rectifier is in the appliance; if it lists an output of 5-7 VDC, the rectifier is in the charging unit. The nickel-and-cadmium, or nicad, batteries used in appliances can be recharged hundreds of times, but they will eventually wear out.

Battery-operated appliances use small direct-current motors. Because direct-current motors are simple and efficient, they can also be found in some appliances that have cords. A hair dryer, for example, has a cord but powers its blower with a DC motor. Any appliance that has a DC motor has a rectifier as well.

If the rectifier in an appliance or a battery charger fails, the appliance will not function at all. To test the rectifier, set a multitester at RX1 and touch one probe to each lead of the rectifier; then reverse the probe positions. The reading should be high in one position and low in the other; if not, the rectifier is defective.

Several personal-care appliances—hair dryers and electric rollers among them— employ heating elements. Such an appliance will have a fuse to protect it against overheating if the thermostat fails. The fuse is very likely blown if the appliance will not heat at all; if the appliance does get slightly warm, the trouble is in the thermostat.

Other personal-care appliances are used with or near water, posing special hazards and repair problems. Appliances that heat water, such as vaporizers and steam irons, will need to be periodically delimed (page 36) to keep them from being clogged with mineral deposits. When repairing an electrical appliance that uses or moves water, avoid shock by being sure the appliance and your hands and feet are dry. Never immerse any appliance or set it in a wet spot while it is plugged in or while you are testing it. And make sure you never use any electric appliance, such as a hair dryer or a manicure set, while you are having a bath.

A Little Black Box That Recharges Batteries

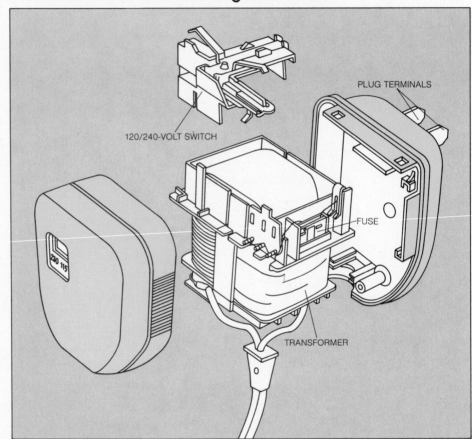

Anatomy of a battery charger. This compact device receives current from either a 120- or a 240-volt circuit in your house. Resistance from the transformer reduces the current flow to between five and seven volts of alternating current. This low-voltage alternating current passes through a rectifier—in this case in the appliance, but sometimes inside the charger—which changes it to the direct current that charges the nicad batteries in the appliance. At the 120-volt setting, current passes through one transformer coil; at the 240-volt setting, it must pass through both coils to be sufficiently reduced. The excess voltage is dissipated as heat—an operating battery charger normally is warm to the touch. A fuse, which protects the device from power surges, is also part of the charger.

If the batteries and rectifier are sound but the appliance does not recharge, check the charger for a blown fuse, either visually or with a continuity tester (page 10). Replace a bad fuse by clipping or soldering a new one in place—in this charger, one lead is clipped under the plug terminal and the other is soldered to the transformer terminal. Also check the charger's power cord for continuity (page 10) and replace it, if necessary, by soldering a new one to the cord terminals. If the transformer coils are burned or discolored, replace the entire charger.

Electric Shavers That Take to the Road or Stay at Home

A battery-operated cordless shaver. This rotary-head shaver is typical of cordless shavers in that it uses a pair of 1.5-volt nicad batteries to power a small direct-current motor that moves the blades. The way this particular version works is that a gear on the motor shaft engages three other gears, and they in turn rotate the trio of circular blades; on some of the other brands, the motor shaft moves a lever that pushes the blades back and forth. There is a rectifier in the stem of this shaver, which converts the alternating current from a charger into direct current for the batteries.

If the shaver is fully charged but runs only for a short time, the batteries need to be replaced. Depending on the model, the batteries may clip into place with spade connectors, or they may have to be soldered in. If the shaver will not run at all and the charger is functioning, the batteries probably are dead. Before replacing the batteries, however, do a resistance check on the rectifier and inspect the switch for contacts that are broken or encrusted with hair. If a shaver with a DC motor runs haltingly, check the brushes on the motor for wear *(page 103)*. These will occasionally need to be replaced.

A cord-powered shaver. Like most shavers that plug into a wall outlet, this model has a small universal motor *(page 18)*. The motor shaft engages levers that move the blades back and forth. Other cord shavers have rotary blades like those of the shaver at left.

If a cord shaver does not run at all, check its cord for continuity *(page 10)*. Also check the switch—on this model and most others, a visual inspection will tell you if the switch is making contact when it is turned on. Clean the switch of any debris. If the shaver stops running when tilted in certain directions, the brushes on the motor probably need to be replaced *(page 103)*. In some cases, however, the brushes may be only loose; in such a case the brush holders can simply be bent to tighten them.

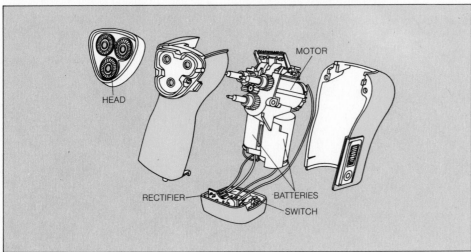

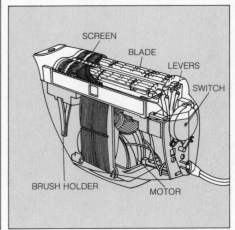

Routine Shaver Maintenance

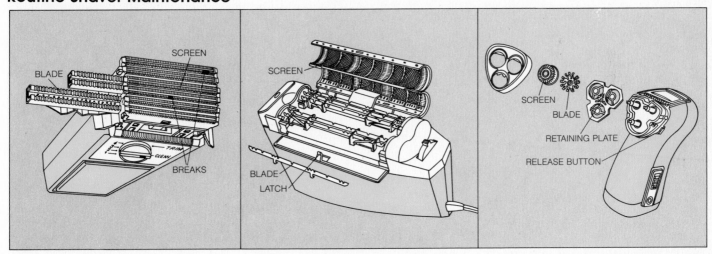

Replacing shaver heads. There are three ways in which shaver heads are commonly attached. When the selector knob on the shaver at left, above, is set on CLEAN, the head pops up and the blades can be pushed out at either end of the head and the screen can be pulled up and off. On the shaver at center, there is a small latch on the side of the shaver head that re-

leases the screen and exposes the blades, which can be unhooked when they are depressed and pushed to the side. The head of the rotary shaver *(above, right)* releases at the press of a button. This action exposes a retaining plate that can be lifted off to free the circular blades—each with its individual screen—when it is time for them to be replaced.

Even a slight flaw in the screen or blade can cause an electric shaver to nick. If you drop a shaver, check immediately for tiny breaks or dents in the screen and replace the screen if you find any. Periodically open the head of your shaver, and brush out the residue inside. A build-up of hair particles can dull the blades, clog the switch or even burn out the motor.

Hair Stylers That Use Heat

Hand-held hair dryers. Both the pistol-grip hair dryer at left and the more compact version at right have a small DC motor that turns an impeller, forcing air past a heating element and out a vent. A multiposition switch controls both the heat setting and the impeller speed. A fuse and a thermostat, attached to the heating element, provide double protection against overheating. A rectifier changes incoming alternating current into direct current for the motor.

The thermostat will automatically turn the dryer off if the appliance begins to overheat. If this happens, you should wait at least 10 minutes to give the dryer time to cool off. Then, if the dryer will not restart, check for hair or dirt lodged between the electrical contacts of the thermostat. If the contacts are clean, test the fuse for continuity and check visually for broken coils in the heating element. On some models the fuse can be replaced separately, but usually the

heating element, the fuse and the thermostat must be replaced as a unit.

Unfamiliar rattles and whines may be caused by a broken or bent impeller. On most units, replacing the impeller entails replacing the motor as well. On the model at right, however, the impeller can be removed separately. When you replace any part, it is a good idea to clean the dryer thoroughly before you reassemble it.

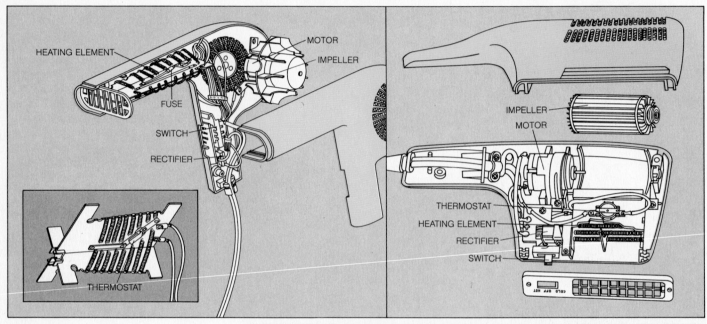

Electrically heated hair rollers. A wire heating element sandwiched between metal plates under the top of this simple device heats spindles, which in turn transfer the heat to aluminum cores in the plastic rollers. A thermostat controls the temperature, and a fuse protects the circuitry should the thermostat fail.

The only problems this appliance can give you are that it will not heat at all or that it will not get hot enough. The latter problem is caused by a thermostat that cuts off at too low a temperature; replace the thermostat. If the rollers do not heat at all, use a multitester to check for continuity on the cord, the heating element, the fuse and the thermostat. Replace the component that does not show continuity.

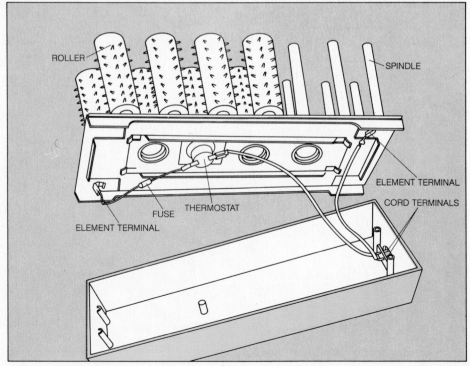

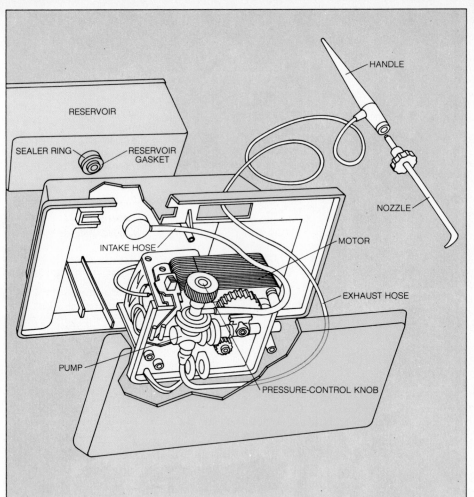

HANDLE

RESERVOIR

SEALER RING   RESERVOIR GASKET

INTAKE HOSE

NOZZLE

MOTOR

EXHAUST HOSE

PUMP

PRESSURE-CONTROL KNOB

An Oral Irrigator for Teeth and Gums

A dental irrigator. Water or medicinal solutions in the reservoir of a dental irrigator are pulled through a flexible intake hose by a pump powered by a tiny, long-lasting motor. The pump pulses 1,000 jets of water per minute through an exhaust hose and out the nozzle of the irrigator handle. A pressure-control knob adjusts the force of each jet to as much as 80 pounds of pressure per square inch.

With water under such high pressure, leaks can develop in the pump, the hose connections or the gaskets that seal the unit—most commonly in the reservoir gasket. A leaky pump should be repaired by a professional. But a leaky reservoir gasket is easily replaced: Pry off the sealer ring that holds it in place and insert a new gasket. To replace the intake hose, remove the bottom of the appliance and lift the motor out of the appliance housing to expose the hose connections. The new hose can be pushed onto the ends of the hose fittings on the pump and the reservoir outlet. When you remove the bottom of the irrigator, though, be careful not to change the position of the pressure-control knob.

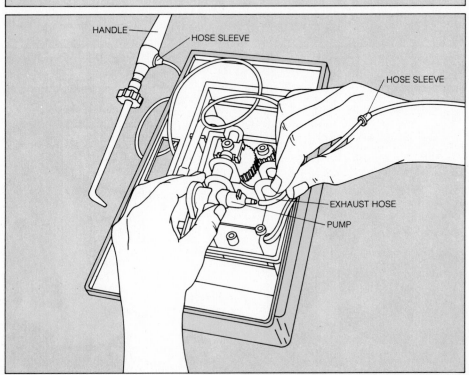

HANDLE   HOSE SLEEVE

HOSE SLEEVE

EXHAUST HOSE

PUMP

Replacing the exhaust hose. Remove the bottom of the irrigator and pry off the plastic sleeve that holds the hose around the pump outlet; slip the hose off the outlet. Disconnect the other end from the handle in the same way. Pull the hose, with its plastic sleeves, out of the housing, and replace it with a new hose, fitted with new plastic sleeves. Push the hose onto the pump and handle outlets, then force the sleeves over them to secure the connection.

If the handle leaks where it connects to the removable nozzle, replace the handle. Pry off the sleeve that connects the exhaust hose to the handle, and insert a new handle.

A Shower Head That Massages

Maintaining a shower head. A mechanism sealed inside the head of these shower attachments causes a pulsating, massaging action. By turning a control ring you can speed up or slow down the pulsations. Both the hand-held attachment *(left)* and the wall-mounted version *(right)* are made up of parts that simply screw together, and so any part that is broken can be replaced. To ensure a strong spray, you should periodically clean the filter screen. In the hand-held attachment, the screen is located between the elbow and the pivot ball, which is held in place by a threaded collar; unscrew the collar to remove the screen. On a wall-mounted fixture, unscrew the shower head from its base to remove the screen. If the shower head becomes encrusted with mineral deposits, you can clean it off with vinegar and a stiff brush.

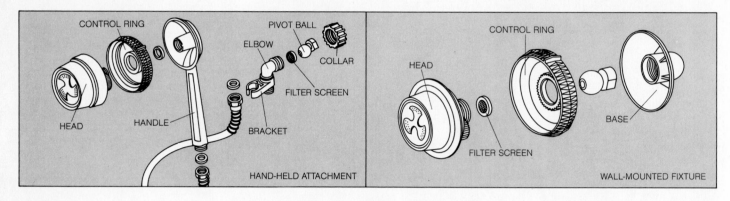

Treatments That Keep an Iron Steaming

The intricacies of a steam iron. The heating element of an iron, located inside the soleplate, is regulated by a temperature-control lever on the handle. At the higher temperature settings, water drips from a reservoir into the vapor chamber; there it is converted into steam and escapes through vents in the soleplate.

Any problem involving the complex inner workings of a steam iron, such as leaks or inaccurate temperature control, should be repaired by a professional. A steam iron's most common problems, however, can be remedied at home. If mineral deposits build up in the steam vents, the iron will not steam or the steam will sputter. Loosen the deposits by filling the iron with vinegar and running it at the lowest setting. Then flush the iron thoroughly with clear water. If the problem recurs, switch to distilled water.

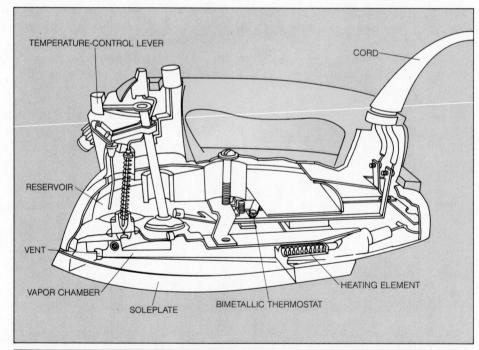

Replacing the power cord. Remove the iron's backplate by taking out the screw at the center of the plate. Slide back the strain-relief sleeve, and loosen the screws holding the cord connectors to the terminals on the iron. To avoid loosening the terminals, steady each one with long-nose pliers as you release the screws. Attach a new iron cord fitted with the same connectors as the old one. If the new cord does not have its own strain-relief sleeve, use the old one, sliding it on before connecting the new cord.

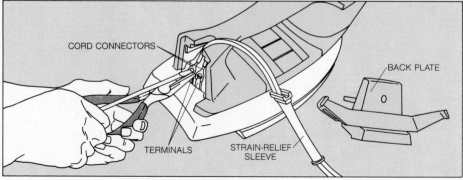

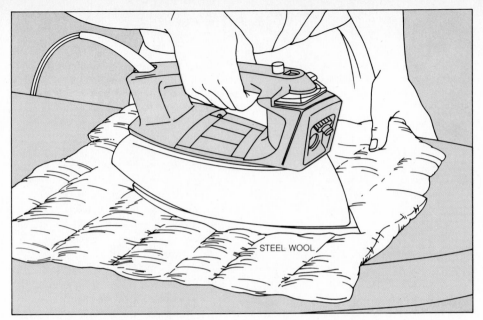

STEEL WOOL

Cleaning an uncoated soleplate. Tiny fibers on the surface of synthetic-fabrics can melt under the heat of an iron and adhere to the metal surface of an uncoated soleplate, causing a resin build-up. This coating, which becomes tacky when hot, causes the iron to drag and stick to the clothing. To remove the resin build-up, set the iron at a synthetic-fabric setting and cut off the steam. Then iron over a layer of medium steel wool with a protective pad of cloth beneath it. If your iron has an aluminum soleplate, be particularly careful to avoid scratching it. When the soleplate looks clean, allow it to cool, then buff it with mild scouring powder and a damp cloth; this will remove any oxidation or mineral deposits that remain. Rinse the soleplate well, then heat the iron to a warm setting and run it over a sheet of wax paper a few times.

Devices That Moisten the Air

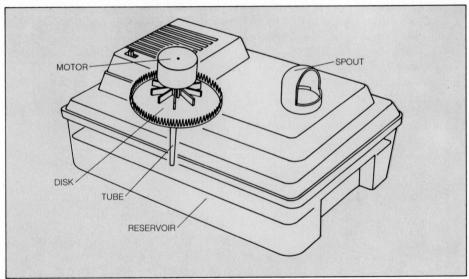

MOTOR

SPOUT

DISK

TUBE

RESERVOIR

A cool-mist sprayer. In this version, a motor spins a tube-and-disk atomizing assembly that pulls water from the reservoir and disperses it by centrifugal force into fine, cool droplets that exit through the spout. The moist interior of this device is an inviting habitat for bacteria. After every few days of use, disinfect the reservoir by filling it with water and ½ cup of laundry bleach, then plugging the spout with a rag and running the machine for 90 minutes. Rinse with clear water. Periodically clean mineral deposits from the moving parts with vinegar and a stiff brush. If the mist from the machine leaves a chalky coating on surrounding furniture or floors, use distilled water in the reservoir.

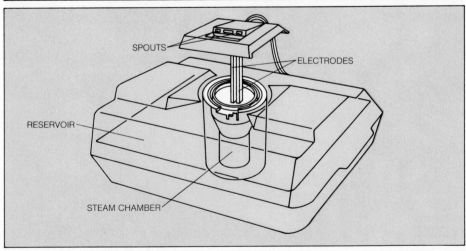

SPOUTS

ELECTRODES

RESERVOIR

STEAM CHAMBER

The vaporizer. In this device, electricity from the power cord passes directly into two electrodes immersed in water inside a steam chamber. The water completes the circuit by conducting current between the electrodes. Since only a small amount of water flows into the steam chamber from the reservoir at any given moment, the water in the chamber boils quickly and escapes through the spouts as steam.

The most common problem in a vaporizer is caused by mineral deposits, which collect on the electrodes. Every few days of use, scrape off the deposits with an old screwdriver or with sandpaper. If the water is slow to steam, add a teaspoon of salt to make it more conductive.

111

Cool Relief with a Room Air Conditioner

Nowadays the cooling effects of an air conditioner are taken so much for granted that an unexpected malfunction seems akin to a natural disaster—like a heat wave or a drought. Happily, an air conditioner works in far less mysterious ways than the weather does. Its most common problems can be diagnosed quickly with a continuity tester, and the faulty part can be replaced with a screwdriver or a nut driver. Most minor ailments can be cured with routine maintenance procedures that also help to prevent trouble from recurring.

Like a refrigerator *(page 58)*, an air conditioner works on the physical principle that matter absorbs heat when it evaporates and emits heat when it condenses. An air conditioner installed in a window or through a wall converts the room inside into a giant walk-in refrigerator. The unit itself is divided by a metal partition into distinct indoor and outdoor compartments. Refrigerant flows between the compartments in a continuous length of metal tubing. Inside, the refrigerant picks up heat and the tubing functions as an evaporator; outdoors, the refrigerant surrenders its heat

and the tubing functions as a condenser.

When an air conditioner loses its cooling power, it is often because grime has accumulated on the evaporator and condenser. Both should be cleaned thoroughly at least once a year. A relatively new unit can be cleaned with a brush attachment on a vacuum cleaner, but an older unit or one that is very dirty should be scrubbed with water and detergent.

To give an air conditioner this kind of full-scale cleaning, disconnect the unit and move it outdoors. Take off the front grille and air filter, remove the metal housing and cover the electrical components and fans with aluminum foil or plastic film. Then gently swing the free ends of the condenser and evaporator—the ends opposite their connections to the compressor *(below)*—a few inches away from the unit. Spray them hard from both sides with a garden hose, and carefully scrub the metal fins and tubing with a mild detergent and a brush. Let the unit dry completely before assembling it, moving it back indoors, and plugging it into its power source.

The air filter behind the front grille should also be periodically cleaned with

soapy water. On some models this filter is made of fiberglass or a similar material, and the entire filter should be replaced about once a month during the cooling season. Replace a foam filter when holes wear through it.

If a good cleaning does not improve the cooling power of an otherwise functioning unit, there probably is a leak in the refrigerant coils. Do not attempt to repair the refrigeration system yourself; take the entire air conditioner to a professional and have it flushed out, repaired and recharged.

Sometimes an air conditioner that cools adequately will develop annoying noises. Fan bearings that grind or squeal spell trouble ahead if they are not oiled. Check the owner's manual for instructions on how to lubricate them. If your model has sealed bearings that cannot be oiled, you will have to replace the entire fan motor.

Locate the source of other fan noises by disconnecting the unit, removing its cover and turning the fan blades by hand to see if they are hitting other parts of the machine. On some units you can reposition the fan blades by moving them for-

Anatomy of an air conditioner. The cooling action of this typical room air conditioner takes place amid the finned evaporator coils located behind the air filter and grille. A fan behind the coils draws in the room air, circulates it over the refrigerated coils and then expels it—cooler, drier and cleaner—back into the room. Adjustable louvers direct the flow of cooled air. Meanwhile the heat drawn from the room air by the refrigerant in the evaporator coils is carried to the condenser, on the opposite side of the partition. Outdoor air, circulated through the condenser coils by a second fan, carries the heat away.

The heart of the cooling system is the compressor, which pumps refrigerant from the evaporator to the condenser and back again. The compressor motor is enclosed in a metal shell and is kept from overheating by an overload protector attached to the shell. A capacitor stores up electricity to help the compressor start, and a thermostat cycles the compressor on and off to regulate the cooling. The thermostat's sensor, attached to the evaporator, detects changes in air temperature. The motor that drives both fans runs independently of the compressor and is controlled by the setting of the master switch.

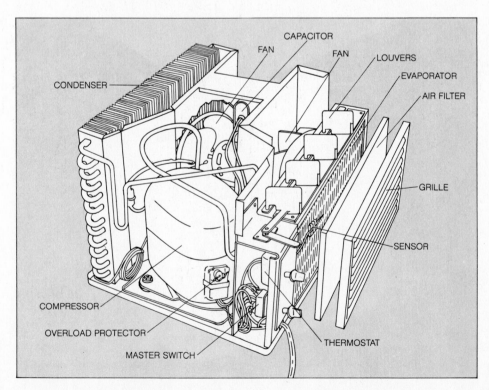

ward or backward on the shaft, or tighten loose blades by adjusting a setscrew at their base. On models that have the blades held to the shaft by a rubber hub, you may be able to eliminate unnecessary noise by installing a new hub; on other models, the entire fan assembly will have to be replaced.

Two other common sources of noise are the refrigerant tubes and the compressor. A rattling noise is sometimes caused by a tube that vibrates against another part of the machine; this noise can be silenced if the tube is either gently bent away from the part it is touching or padded with a piece of sponge. A thumping noise may mean that the mounts for the compressor need to be adjusted. In some cases the rubber pads beneath these mounts deteriorate and must be replaced.

Another annoyance that is easily eliminated is having condensation water drip inside the house. Make sure that the air conditioner tilts slightly outward—about ¼ inch per horizontal foot, raising the inside edge if necessary with thin wooden wedges. If the unit already is properly tilted, check that the collector pan underneath the evaporator coils is clean and that its drain to an outside pan is not clogged with debris.

More serious malfunctions generally involve the electrical system, and treating the problem begins with identifying the part that has failed. If the air conditioner does not operate at all, check the fuse or circuit breaker at the main service panel, and test the electric cord for continuity (page 10). If the unit is receiving power, test the master control switch for a faulty circuit. Also test the thermostat, another possible source of trouble. On some models a defective thermostat will shut down the unit completely; on others, it may stop the compressor while the fan continues to run.

Most often, however, it is either the fan or the compressor that fails. If air blows through the unit but is not cooled, then the problem lies with the compressor. Alternatively, the coils in the machine may grow cold and the compressor continue to hum, but no air will circulate. In this case, the fan motor and its capacitor are suspect (page 19).

When the compressor fails to operate, first test to make sure that it is receiving enough voltage to start it. If the unit is plugged into a double receptacle, you can perform this voltage test (page 12) by carefully inserting the probes of a multitester into the second outlet. Otherwise, touch the probes to the prongs of

the air conditioner's plug after partially withdrawing the plug from the outlet. Note the voltage reading, then turn on the air conditioner and watch the drop in voltage at the moment the compressor tries to start. If the voltage reading drops more than 10 per cent below the voltage that is specified on the unit, the problem is in the wiring of the house, not in the air conditioner.

But if the voltage is adequate, the problem may be in the capacitor connected to the compressor. With power off, discharge and then test the capacitor (page 19). If the capacitor is operating properly, move on to test the compressor motor and its overload protector (page 114). You can replace the latter if it is defective, but replacing the compressor is a job for a professional. It may also be so costly that it will warrant buying a new air conditioner instead.

If all of the components of the compressor check out and it does not have a starting capacitor (below), you can give it an extra boost of energy by installing a hard-start device. This attachment stores power to help the compressor start. Sometimes called a solid-state start kit, this kind of device is sold complete with the necessary leads, by dealers who carry appliance parts.

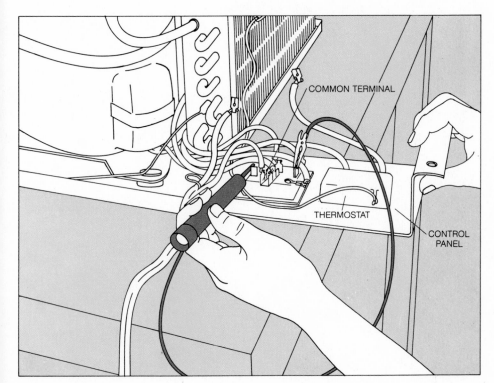

Tracing a Problem through the Master Controls

Checking the master switch. With the unit unplugged, unfasten the control panel and pull it far enough out to expose the back of the control switch. Examine the switch. If you find any loose or burned terminals, replace the switch.

If all of the connections appear to be sound, test the switch for continuity, using the following procedure. Turn the switch to one of the cool settings. With the power still off, remove the wire that connects the thermostat to the switch, and clip one lead of the continuity tester to that terminal. Then trace the wires running from the electric cord. One will be connected, along with several other wires, to a common terminal. The other will have its own terminal. The latter is the hot wire; disconnect it and touch that terminal with the probe of the continuity tester. If the switch does not show continuity, disconnect all the wires, marking them with tape or wax pencil as you go, and replace the switch.

COMMON TERMINAL

THERMOSTAT

CONTROL PANEL

Testing the thermostat. Allow the room temperature to reach at least 75°F.; then, with the unit unplugged, uncouple both wires from the thermostat terminals. Connect the continuity tester in their place. Spin the temperature-selection knob through its complete range, from the warmest setting to the coldest. The continuity tester should light as the switch is turned; if it does not, replace the thermostat.

Also inspect the metal sensor on the evaporator, which is connected to the thermostat. If you find that the sensor has been severely bent or pinched, or if it is broken, you will have to replace the entire thermostat assembly.

Troubleshooting Compressor and Motor Connections

Testing the motor and overload protector. With the unit unplugged, remove the cover of the terminal box on the compressor. Without detaching any wires, connect the continuity tester to the two terminals on the overload protector clamped inside the box. If the overload protector does not show continuity, replace it.

Scrape a little paint off the compressor's shell and detach the wires from the three motor terminals. Touch one probe of a multitester *(page 12)* to the exposed metal on the shell and touch

the other probe in turn to each motor terminal. If there is continuity, the compressor has short-circuited; replace it or buy a new air conditioner.

If neither test reveals a problem, test for continuity in the compressor motor itself. There should be continuity when you touch one multitester probe to the common terminal (where the lead from the overload protector fastens) and touch the other tester probe, in turn, to each of the other terminals. If not, the compressor or the entire unit must be replaced.

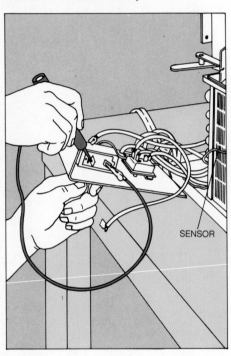

SENSOR

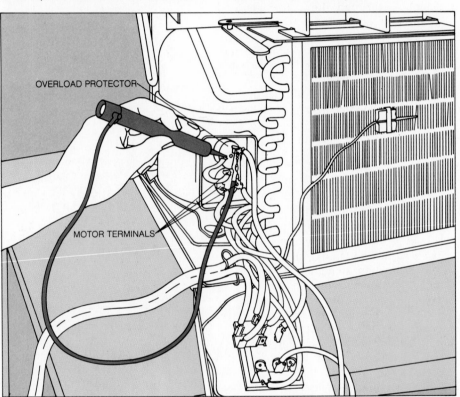

OVERLOAD PROTECTOR

MOTOR TERMINALS

Installing a hard-start device. Attach the insulated connectors on the wires of the hard-start device to the terminals on the spool-shaped starter. Fasten the free ends of the wires to terminals on the capacitor. On a capacitor with two terminal clusters, such as the one illustrated here, attach one wire to a free terminal on each cluster. On a capacitor that has three terminal clusters, one cluster will be attached to the fan motor. Find that cluster, then attach the hard-start device to terminals in the other two clusters. Fasten the hard-start device against the side of the capacitor, using the clip provided.

If a single starter fails to correct your compressor problems, wire an additional hard-start device to the same terminal clusters. If all of the terminals in the clusters are filled, fasten the wires of the second device to the piggyback terminals on the wires of the device already in place.

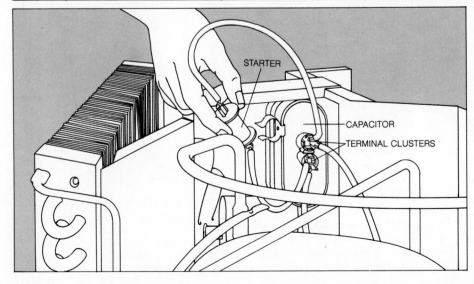

STARTER

CAPACITOR

TERMINAL CLUSTERS

A Machine to Heat and Cool

With the addition of two components—a reversing valve and a defrost thermostat—a room air conditioner will do double duty, becoming a heater as well as a cooler. Machines of this sort, which are called heat pumps or reverse-cycle air conditioners, undergo this unlikely metamorphosis by reversing the flow of refrigerant through the condenser and evaporator coils. The refrigerant then evaporates outdoors and condenses indoors. Even in cold weather, the air outside will give up heat to the refrigerant, which is even colder.

Keeping a heat pump running smoothly requires the same maintenance needed for a standard cooling unit. The filter must be cleaned monthly and the fans lubricated on the timetable prescribed by the manufacturer. Minor adjustments to cure noises and leaks are also identical, and major breakdowns tend to involve the same components as for a cooling unit. A faulty compressor or capacitor or a burned-out fan motor will, for example, prevent the unit from either heating or cooling. When something goes wrong, switching the machine briefly to the opposite mode will often confirm that the source of the problem is a component common to both operations.

If the unit fails to shift modes, the reversing valve is at fault. You can test and replace the solenoid that controls the valve, but the valve itself must be serviced by a professional—it is part of the sealed refrigeration system.

If the machine's only symptom is that it heats poorly, the problem may lie in the defrost thermostat. Inspect the outside coils for ice. In cold weather, condensing water will freeze on the coils, blocking the transfer of heat. Normally, the defrost thermostat corrects this condition by temporarily deactivating the reversing valve and thus transforming the outdoor coils into a condenser until the ice has melted. At the same time, the thermostat switches off the fans so that cold air will not be blowing into the house. Iced coils are a sign that the defrost thermostat is not functioning. Be sure that the coils are free of ice before you begin testing the thermostat.

Tracking Down a Heat-Pump Problem

Checking the reversing valve. Unplug the heat pump and remove its cover. Locate the solenoid, which activates the reversing valve; the solenoid is a plastic cylinder, and it will be mounted near the larger metal cylinder of the reversing valve. Trace the wires coming out of the solenoid to their terminals on the defrost thermostat and the master control switch. Disconnect the wires (it may be necessary to remove the control panel before you can do this), and test the solenoid for continuity (page 17). If there is no continuity, the solenoid must be replaced.

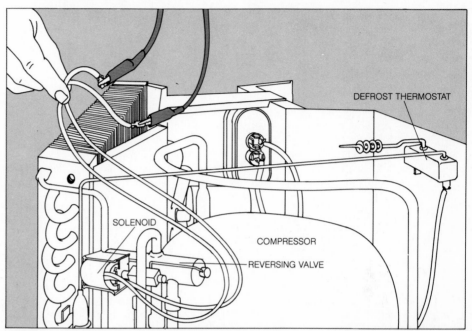

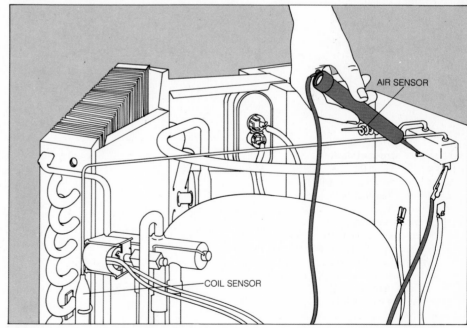

Tracking trouble in a defrost thermostat. With the unit unplugged, remove the two wires from the defrost thermostat and test its terminals for continuity (page 16). If the terminals do not show continuity, replace the thermostat and both of its sensors; one of them is attached to the outdoor coils, the other is suspended behind the outdoor fan. If there is continuity, inspect the sensor tubing for breaks and dents. Also make sure that the outdoor sensor is firmly attached to the coils. If the sensors are damaged, you will have to replace the entire thermostat.

Service for a Dehumidifier

A dehumidifier uses several of the components of an air conditioner to dry the air—but without cooling it. A compressor pumps refrigerant through a sealed system of metal coils, a fan draws the room air over the coils, and electrical switches and circuitry control the action. Properly maintained, a dehumidifier should operate problem-free for many years. Vacuum the coils and clean the fan blades annually, lubricate the fan motor as the manufacturer instructs, and tighten any loose mounting screws if the machine develops a rattling noise.

The first step in servicing a malfunctioning unit is to ascertain which part has failed. If the dehumidifier will not run at all—or runs constantly, even when the room humidity is low—the problem lies in the electrical system. If the dehumidifier shuts down, first be sure that power is reaching the machine: Check the circuit breaker or fuse at the main service panel, then test the wall outlet *(page 12)* and electric cord for continuity *(page 10)*. If the power checks out, test the overflow-prevention switch and the humidistat for continuity. (Unplug the machine for any continuity test.)

If the dehumidifier is not moving the air, test the fan motor for continuity, placing the probes at the ends of its lead wires, usually located inside a compressor control box *(right)*. If the fan motor is defective, it can be replaced.

If the fan is running but the coils are not cold, check the compressor motor for continuity. Test either at the terminals on the side of the compressor *(below)* or at the ends of the wires that connect the compressor to the relay switch that starts the compressor motor—usually this switch is inside the compressor control box. A faulty compressor is usually not worth replacing; it is more economical to buy a new dehumidifier.

If the compressor motor does show continuity and the coils are not cold, the problem is either the overload protector or the relay switch that starts the compressor motor. If the overload protector is attached to the side of the compressor, you can test it for continuity. On most units, however, the overload protector is built into the compressor control box along with the relay switch, and it is diffi-

cult to test the two components independently. Rather than trying to isolate the malfunctioning part, it is simpler to replace the entire control-box assembly. If the coils still will not get cold, the problem may be in the refrigerant level. Do not attempt to check or replace the refrigerant yourself; take the unit to a professional.

A frequent complaint is that the coils of the dehumidifier become covered with ice. It is normal for the coils to be covered with frost for as long as 30 minutes after you switch on the machine. If the ice stays longer than 30 minutes, there may be dirty coils, a nonfunctioning fan, or a defective humidistat. But very often the icing problem is not in the machine, but in the atmosphere. For a dehumidifier to operate properly, the temperature of the air around it should be above 65° F. Below that temperature the coils must become so cold in order to condense water vapor in the air that the moisture freezes before it can run off into the drip pan. There is no solution to this problem except to avoid running the machine at low temperatures.

A Simple Process to Take Moisture Out of the Air

Anatomy of a dehumidifier. The moisture-collecting coils on a dehumidifier are kept cold by the refrigerant inside them. A fan draws air over the cold coils, causing moisture to condense on the coils and drip into a pan below. Meanwhile the heat absorbed by the refrigerant is expelled by the condenser coils. Because these hot coils are next to the cold moisture-collecting coils, the dehumidifier has no effect on the temperature of the air. But the air feels cooler and more comfortable because it is drier.

Cycling the machine on and off is a humidistat—an adjustable switch that responds to changes in humidity and turns the machine on and off. When the drip pan is full, a rubber float triggers an overflow-prevention switch, which cuts off power to the fan and the compressor so that no more water will collect. This switch also activates a warning light on the cabinet front to indicate that the drip pan should be emptied. The electrical components that start and stop the compressor are in a control box mounted on the side of the compressor.

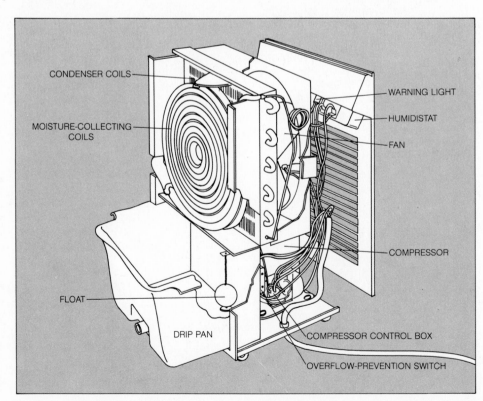

CONDENSER COILS

MOISTURE-COLLECTING COILS

WARNING LIGHT

HUMIDISTAT

FAN

COMPRESSOR

FLOAT

DRIP PAN

COMPRESSOR CONTROL BOX

OVERFLOW-PREVENTION SWITCH

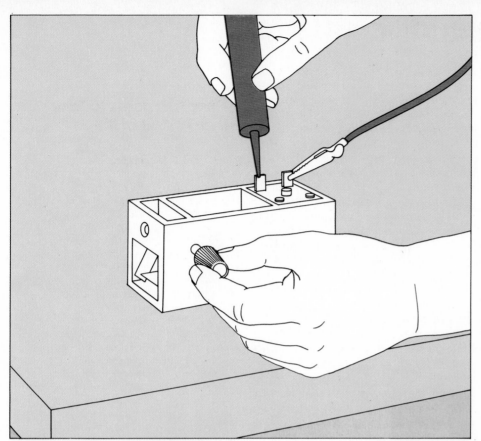

Testing the Humidistat and the Overflow Switch

Testing a humidistat. With the machine unplugged, remove its cover and locate the terminals on the humidistat. Remove the humidistat from its mount, if necessary, to gain access to the terminals. Turn the selector knob to OFF and clip one wire of a continuity tester to one terminal. Touch the tester probe to the other terminal, at the same time turning the selector knob with your free hand. The humidistat should show no continuity at first, but it should register continuity as you turn the knob. If it fails either of these tests, replace the humidistat.

If the terminals of the humidistat are encased in a plastic cover and are inaccessible for testing, trace the wires from the humidistat to their connections with the relay switch, inside the compressor control box. Disconnect these wires from their terminals on the relay switch, and test the wire ends for continuity while you are rotating the humidistat selector knob.

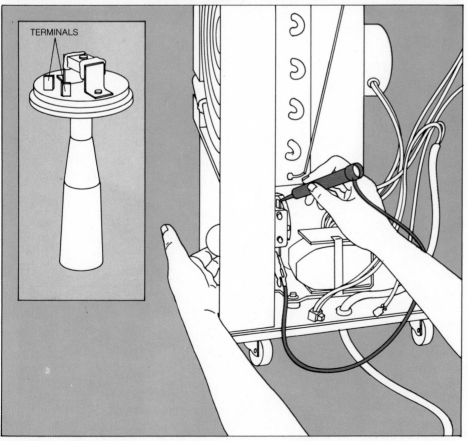

TERMINALS

Checking the overflow-prevention switch. With the machine unplugged, remove the wires from the overflow-prevention switch and test the switch terminals for continuity *(page 16)*. Test it first with the float in the down position, then lift the float and test it again. The switch should have continuity in the down position and no continuity in the raised position. If it fails either of these tests, replace the switch.

Another type of overflow switch is mounted directly above the drip pan and has a rubber tube that extends down into the water *(inset)*. To test this type of switch for continuity, touch the probes of a continuity tester to the switch terminals and have a helper fill the drip pan with water. The switch should show continuity when the pan is empty and no continuity when the pan is filled. If it is impossible to reach the switch terminals with the switch in place on the dehumidifier, remove it and test for continuity by lowering it into a pan of water.

A third kind of switch that guards against overflow is mounted on the dehumidifier below the drip pan; it is activated by the increasing weight of the water in the pan, turning off the machine when the pan is full. To test this switch, simply press down on the empty drip pan to simulate the weight of the water.

Humidifier Maintenance Chores

A portable humidifier is basically a fan that blows air through a wet pad to add moisture to dry air. Although the pad may be kept wet by a variety of means— by turning it on rollers or on a drum through a water reservoir, or by pumping water onto it *(opposite, bottom)*— all humidifiers work by evaporation.

The principal problem with humidifiers is maintaining cleanliness. Humidifiers collect mineral deposits from the evaporating water, and they need to be cleaned periodically. How often you must clean one depends on the quality of your water. If the water is very hard, the humidifier should be cleaned weekly; if the water is soft, an annual or semiannual cleaning will be sufficient.

To clean the evaporation pad or belt, take it out of the humidifier and remove surface deposits with a brush, then flush water through the pad from the clean side to the clogged side. For stubborn scale, soak the pad in a vinegar solution overnight, using ¼ cup of vinegar to each quart of water. Do not stretch or wring the pad, and if it is badly worn or misshapen, replace it.

The same technique of brushing and soaking can be used to remove mineral deposits from metal parts, although the soaking solution can be stronger: up to 50 per cent vinegar. One exception is the float mechanism, which turns the humidifier off when it runs out of water. Some floats are designed to be pulled off the float arm and replaced when they become encrusted with minerals.

The reservoir inside a humidifier also needs cleaning. It may collect algae and slime, especially in soft-water areas. To avoid this problem, never leave water standing in an unused unit. When you do fill the reservoir, add the water purifier specified by the manufacturer, and continue to do so at every filling. To clean the reservoir, sponge it out with a mixture of warm water, mild detergent and a chlorine bleach.

To maintain the fan, keep the blades free of dust and lubricate the motor at the intervals specified by the owner's manual. If you hear grinding noises from the fan motor, the motor bearings are badly worn and the fan should be replaced. Rattling noises from a fan blade

with a rubber hub indicate that the hub is worn. To remove the hub for replacement, pull the blade-and-hub assembly off the drive shaft; then push the hub out with your thumbs, being careful not to bend the blades.

A humidifier's electrical parts rarely fail. If the unit does not run, check first to make sure there is water in the reservoir; if the reservoir is empty, the float mechanism will have turned the unit off. Next test the lead wires of the fan motor for continuity *(page 11)*. Test a float switch for continuity as shown on page 117. Finally, if the humidity remains low even at the highest setting, the humidistat is likely to be faulty. Test the humidistat for continuity as shown on page 117.

Treatments for Three Types of Humidifiers

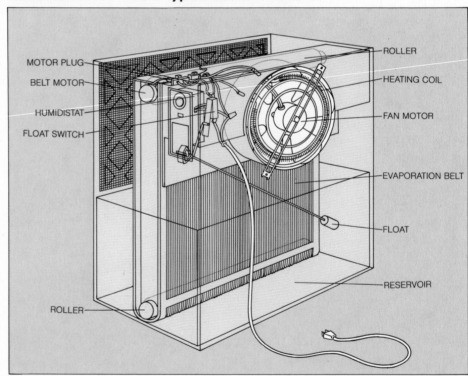

MOTOR PLUG
BELT MOTOR
HUMIDISTAT
FLOAT SWITCH
ROLLER
ROLLER
HEATING COIL
FAN MOTOR
EVAPORATION BELT
FLOAT
RESERVOIR

A belt humidifier. The evaporation pad in this humidifier is a continuous, spongelike belt turned by two rollers, one of which is mechanized. The rollers dip the belt into a water reservoir, then lift it up to the fan, where air, warmed by a heating coil, is blown through the wet belt, thus evaporating the moisture and sending humidified air into the room. A humidistat switches the unit off and on in response to changes in the room's humidity. A float switch turns the unit off when the reservoir runs dry.

Both the rollers and the evaporation belt are designed so that they can be removed from the unit for cleaning or replacement; the rollers uncouple from their frame, and the evaporation belt slides off them. If the belt does not turn but the fan runs, the belt motor that turns the mechanized roller at the top of the unit has probably failed. To test it, unplug the belt motor from the unit, remove the roller-frame assembly, and plug the motor into a standard wall outlet. If it does not run, replace it.

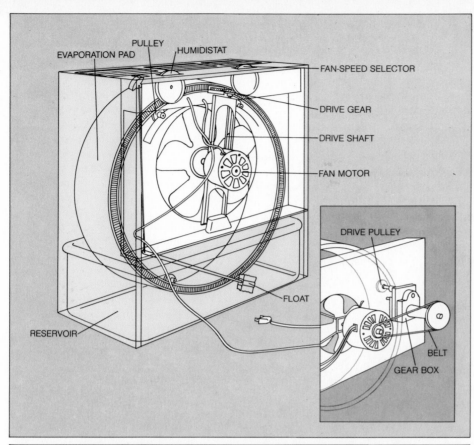

A drum humidifier. In this version, the evaporation pad is wrapped around a plastic drum that is turned through the water reservoir by a drive gear or by a rubber belt *(inset),* either of which is connected to the fan motor. The drum rotates in front of the fan, which bounces air off a plastic drumhead, forcing the air out through the water-soaked evaporation pad. The drum is supported by three plastic pulleys.

The drum, the evaporation pad and the fan blades all are accessible for cleaning or replacement. Simply lift the drum off its pulleys; the evaporation pad then slides off the drum. To replace a worn drive gear, pull the old gear off the drive shaft. To replace a worn belt on a belt-driven drum, slip the old belt off its pulleys. To replace a worn drive pulley, loosen the setscrew that holds the pulley on the gearbox shaft. To detach the gearbox, remove its mounting screws.

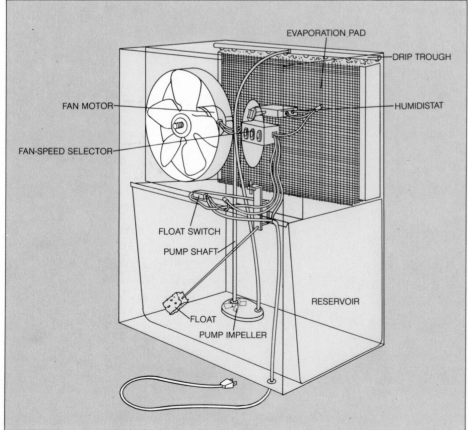

A pump humidifier. A flexible rubber tube connects the shaft of this humidifier's pump to the drive shaft of the fan motor. The pump lifts water from the reservoir through a rubber hose to a drip trough at the top of the unit. From there, the water trickles down into a stationary evaporation pad and evaporates in the airflow created by the fan.

To clean or replace the evaporation pad, tilt back the hinged access panel and slip the pad out of its frame. Clean the holes in the drip trough with a stiff wire, and replace the rubber hose if it is cracked or brittle.

If the pump becomes clogged with minerals or sediment, remove the reservoir cover and unscrew the pump housing from the bottom of the reservoir. Take off the pump shaft and the impeller and clean them with mild detergent and warm water. Check the rubber tubing connecting the pump shaft with the fan motor. If it is cracked or broken, replace it.

Keeping a Window or Oscillating Fan Twirling

A fan is too simple a device to fail often, but when one does cause trouble—by making worrisome noises or not working at all—repairs are straightforward. The typical fan is little more than a one-piece propeller-like blade spinning on a motor shaft, and even an oscillating fan presents only one complication—the gear mechanism that makes it swivel.

Noise is a common problem with fans. If your fan rattles or vibrates too much, first make sure it is not resting on or against an uneven surface. Place an oscillating fan on a cushioned surface; insert a cardboard shim between a window fan and the window frame. If the fan still rattles, check for loose parts—a nameplate, perhaps, or screws or clips that secure the blade guards, the switch knob and the carrying handle. To isolate a noise, hold your hand against the suspected part with the fan running—the noise should stop. Tighten all screws, bend clips so that they clasp firmly, and reglue loose nameplates.

If the noise persists, disconnect the fan, remove the blade guards or grilles, and tighten the setscrew that fastens the hub of the metal blades to the shaft or the spinner that keeps a plastic blade unit in place. Also, you may need to pry off a C clip and tighten washers that hold a fan-blade unit on the motor shaft. If a metal-bladed fan is dropped or tipped over, denting its grille or guard, straighten the grille or guard. But if the blade is bent, the entire blade unit must be replaced. Though straightening may decrease the noise, fan blades must be precisely balanced; an imbalanced one will cause vibration. This in turn will cause the fan to "walk," or shift position, and cause extra wear on the motor.

If the fan does not work at all, examine the electric cord first for signs of wear or damage. Then disconnect the cord from its terminals on the fan and test the cord for continuity *(page 12)*. Also, a defective on/off switch may either cause a fan not to operate, or allow it to operate at only one speed. Check the switch for continuity at each setting. If there is no continu-ity at one of the settings, replace the switch, marking the positions of the wires before removing the old switch.

If an oscillating fan does not swivel smoothly back and forth, the cause may be stripped gears. Turn the fan off, set the oscillating control to ON and try to swivel the fan by hand; it should not move. If it does, remove the motor housing and inspect the gear assembly. If the assembly seems worn, replace it.

If the fan spins too slowly, turn it off and spin the blade with your finger. If it drags, the motor may need oiling. Some older fans have oil holes in the motor housing; squirt a few drops of light oil, such as sewing-machine oil, in the holes and start the motor for a few seconds. For older fans without oil holes, squirt penetrating oil on the motor shaft. Fans of more recent design have sealed lubrication and cannot be oiled.

If the fan hums but the blades do not move, test the motor for continuity with a multitester *(page 11)*. A defective motor should be repaired by a professional.

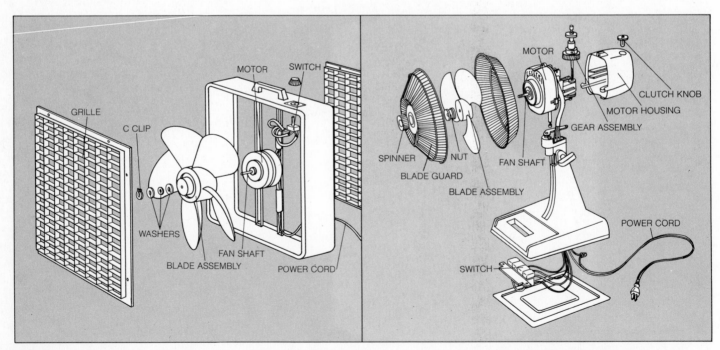

Two types of fans. In a window fan *(above, left)*, a motor turns a one-piece blade unit that is held to the motor shaft by C clips and washers or by a setscrew. For safety, the blade unit is covered by grilles on both sides of the fan hous-ing. A switch regulates the speed of the motor and the direction of rotation.

The assembly of an oscillating fan *(above, right)* is the same as that of a window fan, except that the blade unit may be held to the motor shaft by a spinner and a nut, if not by a setscrew. The blades are surrounded by front and rear blade guards that are screwed or clipped together. A gear assembly allows the fan to pivot.

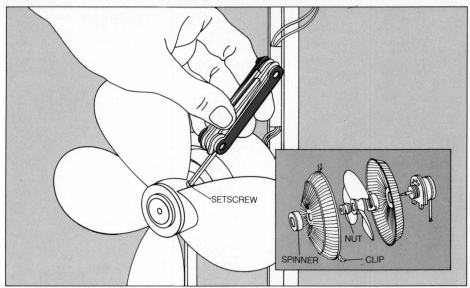

Replacing a blade unit. To replace a metal blade unit, disconnect the fan, remove the blade guards or the front grille, and loosen the setscrew holding the blade unit to the motor shaft. Remove the damaged blade unit and slip a new one onto the shaft, placing it so that the setscrew hole in the blade unit is seated against the flat part of the shaft. Fasten the setscrew.

To replace a plastic blade unit *(inset),* pry off the clips with a screwdriver, remove the blade guards and unscrew the plastic spinner, using channel-joint pliers, if necessary, to loosen the spinner. After replacing the blade, you may need to replace the spinner-and-nut assembly as well.

SETSCREW

SPINNER   NUT   CLIP

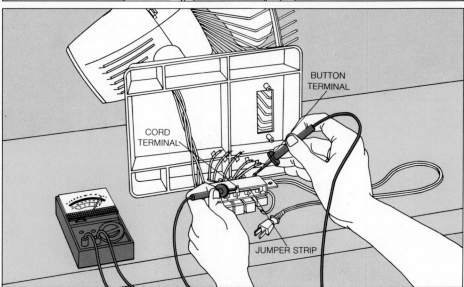

Testing a multispeed switch. Remove the bottom plate or grille and pull off the switch housing. Test the switch for continuity *(page 10)* by first disconnecting the wires to the switch, recording the wire locations. Set the switch to the first speed, and place one tester probe on the terminal to which one wire of the electric cord was connected; on a push-button switch, this terminal will be a jumper strip. Place the other probe on the terminal for the speed you are testing; it should show continuity. Repeat the test for each speed by setting the switch to that speed and moving one probe to the appropriate terminal while leaving the other probe on the electric-cord terminal. There should be continuity at every speed; if not, replace the switch.

BUTTON TERMINAL

CORD TERMINAL

JUMPER STRIP

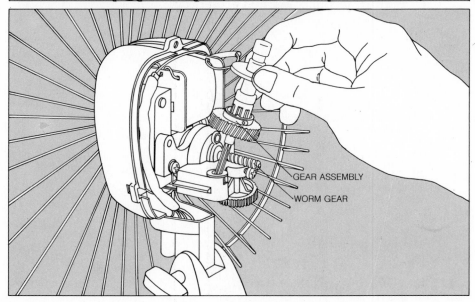

Checking an oscillating fan's gears. Remove the clutch knob and unscrew the motor housing. Lift the gear assembly out of its mounting and check the gear teeth for wear; if they look worn, replace the entire assembly. Then check the teeth of the worm gear on the motor shaft for wear; if these teeth look worn, have the worm gear replaced by a professional.

GEAR ASSEMBLY

WORM GEAR

Warmth Restored to a Faulty Space Heater

A portable electric space heater is a simple appliance—even the most elaborately designed model has only a few working parts. There are a control knob to turn the unit on and off, a heating element to radiate heat, a thermostat to regulate temperature and, on some models, a fan to blow heated air into the room.

Heating elements take different forms—some are made of thin steel ribbon, some are wire coils, others have wires encased in quartz rods—but in general, space heaters all work in the same way. If a heater will not heat at all, make sure the problem is not a blown fuse or a tripped circuit breaker, then start your troubleshooting with the power cord.

First unplug the cord and examine it for signs of wear. A frayed power cord not only may interrupt the flow of current to the heater; it is a fire and shock hazard and should be replaced immediately. Even if you can see no damage, the cord still may be the culprit. Remove it and test it for continuity (page 10).

To test or replace the power cord or any other malfunctioning part you must get inside the heater—and that may require more ingenuity than making the repair does. On some heaters you can simply remove screws along the front grille, pull the control knob off its shaft, and remove the faceplate and cover. On other models you must remove screws on the back and underside of the unit; on still others you must remove a side panel, disconnect wires to the thermostat, and slide the control panel and grille out.

With the inside of the heater exposed, you can remove the power cord for testing. Loosen the cord connections in the heater, then release any strain-relief device by rotating it a quarter turn with pliers (page 40). If the continuity test indicates that the cord is defective, replace it with a cord that has wires of the same gauge; if you are not sure of the gauge, check with an electrical-parts shop or the manufacturer, because an inadequate power cord is hazardous.

If the power cord is functioning and undamaged, reconnect it but do not plug it in; then check all of the wires inside the heater visually for breakage, burned spots or loose connections. Replace any damaged wires and tighten loose connections as necessary.

The next two parts to check are the thermostat and the heating element. If the contacts on the thermostat are dirty, clean them as shown on page 124. If they do not close completely when you turn the control knob to ON, replace the thermostat. To remove the old thermostat, you may have to use a wrench to loosen a large hexagonal nut on the control-knob shaft; on other models, just remove the screws that secure the thermostat.

If the thermostat is working but the heating element is not, disconnect the wires from the heating-element terminals—you will find one at each end—and test the element for resistance with a multitester (page 15). Set the tester at RX1 and touch the tester probes to the element terminals. If the meter reads between 5 and 30 ohms, the element is working. If the meter needle does not move, indicating no continuity, remove and replace the element. If it is a ribbon-type element, replace it as shown on page 125. A coiled element can be unscrewed and lifted out for replacement; a quartz heating rod simply slips in and out of two sockets.

If your space heater has a control switch with settings for HIGH, MEDIUM and LOW and the heater works at one setting but not another, the switch probably is at fault. The surest way to isolate the problem is to perform a continuity test on the switch (page 16). But if the element fails to heat at any setting, it is very likely that you will need to replace the control switch.

Space heaters with fans may become unusually noisy if either the fan or its motor malfunctions. You may need only to lubricate the moving parts; more severe problems call for a continuity test and possible replacement of the entire motor-and-fan assembly (page 124).

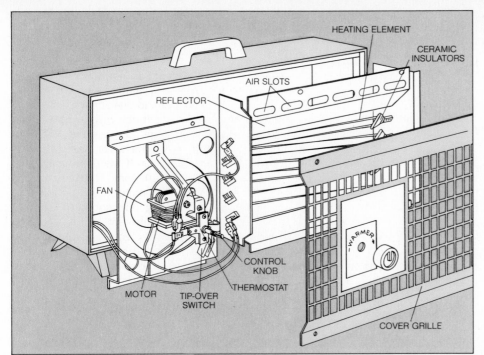

Three Types of Portable Electric Heater

Anatomy of a fan-forced space heater. A fan-forced heater warms a room in two ways. When the control knob is turned to ON, current activates the fan motor and the contacts of the thermostat close. The thermostat then activates a ribbon-like nichrome (nickel-chromium) heating element (*page 124*) woven between ceramic insulators. This heating element, with the aid of an aluminum reflector, radiates heat through the cover grille into the room. Meanwhile, the fan blows air against the back of the reflector; this air, warmed by the hot aluminum, is blown out into the room through the slots above the heating element.

When the heating element reaches a prescribed temperature, contacts on the thermostat separate, interrupting the flow of current. The tip-over switch—a weighted arm that swings on a pivot—automatically separates the thermostat contacts if the heater falls over.

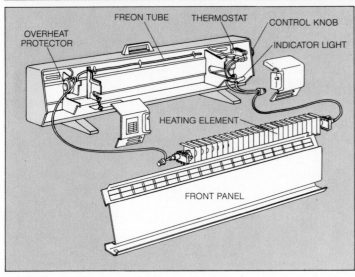

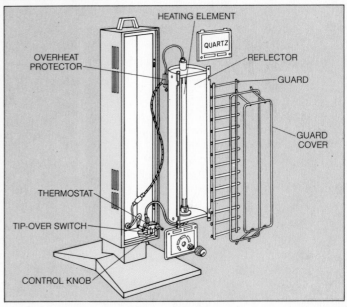

Anatomy of a baseboard heater. The baseboard heater, so named because it fits inconspicuously against a baseboard, has a coiled heating element activated when a control knob on one end of the unit is turned to ON, forcing the contacts on the thermostat to close. When the element heats to its prescribed maximum temperature, an overheat protector (signaled by a freon-filled tube on the rear of the unit) interrupts the flow of current and allows the element to cool. When the minimum temperature is reached, the thermostat contacts close again and the element reheats.

A red indicator light signals whether the unit is turned on or off. A front panel with a grille encloses the unit for safety, but it allows the heated air to flow into the room.

Anatomy of a quartz heater. The heating element in this space-saving upright heater consists of nichrome wire encased in a quartz rod. The element is activated when the control knob is turned to the on position and the thermostat contacts close. A tip-over switch beside the thermostat shuts off the current if the unit falls; an overheat protector at the top of the heater keeps the element from heating beyond a prescribed maximum temperature.

There is a curved metal reflector behind the element, which increases the efficiency of the unit by directing radiated heat into the room through the guard and the guard cover enclosing the front of the heater.

Thermostats, Tip-Over Switches and Heater Fans

Checking the thermostat. If the heating element does not heat, unplug the heater and remove the panels that cover the thermostat, then examine its contacts. If their facing surfaces appear dirty, burned or corroded, slip a folded piece of fine sandpaper between them and gently sand them clean.

If cleaning does not solve the problem, examine the contacts with the control knob turned to the on position. If the contacts do not touch, you will need to replace the thermostat. Label the two thermostat wires so that you can return each of them to the proper terminal; then remove the mounting screws, take out the old thermostat, and install a new one.

Testing the tip-over switch. To test the tip-over switch in a fan-forced or a quartz heater, plug in the heater, allow it to warm up, then tip the unit onto its back. If the heating element does not begin to cool immediately, unplug the heater, let it cool, and remove the panels necessary to expose the thermostat. With the heater upright, push the arm of the tip-over switch back and forth so that the switch lever forces the contacts apart. If the arm does not swing freely or if the contacts do not separate, the tip-over switch should be replaced. On most heaters the tip-over switch is part of the thermostat; if so, replace the whole assembly.

Help for a heater fan. If a heater fan will not turn, unplug the unit and remove outer panels as necessary to check for wires or other obstructions that may catch on the blades. If the blades are not blocked but move stiffly, coat the fan shaft with a silicone-spray lubricant. If the blades spin easily but the fan does not work, check the motor for continuity. Disconnect the motor lead connected to the heating element and hold the tester probes against the other motor terminal. If there is no continuity, remove the connectors from all the motor terminals, unscrew the motor assembly from its mounting, and install a new motor-and-fan assembly.

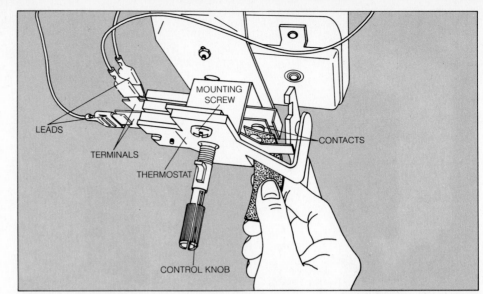

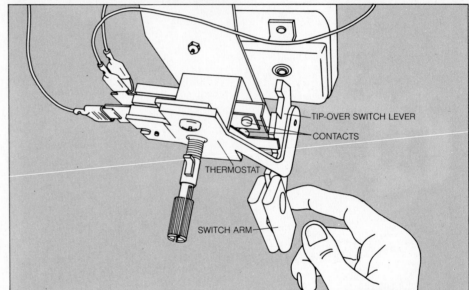

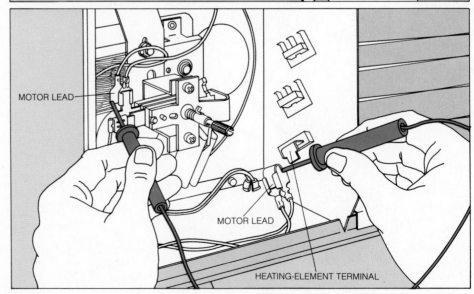

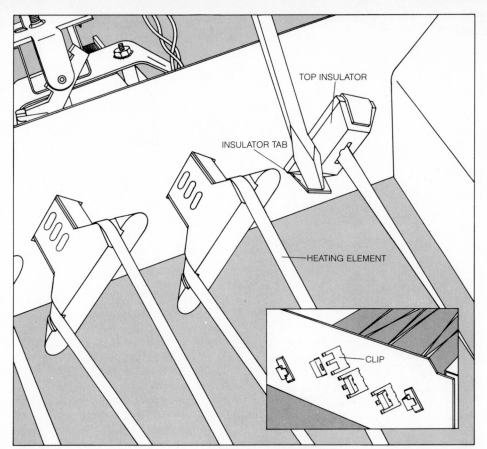

TOP INSULATOR

INSULATOR TAB

HEATING ELEMENT

CLIP

Replacing Two Kinds of Heating Element

Threading a ribbon-type element. With the unit unplugged, draw a diagram showing the installation pattern of the ribbon heating element, then disconnect the wires at both ends of the element. With a screwdriver, push back the tabs that secure the insulators at both ends of the element; pull the element out of the unit.

Wearing rubber gloves to keep moisture from damaging the new element, position an end insulator in its slot and bend the tabs back into position to secure the insulator. Then, following the diagram you made, thread the ribbon back and forth around the remaining insulators. Secure the second end insulator as you did the first. To adjust the tension of the element at any point, pull out the clip that anchors the ceramic insulator *(inset)* and reinsert the clip in another hole.

Replacing a baseboard heater's element. With the unit unplugged, remove the heater cover and expose the wires connected to the terminals on both ends of the coiled heating element. Disconnect any wire caps on the wires from these terminals, then remove any retaining screw that locks the heating element in place. Lift out the old element and replace it with a new one, fastening the wires securely.

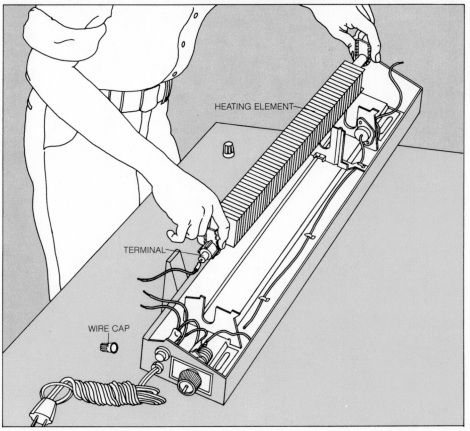

HEATING ELEMENT

TERMINAL

WIRE CAP

Picture Credits

The sources for the illustrations in this book are shown below. The drawings were created by Jack Arthur, Roger Essley, Charles Forsythe, William J. Hennessy Jr., John Jones, Dick Lee, John Martinez and Joan McGurren. Credits for the illustrations are separated from left to right by semicolons and from top to bottom by dashes.

Cover: Fil Hunter. 6: Fil Hunter. 9-12: Eduino J. Pereira from Arts and Words. 13-19: Frederic F. Bigio from B-C Graphics. 20-24: Wagner/Graphic Design. 25-30: Edward L. Cooper. 31-32: Adsai Hemintranont. 34: Fil Hunter. 36-43: Frederic F. Bigio from B-C Graphics. 44, 45: Gerry Gallagher. 47-53: John Massey. 54-57: Forte, Inc. 59-66: Eduino J. Pereira from Arts and Words. 67, 68: William J. Hennessy Jr. 69: from Oscar E. Anderson Jr., *Refrigeration in America.* Copyright 1953 by Princeton University Press, copyright © renewed 1981 by Princeton University Press. Published for the University of Cincinnati, reprinted by permission of Princeton University Press and the University of Cincinnati. 70: Fil Hunter. 73-79: Frederic F. Bigio from B-C Graphics. 80-87: Walter Hilmers Jr. from HJ Commercial Art. 89-94: Frederic F. Bigio from B-C Graphics. 95: Elsie J. Hennig. 96, 97: Frederic F. Bigio from B-C Graphics. 98, 99: Arezou Katoozian. 100-103: Walter Hilmers Jr. from HJ Commercial Art. 104: Fil Hunter. 106-111: William J. Hennessy Jr. 112-119: Elsie J. Hennig. 120-125: Snowden Associates, Inc.

Acknowledgments

The index/glossary for this book was prepared by Louise Hedberg. The editors wish to thank the following: The Alexandria Armature Works, Alexandria, Va.; Mr. and Mrs. Gerald F. Allard, Stratford Hall Plantation, Robert E. Lee Memorial Association, Stratford, Va.; The American National Standards Institute, New York, N.Y.; The American Society of Mechanical Engineers, New York, N.Y.; Appliance Parts, Inc., North Minneapolis, Minn.; The Association of Home Appliance Manufacturers, Chicago, Ill.; G. C. Bender, Alexandria, Va.; Mrs. Joanne Boyer, Stratford Hall Plantation, Robert E. Lee Memorial Association, Stratford, Va.; Donna R. Braden, The Edison Institute, Dearborn, Mich.; Nancy C. Campbell, Director of Interpretation and Education, Sleepy Hollow Restorations, Tarrytown, N.Y.; Division of Costumes, National Museum of American History, Smithsonian Institution, Washington, D.C.; Division of Electricity and Modern Physics, National Museum of American History, Smithsonian Institution, Washington, D.C.; Meryle Evans, New York, N.Y.; John T. Franklin, Lindsay Franchised, Inc., Arlington, Va.; General Electric Company, Appliance Motor Department, De Kalb, Ill.; Basil Haley, Culligan Water Conditioning of Greater Washington, Vienna, Va.; Robert Helton, Appliance Fix-It, Bailey's Crossroads, Va.; Paul Holtzman, Philadelphia, Pa.; Institute of Electrical and Electronics Engineers, New York, N.Y.; Barbara Jansen, Textile Division, National Museum of American History, Smithsonian Institution, Washington, D.C.; Walter Johnson, Electric Shaver Shops Virginia, Inc., Bailey's Crossroads, Va.; Mary Jones, Sleepy Hollow Restorations, Tarrytown, N.Y.; Joan Koslan-Schwartz, Vienna, Va.; Felice Jo Lamden, Delaware Art Museum, Wilmington, Del.; William Lance, Service Manager, Culligan Water Conditioning of Greater Washington, Vienna, Va.; Daniel W. McNew, Culligan Water Conditioning of Greater Washington, Vienna, Va.; Alice Malone, Public and Academic Programs, National Museum of American History, Smithsonian Institution, Washington, D.C.; National Appliance Association, Kansas City, Mo.; National Appliance Parts Suppliers Association, Chicago, Ill.; National Housewares Manufacturers Association, Chicago, Ill.; Sharon L. Pala, Public Affairs, Hoover Company, North Canton, Ohio; Geraldine Sanderson, Public Affairs, National Museum of American History, Smithsonian Institution, Washington, D.C.; Lieutenant Commander Kirk Y. Saunders, South Mills, N.C.; Dr. Romeo Segnan, Department of Physics, American University, Washington, D.C.; Ann Serio, Division of Domestic Life, National Museum of American History, Smithsonian Institution, Washington, D.C.; James C. Sutherland, Stratford Hall Plantation, Robert E. Lee Memorial Association, Stratford, Va.; Eloise Waite, Washington, D.C.; Whirlpool Corporation, Consumer Affairs Training, Benton Harbor, Mich.; Wisconsin State Historical Society, Madison, Wis. The editors would also like to express their appreciation to Edgar Henry and Mark P. Schaffer, writers, for their help with this book.

Index/Glossary